❡ HOT ROX! ❡

"This bittersweet story, set in the cruel world of the very rich, will leave you somewhere between tears and laughter and with an unexpected sense of inner strength."

> Pat Booth
> Author of *Palm Beach* and *The Sisters*

"[Roxanne Pulitzer] has turned a sordid and sorry spectacle into a riveting cautionary tale."

> *New Woman*

"Might not win the Prize Pulitzer, but does have the dish heavenly."

> *The Village Voice*

ROX IS ON A ROLL:

Her first sexual experience with Peter Pulitzer created such an overwhelming physical release that "it reminded me of how sharks quiver when they're about to attack."

On her twenty-eighth birthday, a party guest appeared with a silver tray bearing a message "Happy Birthday Rox" spelled in lines of cocaine.

Dinner with Palm Beach notable Patrick Lannon, the former chairman of the board of ITT, resulted in a *tour à deux* to a room containing his private pornography collection, including whips, chains, and handcuffs.

⟦ROX REVEALS:⟧

She would dress up in provocative outfits and perform striptease for hubby Pulitzer—and each Christmas, they would exchange X-rated gifts.

The infamous *ménage à trois* included her husband and her friend Jacquie Kimberly, the young wife of the Kleenex tissue heir... champagne and cocaine helped ease the awkward moments.

During her six-year marriage, she received a $1,000 monthly allowance from her husband. "This way," he told her, "if you want to go shopping or see a movie, you don't have to ask me for money."

THE PRIZE PULITZER

Roxanne Pulitzer

with Kathleen Maxa

BALLANTINE BOOKS ● NEW YORK

*With all my love to Mac and Zac,
to help you one day understand.*

Library of Congress Catalog Card Number: 87-40191

ISBN 0-345-35930-5

This edition published by arrangement with Villard Books, a division of Random House, Inc.

Manufactured in the United States of America

First Ballantine Books Edition: March 1989

All our final decisions are made in a state of mind
that is not going to last.

*—MARCEL PROUST

Acknowledgments

Thank you to my family, for being so supportive.

And to the following friends for all their love and help: Roberta Cusumano, Pat Booth, Margaret Campbell, Patrick Wachsberger, Sherry and Jim Vrooman, M., Judge Mary Lupo.

To my editor, Peter Gethers.

A very special thank-you to my dearest friend, Lorraine Odasso.

Author's Note

In the course of writing this book with Kathleen Maxa, we went through the court transcripts at great length, several thousand pages of them. Especially on the subjects of sex and drugs, there was a great deal of contradictory testimony. I have tried to be fair to those people, in particular Herbert, whose testimony and memories substantially differ from mine. The judge, it must be noted, certainly believed Herbert. But just as certainly, I stand by my account in this book and consider, at long last, that I have told my tale and told it 100 percent truthfully.

As we all know, lawyers seem to rule the world these days. So, while editing the book, I wound up removing several incidents and anecdotes for legal reasons too numerous to recount. As a result, there may be a gap here and there in motivation or even, once or twice, logic. I don't think that damages my credibility. All it does is keep me from spending the rest of my life in court.

Conversations that are not quoted directly from the court transcripts are recounted to the best of my recollection. Again I tried to make them as fair as possible and I consider them all to be accurate and truthful.

I would also like to note that I have left out several of the unpleasant incidents that happened to or between Herbert and me—things I testified to at the trial—because I am sure that one day our children, Mac and Zac, will read this book. I want them to understand what happened, but I do not want them to think of their father, or their mother for that matter, with anything less than complete love and respect.

¶{One}¶

It wasn't easy establishing myself as Palm Beach's leading practitioner of "gross moral misconduct," to borrow a phrase from the court's final judgment in my divorce.

I had a lot of competition. The town's reputation as a kind of Buffet Society Babylon speaks for itself.

I also had a lot of help creating this and other misconceptions about me, including that titillating but—I hate to disappoint you—untrue newspaper report that I slept with a trumpet.

The press deserves some recognition for casting me as a sex-crazed, cocaine-addicted disciple of witchcraft. And, of course, my ex-husband, Herbert Pulitzer, provided me with my big moment: defendant in the most one-sided marital split since Henry VIII axed Anne Boleyn. She lost her head; I managed to keep mine but lost everything else—my husband, my home, my so-called friends, my reputation, and, most devastating of all, my children.

Sadder but wiser, I've learned that the rules are different in Palm Beach, just as the rich are different. Both are more ruthless.

But you don't have to trust only me on this. F. Scott Fitzgerald picked up on it long before my introduction to the silver-spoon set.

"Let me tell you about the very rich," he wrote. "They

are different from you and me. They possess and enjoy early, and it does something to them, makes them soft where we are hard, and cynical where we are trustful, in a way that, unless you were born rich, it is very difficult to understand. . . . They think deep in their hearts that they are better than we are because we had to discover the compensations and refuges of life for ourselves. Even when they enter deep into our world or sink below us, they still think that they are better than we are. They are different."

My story is about that difference and my failure to appreciate it—whether out of foolishness, love, passion, or all three.

For nearly eight years I lived a fairy tale among the very rich. I married a man who was one of the most handsome, glamorous, coveted men in Palm Beach, a man who was born to a name that commanded the kind of power most people spend a lifetime trying to attain.

We lived a life that was beyond the quotidian demands and financial considerations that govern most people's lives. And because of that, I came to think my life was also beyond reproach.

What is it about being so carefree that has a way of making you so careless?

I don't claim to have all the answers. But I believe that my loss of perspective had as much to do with immaturity as with materialism. It had to do with a loss of faith in myself and the values in which I was brought up, more than an addiction to drugs or the finer things in life. When you lose a sense of who you are and where you've come from, you lose everything.

My fall from grace, I believe, qualifies me for a level of candor in describing a style of life among a group of people in a town not given to honest self-appraisal. I am no longer dazzled or intimidated. I have seen and experienced the wreckage that carelessness can make of people's lives.

But mine is not finally a story of loss or failure. It is a story of survival, of coming to terms with myself, my mistakes, and the crooked hand that fate seems to deal, although it is my firm belief that we make our own destiny. It is also, underneath the sensational headlines, the glitz and glamour, a story filled with humor and affection. As far as my children, Mac and Zac, are concerned, it is also a tale of great love. And, as hard as it is for me to admit now, there was certainly great love where Herbert was concerned, too.

Although it would be easy for me to cast Herbert as the villain and me as the victim, it wouldn't be honest. Unwittingly, I provided him with plenty of ammunition with which to ruin my reputation in court and in the press. Unintentionally, I also provided him with the motive to do it: anger. Unfortunately, I allowed myself to lash out against him, to break confidences and publicly say things of which I am still ashamed and which I will always regret.

A contested divorce by definition is emotional warfare. It is sometimes savage, particularly when child custody is involved, and always brutal. But it is never rational or fair. Ultimately the only thing it ever proves is which spouse has the best lawyer and the deepest pockets.

But how many people understand that before it's too late? I sure didn't.

And that lack of understanding cost me.

It cost me my children.

That's one of the reasons I'm writing this book. I think the good times make for entertaining stories. But the bad times should teach people some valuable lessons—lessons I certainly learned the hard way.

I know that I sometimes seem aloof. I'm not sure why this attitude comes through, but I know it does, especially when I feel that I'm being challenged or threatened. My body language just gives off these "don't tread on me" signals and I take on this "go to hell" attitude. It's a self-defense mechanism that I have—a wall comes down, my defenses go up, and I come off cocky, invulnerable, hostile. It's not really me, but there's no question that it's my way of coping sometimes.

I first realized this when I saw myself on television during the trial and I thought: *That girl's not me.* I know that the judge picked up on it, for he commented on it in his final decision: "Frankly, the court was somewhat relieved when, toward the end of the eighteen day trial, the wife finally broke into tears, necessitating a brief recess, indicating that she was, after all, capable of human emotion and concern."

Later, well-meaning friends told me, "You came across as so cold, as if you had your claws out. If you had just relaxed and been yourself! As it was it looked like a private ego war between you and Herbert."

Relaxed I wasn't. No question. How do you relax when you are going through a divorce that is the subject of the sort of media blitz usually reserved for Senate impeachment proceedings? Or when the most intimate moments of your married life are publicly broadcast? Or when your religious beliefs are maligned and ridiculed? Or when your worthiness as a mother is being challenged in open court? Believe me, there is no worse feeling than being accused of being a bad mother.

I was stunned and hurt and angry. But mostly, I was disbelieving. I just couldn't grasp that this was really happening to me. And the video cameras in the courtroom only reinforced the unreal quality of the entire eighteen day trial. I felt like a contestant on the TV show *This Is Your Life,* only they had mistakenly confused my life with that of some other woman—a cocaine-crazed, promiscuous unfit mother.

I knew that wasn't me. And the allegations were so ludicrous, the people making them so obviously prejudiced, I really didn't believe that anyone else took them seriously either. Certainly not the judge, anyway.

In my mind, the trial was just the latest round in a stubborn contest of wills between Herbert and me that had been continuing on and off for months—one minute we were at a standoff, the next we were reconciling. The issue, as it probably is for many troubled couples, was the balance of power within our marriage. After seven years, I had begun to rebel against the degree to which Herbert had always dominated me. But I still loved him. And I know this sounds crazy, but I believed he still loved me—right up to and even throughout the trial.

At the time I just didn't appreciate that once the lawyers became involved, Herbert's and my emotional power struggle would escalate into a battle in which custody of our children was his side's ultimate weapon. Once the courts became involved, it became a battle for public opinion, too, as each side sought to portray the other as an unfit parent.

My marriage unraveled, typically, over many months and many confrontations. But the incident that sticks in my mind as the dangling thread that started it all took place one autumn night in 1980 during an evening out with friends.

Following one of those stuffy black-tie dinners around which Palm Beach revolves, we all decided to go dancing at one of the then popular discos across the bridge in West Palm Beach. We had been there only a short time when Herbert, who did not much like to dance, said he wanted to go home. I wanted to stay. The cocaine and champagne were flowing, as they often did in those days, and we were all having a good time.

But Herbert and I had this agreement in our marriage that we would always go home and to bed together. We had never broken it. Ours was not a typical marriage. Herbert did not have a regular job; therefore we were together day after day and night after night for five years. So when Herbert halfheartedly said, "Why don't you stay?"—as he often did for public appearance—he was also putting me through one of his habitual tests. This night for some reason his challenge struck the wrong chord in me. He was like a father giving a child permission to eat a second candy bar, even as he shakes his head in disapproval.

For the first time, I chose to stay, to ignore his disapproval and to give in to the urgings of the others in the group: "Come on. Don't go home. It's not even midnight. You can ride home with one of us."

But I was also giving in to a newly emerging need to assert myself in the face of Herbert's long-accepted authority over me. Until now, he had always set the mood, made the decisions, and called the shots in the marriage, and I had always gone along. But after six years of anticipating Herbert's needs, wants, and moods, I was beginning to feel like reserving the right to make a few choices based on what Roxanne wanted. Not many, just a few.

Staying out that night was one of those choices. But I surprised myself by making it, because there was a time when I never thought I would do anything to risk Herbert's disapproval.

I guess I felt guilty, because after he left and I figured he was home, I called him from a pay phone at the disco to tell him that I missed him. I asked him if he wanted me to come home. "Don't be silly," he said. "I'm just tired tonight and I don't feel like dancing."

I hung up the phone and was still debating whether to call a taxi and leave when someone asked me to dance. A few more glasses of champagne and all of a sudden the disco was closing and the party was moving to the house of one of the couples. I thought I'd stay another hour, but the next thing I knew it was daylight.

When I saw the dawn breaking, I was panicked, knowing that Herbert would be furious. It was one thing to stay out an hour or two later, and quite another to stay out all night.

Minutes later, when I arrived home with my friend Inger, Herbert was gone. Figuring that he must have gone over to the boat in a huff, we drove over to the marina. There was Herbert sitting on the edge of the *Sea Hunter*, varnishing the deck.

He didn't even look up when our car pulled in. I knew he was really mad. Herbert didn't get that mad at me very often, and when he did, it terrified me. He didn't have to say anything. His wrath was as palpable as a leather belt on the backside.

Finally, after what seemed like an interminable silence, he lit into me, his voice tinged with disgust. "You're supposed to be here varnishing the boat with me, and look at you. You haven't slept all night. You're hung over and still high."

I started to cry, because I was all of those things.

"I've had it with the drinking and drugs," he continued. "That's why you didn't come home. We're not going to do it anymore." This was the beginning of a frustrating syndrome—sometimes absolutely no drugs, sometimes they were fine.

Inger rushed to my defense. "Come on, Herbert," she said. "What's the big deal? Roxanne hasn't done anything wrong. She's been at my house since the club closed."

I knew she was only making the situation worse. "I think you'd better leave," I told her in what I thought were no uncertain tones. But she kept right on scolding Herbert for being unreasonable, unaware that she was digging a deeper grave for me. Now the issue would be my wild friends, as well as the hour.

"Inger, you had better leave!" I repeated. Finally, she took the hint.

Then I picked up one of the paintbrushes. Still dressed in my evening clothes and exhausted, I began varnishing in silence alongside Herbert. Hours later, when he decided I'd been punished enough, he said it was time for us to stop.

Over the next year and a half there would be many more confrontations and reconciliations, more anger-provoking defiances and emotionally exacting punishments. A pattern began to emerge.

But that night at the disco, when I first chose pleasing myself over pleasing Herbert, unleashed the frustrations, insecurities, self-deception, and psychological game-playing that ultimately drove us apart. The frayed emotional edges of our relationship were beginning to unravel our marriage.

Like a lot of couples who don't make it, we tried to pretend that those negative feelings weren't real, that they were just passing figments of our angry imaginations, emotional gremlins. After all, we still loved each other, were still sexually attracted to each other, still preferred each other's company.

But the emotional gremlins were very real. The fantasy was falling in love and believing that love guaranteed living happily ever after. In retrospect, I realize that it was a dream, not a reality, that I was trying to live.

I was an aspiring Cinderella when I met Herbert Pulitzer, Jr.—nicknamed Peter, for some unknown reason. There's no getting around it: I was chasing my gender's version of the American dream—being swept off my feet by a handsome, successful Prince Charming with enough money to take care of me in the security and comfort I envisioned as my birthright.

But I didn't marry Herbert Pulitzer for his money or his name. The fact is that those who have tried to characterize me as a gold digger are really selling Herbert short. I married him because he was the sexiest, smartest, funniest, strongest, most intriguing and interesting man I had ever known. At the time, I couldn't imagine being more in love.

I was totally devoted to that man, totally content to let my life completely revolve around him. Not only was he my Prince Charming, he was my teacher and best friend. But my worship of Herbert was inevitably bound to lead to disillusionment.

The failure of our marriage, I realize now, cuts right to the bedrock of my personality. Like a lot of young women, I was eager to relinquish myself to romance and dependency without even realizing just what I was giving up. Lacking the self-confidence to test myself, I opted for love and marriage. The only problem was that I grossly under-estimated my need for independence and my capacity for personal growth.

It wasn't until long after the divorce and after I learned to cope with the devastating grief of losing custody of my children that I realized just how strong I really am. In a sense, the wrenching aftermath of my divorce turned out to be the test I needed to prove myself to myself.

I never would have believed that I would survive the loss of Herbert, much less that of Mac and Zac. And I very nearly didn't. I was totally unprepared for the anguish of losing my children. To no longer be able to share their warmth and laughter and all the little daily rituals and moments that would never be repeated was the most painful shock of my life.

There were times when I was so filled with despair and guilt over being separated from them that I considered ending my life. I probably would have, had it not been for the support of my family and a few close friends. I also knew deep down that I had to stay in this world for Mac and Zac's sake.

So I not only survived, I learned. Over many months of soul-searching, somewhere between the initial shock, the inevitable self-pity, anger, bitterness, and the many tears, I discovered an important fact about myself: I am not a quit-ter. And after I recognized that, I knew it was up to me to make the most of my life from here on.

The first step was redefining my relationship with Mac and Zac, who were then just five years old. The cruelest, most demoralizing aspect of the trial for me was being labeled an unfit mother. All the other allegations made against me by Herbert's side were not as difficult to han-dle. But this one totally shattered me. In my heart, I knew it wasn't true. But for months afterward I tortured myself by reliving every single moment that I had ever left them with the nanny to go off and do something on my own or with Herbert.

Before I could regain my confidence as a parent, I had

to come to terms with just what it was to be a good mother. I found that I had a much clearer image of what a good mother was *not* than what she was. I also had to understand that losing parental control over my children didn't have to mean giving up our deep love for each other.

I decided that in the limited time I was permitted to spend with them, I would strive to be honest, open, loving, and dependable, to do my best to provide them with the warmth, tenderness, and sense of security that only a mother can give. I vowed that I would never make them feel guilty about loving their father or say anything against him. And as difficult as it has been sometimes, I think I have kept that promise to myself in the years since.

The second step in getting my life on track was taking responsibility for my mistakes—never an easy bridge to cross under any circumstances, but especially difficult after a divorce because your ex-spouse makes such a convenient target to blame. Crossing that bridge was the biggest test of my life—the test of my spiritual strength and faith.

Although I don't consider myself a religious person in the conventional Sunday-go-to-church sense, I've always had a strong faith in God and a deep-rooted respect for the mysterious ways in which He works. While my Baptist upbringing instilled in me a strong belief in retribution, beyond that, like a lot of people, I have felt the need to develop and refine my own philosophical framework. I'm sure that for me that need was nurtured by my growing up in a region that has a unique tradition of religious innovation and progressiveness that continues today.

During the middle and late nineteenth century, western New York was the birthplace of a number of religious and other reforms. Joseph Smith, who founded the Mormon Church, organized his first congregation in Fayette, New York, before eventually moving on to Utah. John Humphrey Noyes and his Utopians founded one of the first religious communes in Oneida, New York. The women's suffrage movement got its start in Seneca Falls. And the Chautauqua movement, which began as a traveling series of popular adult lectures and discussions and evolved into the world-famous Chautauqua Institute, was founded within a few miles of my home at Lake Chautauqua, New York.

In those days, before television and mass communication, people regularly gathered at lyceums, revivals, campgrounds, and one another's homes to discuss the news and to debate the issues of the day. And one of the most remarkable and widely discussed events in the area then was the strange rappings at the home of farmer John Fox and his family in Hydesville, New York.

In 1948, shortly after moving into the old cottage, the family began to hear inexplicable late-night knockings in the walls. Eventually, the two Fox sisters established two-way contact with the source of the rappings by devising a code. They claimed to have learned that the knocker was the spirit of a drifter who had been murdered long ago and was buried under the house.

People flocked to the farmhouse to hear the knocks for themselves and to witness the Fox sisters' communication, and the sisters were invited to demonstrate their special capability at the Rochester Lyceum. Scoffers probably outnumbered believers, but investigations by leading citizens could not disprove the sisters' claim, and many of the investigators came away convinced. More important, the Fox sisters' communications with the spirit provided the impetus for open, enlightened investigation of paranormal phenomena, as well as the organization of a religious denomination known as Spiritualism.

Spiritualists believe that spirits of the dead survive as personalities and can communicate with the living through persons known as mediums. Mediums receive messages through a variety of methods with a variety of results. Some assume a trancelike state during which their bodies are actually the receivers for the spirit messages; some communicate through automatic writing, drawing, or speaking—and, yes, trumpets.

The messages can serve many purposes. Some mediums

are spiritual healers and use their gifts to root out the mental and spiritual origins of disease that are beyond the scope of physical medicine. Some practice clairvoyance—the ability to see distant or hidden events and even to predict the future. Others simply provide the reassuring opportunity for people to communicate with their dead loved ones.

The practice of mediumship among Spiritualists is not related in any way that I know of to witchcraft or devil worship or anything of the like. Nor is there anything magical or voodoolike about psychic powers. Spiritualists, as well as many scientists, believe that spirits are part of the natural world, that they have communicated with mortals throughout human history, and that the ability to communicate with spirits is part of the normal makeup of all of us. That ability is more highly refined in some individuals than others, but it is no more supernatural than the gift of, say, perfect pitch.

I also do not consider Spiritualism to be a weird cult. In fact, I find that characterization offensive.

My belief in the metaphysical has evolved slowly since my childhood. The leading center in the world for Spiritualist teaching is located in the lakeside village of Lily Dale, New York, where I resided for several years as a child before my family moved two miles down the road to the hamlet of Cassadaga. Each summer, tiny Lily Dale hosts an old-fashioned camp meeting which attracts thousands of followers from all over the world. They participate in lectures, seances, and workshops on subjects typically ranging from meditation, hypnosis, holistic healing, and mediumship to understanding extraterrestrial messages.

As a child, I seized on these summer-long sessions as opportunities more for mischief-making than learning. Along with whatever cohorts I could enlist, I used to hide out in the bushes surrounding the main outdoor meeting area, "the Stump," and attempt to frighten the assembled with my repertoire of ghostly sounds. But as I grew older, I became captivated by the stories I heard from neighbors and members of my family of their personal experiences with spirit communication, or psychic phenomena.

Billy Turner, one of the leading psychics of his day, was born and raised in my hometown and was a longtime friend and trusted spiritual adviser to certain members of my family. His reputation was so well established that he attracted clients from all over the world, many of them wealthy and distinguished. The late Marjorie Merriweather Post, for example, used to summon Billy to her fabulous Palm Beach estate, Mar-a-lago, to consult with her.

Obviously, there is a lot of opportunity for fraud and it's easy to be duped by fake psychics in the beginning. But I consider myself to be fairly skeptical of any medium's powers until they are thoroughly demonstrated to me. And there is no question in my mind that Billy had a special gift, a legacy from his grandmother, who had also been a medium.

From my first reading with him when I was sixteen until his death several years later, Billy never ceased to amaze me with his ability to recall incidents from my past and even foretell events in my future, including my marriage to Herbert. In the dim quiet of his study, he would don his grandmother's spectacles, assume a hypnosislike trance, and suddenly begin speaking in his dead grandmother's voice. He was a helpful guide to me in weighing important decisions and in evaluating moral and spiritual concerns. Over the years I have also been guided by other reliable mediums.

But I consider seeking the help of mediums to be very different from allowing them and their messages to rule one's life. Unfortunately, there was a point during my divorce when I was so confused and desperate that I did allow one psychic to influence me. In the end I paid a terrible price for trusting her and learned a lesson I shall never forget. But more about that later.

I think it's a mistake to depend too much on spiritual messages, even when they are communicated through a trusted psychic, because I don't believe that all communications are infallible. The spirits themselves are not infallible. To me, psychic messages are just another important source of information that should not be overlooked. I figure that I need all the help I can get in life!

I certainly needed it after my divorce. It was only after much soul-searching and reading during that period, and through the help of trusted mediums, that I felt truly in touch with my spirit guides, the souls who have gone on ahead of me and are concerned for my welfare. Through that long, slow, emotionally healing process, I was able to come to terms with my mistakes and to transcend the anger and pain I had felt.

To me, that is the most important aspect of self-understanding. I believe that unless we assume responsibility for our mistakes, we are doomed to repeat them and to suffer the results until we do—not just this time around, but throughout every subsequent reincarnation of our spirits.

I believe that Herbert and I have gone around and around together before in past lives, repeating the same mistakes over and over, never understanding why, selfishly and stubbornly blaming each other. That's probably why our parting this time was so cataclysmic; it was the cumulative effect of so many earlier failures.

For the first time I feel, at long last, that I am freer of his hold.

And while there's a sad irony in knowing that I would not be on my way to real self-understanding if I hadn't lost custody of Mac and Zac, I believe that ultimately I have gained a far greater capacity to help guide them through the difficult times that inevitably lie ahead as they grow up. My hope is that I can save them from making the same mistakes.

If having lost their daily presence in my life now means that I can help them find themselves and the answers for them later, it will have been worth the price.

❧[*Two*]❧

I grew up in Cassadaga, New York, a one-stoplight hamlet sandwiched between two trailer courts in the Allegheny foothills of western New York. The town is named for one of three connecting lakes, which the Indians christened Cassadaga. According to local legend, the name means "under the rock."

Unfortunately, the significance of the name has long been forgotten. As a child, I liked to believe that "under the rock" referred to some mysterious Indian hiding place or burial mound, and I spent many afternoons in the woods that surround the lake looking for *the* rock. After I grew up and moved away, however, I came to think that in naming Cassadaga, the Indians were referring to the obscurity of the place even then. To the world outside, hailing from Cassadaga was like emerging from under a rock.

Cassadaga prides itself on its immutability. For as long as anyone can remember the population has held steady at about 330 residents, which is just fine with Cassadagans. Not only does this size ensure that everyone knows everyone else's business, but it eliminates the need for an expensive sewer and water system to replace the septic tanks and wells. During the fifteen years since I have resided in Cassadaga, the installation of a push button for pedestrians at the town's one traffic light remains the only public works project that I know of.

In this hardscrabble community of farmers, and factory workers who commute to jobs in nearby "big" cities such as Jamestown and Dunkirk, life goes on but nothing ever changes, except the seasons. During the summer, the village revolves around the marshy lake, which is large enough to accommodate swimmers, water skiers, and fishermen without too much complaining among them. During the long, cold winters, Cassadaga revolves around snow—snow forecasts, snowfalls, snow shoveling, and, thanks to the surrounding hills, snow skiing.

Still, despite its sleepy way of life, Cassadaga is far more home to me than the fast lane in Palm Beach will ever be. It's the place I've always run to when I'm down or when my life is in turmoil—which, thank God, no longer seems to be an annual event. Somehow those long talks across the kitchen table with my mom and the solitary, leisurely walks around the lake make it all better.

Cassadaga is still the standard by which I judge how far I've come and how much farther in life I have to go. I confess I couldn't resist attending the fifteen-year reunion of my Cassadaga Valley High School class at the Jamestown Elks Lodge and that I was nervous about how I, the most notorious divorcée in the class of 1969, would be greeted. As it turned out, my old friends were just as nervous about seeing me again until they realized that I was the same old Rox—one of the first to arrive at the party and one of the last to depart.

I am the third generation of my family to grow up in Cassadaga and the first one to leave, unless you count my father, William Renckens, which I never do, because he just doesn't much figure into my life. My father didn't actually leave anyway, at least not in the sense of making up his mind to relinquish Cassadaga and strike out on his own in the world. He was thrown out of town by my mother, who rightly concluded that Cassadaga wasn't big enough for both of them.

Tired of supporting him and his drinking habit, mother handed him $500—all the money she had in the world—and told him, "Take this money and use it to get as far away from here as you can." He did, perhaps because it was the best opportunity that had ever knocked on his door, perhaps because he knew that once my mother makes up her mind about something, *nobody* changes it.

Many years later I learned that my mother had obtained that $500, which was more than a month's wages in her waitress job, by taking out a loan with a finance company. I don't know whether that bold move was a cumulative response to her years of frustration, or whether it was sparked by the heat of anger after one of their many violent arguments over his drinking. In one of the two recollections I have of my father, one that is etched in my memory forever, I remember him hitting my mother on the back and shoulders with a broom handle while all of us children screamed, "Don't hit her! Don't hit her!"

I do know that her decision to go it alone at age 23 with three young children to support and care for took a lot more courage than I realized until I had to face that prospect myself.

My only other memory of my father is the last time I saw him. I came home from kindergarten one day to find our family car parked in the gravel driveway, its trunk stuffed with boxes and suitcases and tied half closed with a rope. My father was sitting behind the wheel with the car door propped open, waiting. My sister, Pam, who was then two, and my brother, Keith, who was barely a year old, were playing in the tall grass outside of our ramshackle asphalt-sided house.

As I headed for the front door, my mother emerged with a basket brimming with wax-paper-wrapped bundles. For a minute I thought we might all be going on a picnic, except for the sad expression on her face. Then she handed the basket to my father through the rolled-down passenger window. He turned the key in the ignition, backed the car out onto the road, and drove away.

Since my father never said goodbye, and my mother didn't explain where he was going, I didn't understand at the time that he was leaving for good. From then on, he was just gone, never to be talked about or heard from again.

During the publicity surrounding my divorce from Herbert, a reporter in pursuit of juicy copy managed to locate my father at a farm for alcoholics in California. The reporter asked my father what he remembered about me. According to the published story, he replied, "She was a very nice little girl."

There was no doubt that a great deal of the loneliness I experienced as a small child was linked to my father's disappearance. I never did quite get over having no father during my childhood. I wondered a lot about him, and I really longed for a card or Christmas greeting—something from him that I could have treasured.

I remember also having nobody to talk to during most of the day. My mother would have to go to work, and Pam and Keith were two and three years younger than I, so I couldn't talk to them freely either.

I was in charge of them, sometimes baby-sitting alone, from the age of seven on. I soon had to learn responsibility and organization from the adult world. Mine was truly a fast-paced growing-up procedure. At a very young age, however, I developed a strong sense of humor, which to this day I rely on to pull me through difficult times. I loved to play jokes and to laugh. I was always popping out from behind curtains and playing games with my brother and sister as soon as I could take a minute from my chores. On the whole I was an optimist—I felt my cup was always half full, not half empty. In later years this proved to be the other saving grace that helped to carry me through the rough periods.

There were seldom moments I could truly be a child. Taking care of my younger siblings was a full-time job. Despite the love I had for them, it was a lonely job for me.

So it all makes sense that years down the road, the little

girl that never had a chance to be came back for Herbert and ran straight into his arms. Here was somebody strong and trustworthy who would take care of me always—or so I thought. I never anticipated the obvious pitfall that lay in wait for our relationship—what would happen to the foundations of our love when the little girl, warm and secure at last, would inevitably need to grow up, for good this time.

As we got a little older, Pam did most of the cooking and I did all the cleaning and the ironing. Our poor background was the cause of my innumerable flights of fancy away from the real world. It fueled my need for the land of make-believe, and I would often escape into imaginary travels and storybook adventures. These involved very pretty things, like lace and frills, and very attractive people in a wonderful world where all was as it should be—happy, innocent, problem-free. In my fantasy world, no one was ever mean or unfair and everyone was equal, accepted—and loved.

For all my precocious maturity, I was very insecure as a child. I never quite felt good enough, never totally accepted just for myself.

Cassadaga was, and still is, a community which revolves around the family, looks down on divorce, and expects conformity. Growing up without a father contributed to my feeling out of place there. We were the only kids I knew raised by a single parent. I longed to be like everyone else.

Mostly I longed to have a mother who stayed home and baked cookies and sewed dresses like my girlfriends' mothers. But my mother had to work two shifts in order to support us. I hardly saw her. She was gone before I was awake, working from six o'clock into early afternoon at Rush's restaurant. After the lunch crowd, she would come home for a couple of hours before returning for the six-to-midnight shift at the White Horse Inn, a tavern/restaurant and gathering place.

It bothered me that my mother worked in a bar, perhaps because I didn't know how to reconcile her occupation with my strict Baptist upbringing—Baptists opposed drinking as the devil's temptation. If my mother, who never drank herself, saw any conflict between her job and her convictions, she never discussed it with me.

The few other mothers in Cassadaga who worked outside the home were schoolteachers; schoolteaching was low-paying but highly respectable. I sensed that they—and others—disapproved of my mother's job, and I'm ashamed to say that that bothered me, too.

If their disapproval bothered my mom, she kept that to herself, too. My mother is far too independent-minded to worry about what other people say, anyway. I've come to realize that even though her working as a waitress was necessary, she derived a measure of satisfaction from it, too.

Although she is now remarried and could retire comfortably, she continues to work the morning shift as the owner/operator of the Cassadaga Variety Store and Laundromat, which is really a lunch counter with a magazine rack and a few shelves of sundries. From behind a long, worn Formica counter crowned by a large glass jar containing packets of Lance crackers, my mother dispenses advice, jokes, and news to her customers along with coffee, sandwiches, ice-cream sodas, shakes, and sundaes. The morning customers, mostly men, gather over coffee and talk to her about the big buck deer that got away or the layoffs at a local plant.

While my mother was at work, we children were often in the charge of a baby-sitter named Viola, a passive woman who took the job of baby-sitting literally. She sat there and she watched. The one and only domestic task that Viola performed was to cook supper, which consisted of either meat loaf or macaroni and cheese. To this day, I hate both of these dishes.

Viola and I did not get along. She was always nagging me to do things around the house, while she watched TV or ate her way through the refrigerator. Naturally, I thought this division of labor outrageously unjust, especially since as the eldest I already had a considerable share of household chores.

We three children were very different from one another. Keith was the athlete, the active one. Pam was bedridden for a year and a half with rheumatic fever; therefore she was more the indoor type. I was definitely the optimist, the outgoing one, and the most emotional one, too. Later my little brother, Kenny, eight years younger than I am, became the trapper and hunter—Cub Scout type.

My mother's paychecks had to be stretched to make ends meet, and occasionally they didn't stretch that far. Once when she didn't have enough money for more heating oil, we all slept in snowsuits, in the same bed, on and off throughout the winter. When my grandmother learned of this, she was furious that my mother hadn't come to her for the money, even though Grandma must have known that her daughter was not one to ask for anything. My mother would eat soup for a week rather than borrow money until payday.

And yet despite our limited finances, somehow Mom always managed to come through with the really important things we needed, whether it was a new dress to wear in the school play or gear for sports activities or music and singing lessons.

We children understood early on, though, that we would have to earn our own spending money. By the time I was six, I was doing the family laundry and ironing and taking in outside ironing for extra money. When I was twelve, I was completely in charge of my younger siblings while my mom worked. However, in this I was not unrewarded: no more Viola. And I had a new measure of independence.

I know such childhood industry is supposed to mold good character. But in my case, I'm afraid it only instilled in me a distaste for domesticity and the determination to avoid it when I grew up—a vow I used to repeat regularly to anyone within earshot whenever it was my turn to wash the supper dishes.

I always felt it was important to clearly voice my opinions, so I was a straightforward and outspoken child. My mother would just shake her head as though dismayed that I could be so out of touch with reality when she heard me voice yet another of my many farfetched notions about my future.

Traveling the world was one big dream. It wasn't so much that I had particular places that I wanted to see, I just liked the idea of being able to pick up and go wherever I wanted on a whim. It was bohemian and romantic. There were fascinating countries to visit, and I liked to dream up make-believe ones as well. I wanted to see if the world would hold its promise. As a girl, I used to lie awake at night listening to the trucks that roared down Route 60 past my house. I supposed they were headed for distant destinations like Pittsburgh, Chicago, New York, maybe even California, and I imagined visiting those places too.

The one job I did enjoy as a kid was picking grapes with my friends in the vineyards around Cassadaga, a main source for Welch's jellies and jams. To me, picking grapes was a contest of skill and speed, because you were paid according to your productivity. I learned to pick very fast.

Winning has always been a propelling force in me. While other Cassadaga girls my age played house with baby dolls and toy appliances, I trained to become the youngest kid ever to swim the one-mile width of the lake, to be the most accomplished hitter, pitcher, and runner on my Little League team, and to be the best cheerleader in the history of Cassadaga Valley Central High.

I've never been sure what fueled this drive—whether it was a need to get back at those who I felt looked down their noses at me, or just a need to display my natural athletic ability, or both. My mother has told me that when she used to watch me playing sports, my face was so wrenched with determination that I never looked as if I was having any fun. I still have that intensity, that need to go for it and just push myself to my physical limits, whether I'm teaching an aerobics class or playing a set of tennis. I play to win.

Cheerleading was the all-consuming passion of my girlhood. Making the junior and varsity squads was the key to popularity among my peers and one of the few status symbols within my reach. With my best friend, Robin, I practiced constantly for three years before our first tryout in seventh grade. Merely making the team wasn't enough, however. We had to be the best—and we were.

But while being the best was important to me, I also liked to make the rules. I remember more than a few arguments with Robin, who grew tired of always being the first runner-up in our make-believe Miss America contests, while I always insisted on being the winner.

If I had a friend, I wanted to be *best* friends—which to me meant being inseparable. Fortunately, Robin agreed with my interpretation of friendship. But looking back, I'm sure her mother must have thought she was raising Siamese-twin daughters. We did everything in tandem— swimming, water skiing, selling Girl Scout cookies—and we often spent the night together. I would savor those sleep-overs at Robin's house. We would feast on potato chips and Pepsi, a real luxury for me, because we rarely had such treats at our house.

My stepfather entered my life with not much more advance explanation than had accompanied my father's exit, although if I hadn't been so absorbed with the daily dilemmas of preteen puberty, I would have seen his arrival coming. One day, my mother told us that she was marrying Tyrone Ulrich, who was a police officer with the county, and that he was planning to adopt us. They were married a short time later, and soon afterward he became my legal father. So Roxanne Renckens became Roxanne Ulrich.

They had been dating for several years, and more and

more their evenings out together were giving way to weekend outings with us kids, which no doubt was their way of preparing us for their marriage and easing my stepfather into the family. Nevertheless, I felt that he was taking away from me the little time I had with my mother, and I resented him a bit at first.

Eventually my resentment gave way to acceptance. Even I could see that he was good for my mother. He seemed to bring out in her a giddy, almost girllike quality that I had never seen before. She seemed more carefree, more energized, and more concerned about her appearance.

He was a very handsome man and still is. His dark brown hair is turning silver, but his six-foot-two frame is as trim as it was during his days on the police force and his bearing is just as imposing. You don't mess with Ty Ulrich.

While he was dating my mother, Ty always managed to make time for us children. He was a natural and patient teacher and once volunteered to help me collect leaves for a biology project—he spent hours sorting, pasting, and labeling with me. He taught me how to ski and encouraged me to join the junior ski patrol. He taught me how to hunt. And even more than the techniques of aiming and shooting a rifle, he taught me a sportsman's self-reliance and respect for nature.

Many evenings our family dined on pheasant, rabbit, and quail that he and I had bagged just minutes before. "Come on, Rox," he'd call to me as he returned home from work. "Let's go get some dinner." And we would walk out the back door and down the railroad tracks behind our house and rustle up the main course.

Nevertheless, as a teenager who had grown up largely on my own, I found it difficult having someone just come in and take on the role of father permanently. Suddenly there was someone to call Dad, which seemed awkward to me. Even more awkward was living with a man. I wasn't prepared to see him walking around in his underwear or to have him see me in mine, especially now that my body was developing. I felt he was invading my privacy.

As I grew older, I began to chafe at having another authority figure in the family and in my life. I felt he was usurping my role as the second in command in my mother's absence. And just at a time when I most wanted not to be interfered with, to come and go as I pleased, he was laying down curfews, telling me whom I could and couldn't date, and insisting I go along on family vacations.

During one trip to Washington, D.C., I complained and pouted the whole time. While they were taking me around to see the White House, the Capitol, and the various monuments, I was busily scouting each stop for a telephone booth to duck into and call my current romantic crush. And when on the return home they insisted on a scenic detour to Luray Caverns, Virginia, to take in the stalactites and stalagmites, I never let them hear the end of it.

But even worse than being forced to do the family things I didn't want to do, having a stepfather who was a police officer meant that I never seemed to be able to get away with any of the teenage transgressions my friends pulled off with ease. Once my father stopped one of my friends for doing forty-five miles an hour in a thirty-five-mile-an-hour zone. The car was crammed full of kids who were celebrating a high school football victory with a few cans of beer. I can still hear him roar, "Okay, everyone out of the car." And I can still see the furious look on his face when I emerged—the last, but by no means the least culpable, as far as he was concerned. "I want all of you to go straight home," he demanded, "except for you. You're coming with me." They got off, I got grounded.

Another time, a couple of months before my eighteenth birthday, I was sitting at the bar of a favorite high school hangout, drinking a beer and watching a pool tournament with a group of friends, when I felt a tap on my shoulder. I turned around to find my dad standing right behind me. That time not only was I grounded, but he took away my doctored birth certificate.

Somehow, we both managed to get through my teen years without any permanent emotional scars. And my moving out of the house to an apartment of my own at the end of my senior year no doubt helped.

Although I had longed to go away to college after graduation, there simply wasn't the money for it. But that didn't diminish my determination to collect as many credits as I could during high school. To me, extracurricular and scholastic achievement was another form of competition. I was an honors student, and a cheerleader for four years; I sang the lead in two student musicals and served on the student council.

Most girls in Cassadaga were either going steady with a boy by the age of sixteen or desperately trying to. Within weeks after graduating from high school, they were engaged. Then they'd move on to a little postgraduate work as clerk typists or cashiers, or—for the really ambitious ones like my friend Robin—a year at beauty college and Fredonia State University. Their careers generally lasted just long enough to earn the money to pay for a big wedding reception at a local restaurant and a honeymoon in the Poconos. After that, they'd retire to have babies, bake cherry pies, and make payments on their Maytags.

I wanted none of it, and a gulf began to open between them and me—even between Robin and me. I just knew there had to be something more to life than settling down, especially when I hadn't even begun to live yet. I was sure that at any moment fate would intervene and some cosmic encounter with destiny would avail itself.

I had become very aware of boys. Part of me wanted very badly to know more about them, but the other part was quite shy about it.

I remember my first date, when I was about fourteen years old, as a horrifying experience. My mother had allowed me to go out to a movie, and I had spent hours getting ready. This included the wearing of a padded bra to enhance my small chest. But when I walked into the kitchen to meet my date, there, sitting on top of a side counter, were two small, round, very visible telltale foam-rubber pads—I had forgotten to put them in. How I wished the earth would open up! I remained upset the whole evening.

Fortunately, things improved. While refining my cheerleading jumps, I did manage to acquire some more marketable skills: typing and office management. During my senior year, I worked part-time as an executive secretary for a company that made automatic voting machines in neighboring Jamestown, New York. The $65 a week I earned was enough to cover my spending money, keep up the payments on a used 1968 Mustang, and convince me that I was a woman of independent means who was ready for the big time: my own apartment in Jamestown.

My parents didn't approve of the idea at first. But I argued sensibly and successfully that it was more practical for me to live in the same town where I worked. I didn't mention, however, that it was also more practical for me to live in the same town as the young man with whom I was madly in love.

His name was John, and I first met him at Frawley's tavern in Cassadaga, where he played the keyboard in the rock-and-roll band that performed on weekends. I was immediately attracted to his dark good looks and shoulder-length hair; he was the closest thing to a hippie I had ever seen in conservative, flag-waving Cassadaga.

In fact, John wasn't nearly as radical and reckless as he appeared at first. Although only eighteen, he was already a successful professional musician whose weekends were booked with local playing dates far in advance. With those earnings and the savings of his Albanian immigrant parents, he planned to go on to college and a musical career in the recording industry, which he eventually did. It was a goal which seemed incredibly glamorous to me. But even more than the glamour, John's incredible sense of self-confidence drew me. He seemed to know exactly what he wanted from life and how to go about getting it.

With John, I experienced sexual love for the first time,

after months of working up to it in my Mustang and his Corvette. One night, while his parents were away on vacation in Ocean City, we finally had the perfect romantic opportunity for an entire evening alone together. By the time he led me upstairs to his room that night, I was very excited. When he took me in his arms as we lay on his bed, I felt the physical sense of falling in love—like a long, slow slide down a snow-covered slope. Sure, it was fumbling and groping and inexperienced. But it was also sweet and innocent and wonderfully tender. I had never before felt so close to anyone, and I knew he felt exactly the same.

While I admired John's ambitions and plans for his future and believed totally in his talent and ability to realize them, I never thought about how those dreams might not include me. When John went off to college that September, every weekend I could I made the six-hour round trip to Kent State University to be with him. I lived for those weekends together and never really thought beyond them as far as my future with John was concerned.

Then, that spring, I began to suspect I was pregnant. To put it mildly, this was an unwelcome prospect for which I was just not prepared. As much as I loved John, I knew that marriage was out of the question. I wasn't at all sure that I was ready to settle down with a baby. And I knew that our marrying would mean John's having to quit school and give up all his dreams. I could never allow him to do that, although part of me nevertheless wanted to hear him say that he loved me enough to marry me. Because there was really no other choice, I decided to have an abortion. And because I had no one else to turn to for help in obtaining one, I decided to tell John.

I still remember the pained look on his face when he came to my apartment that afternoon. I could tell that something was troubling him as much as my news was troubling me. I decided to wait with my announcement and let him speak first.

"You know, this is not going to be easy for me," he

began, and then proceeded to tell me that he had decided to tour Europe with Santana as a member of the hit group's backup band. "It's not that I don't love you," he said, "but I can't even think of the idea of turning this down. Of course, we'll still see each other when I get back, but in the meantime, you should date other people."

If he had reached into my chest cavity and ripped out my heart, I don't think it could possibly have hurt more. I just couldn't believe that he was urging me to date others. His decision to take the offer to go to Europe I could have handled, even understood. But his breaking up with me in order to do it was devastating.

I was in such a state of shock, I couldn't catch my breath. I just made uncontrollable wheezing sobbing noises as the tears poured from my eyes. The more John offered weak consolations—the summer would be over before we knew it, we would still see each other, etc., etc.—the louder I sobbed and the more the tears streamed. Finally, he just gave up trying to comfort me and left.

I never told him my news.

❧ [*Three*] ❧

I first met Peter Dixon through his older brother, Lloyd, who was my boss at American Voting Machines and the dutiful scion of the family that held controlling interest in the company. For months, the earnest, button-down Lloyd had been trying to fix me up with Peter, the family renegade and party boy.

Shortly after I became his secretary in the fall of 1970, he had defended me against the personnel director's threats to have me fired unless I dropped my hemlines. In my one stab at sixties-style protesting, I stubbornly refused. I told her that I didn't think that the length of my skirts was any of her business or that it affected my business skills. Lloyd supported me.

When I was finally introduced to Peter during a party at Lloyd's house, I thought he was entertaining, charming, and even cute with sandy hair, a boyish grin, and an irrepressible personality. I marveled at his lackadaisical, rather devil-may-care attitude toward college and his studies.

But until John left me heartbroken to depart on his trip to Europe, Peter and I were always just casual friends who shared occasional drinks and confidences at the end of the workday. Actually, I did most of the confiding. Discretion about myself has never been one of my strong suits. I will pour out my heart and problems to anyone within earshot.

Peter was an attentive and sympathetic listener. He was the kind of person who made you feel, no matter how reckless or foolish you had been, that he had made equally dumb mistakes. This was especially reassuring since he was five or six years older than I and much more worldly.

Because he already knew about my relationship with John and because I was desperate, I turned to Peter for help in obtaining the abortion. He lent me the $250, found a doctor, and drove me to the doctor's office in Buffalo, an hour away.

When we arrived, I was relieved to find a modern, respectable-looking medical office instead of one of those seedy back rooms I had heard about. I was immediately ushered into an examining room for an internal examination and a pregnancy test, which turned out to be negative. I left the doctor's office not knowing whether to feel relieved or let down after my weeks of assuming the worst and agonizing over what to do. And I promptly obtained a prescription for birth-control pills, even though I was still so heartsick I was certain that I would remain celibate forever.

Now that I was alone, going out with Peter Dixon seemed a good way to pass the time until I figured out what to do with the rest of my life. Not only did I feel a tremendous obligation to him for helping me through my false crisis, but I also hoped John would come running back to me as soon as he heard of the new man in my life, begging my forgiveness and pledging his undying love. Eventually he did—the only problem was that I was, by that time, hours away from marrying Peter Dixon.

In the meantime, Peter pursued me with diligence. He brought me flowers and candy, indulged my weakness for pistachios by stocking the glass candy jar on my office desk, and always seemed eager for my company. Never before had anyone lavished so much romantic attention on me.

I was also dazzled by his sophistication. He drove a chocolate-colored Jaguar XKE with natural leather interior, and wined and dined me at the best restaurants in Jamestown. When we were out with a group, Peter would always pick up the check, but not in a showy, big-spender way. He was genuinely generous, just as happy to spend his father's money on you as on himself.

I also admired Peter's spontaneity. On a whim, he'd call me to say that the company plane was going to Pittsburgh or New York or Chicago that night and suggest that we fly in for dinner. For someone who had never been on a plane before, this was very impressive.

I believe he was attracted to me because we shared the same hell-bent character. Peter liked to joke that he was the black sheep of the family, and I could certainly relate to a sense of estrangement in that I had never wholeheartedly conformed to Cassadaga.

Peter's errant youth had been played out in direct competition with a "perfect," overachieving older brother, who was eager to measure up to his domineering family's expectations. Lloyd III, who was nicknamed Laddie, had been a bright student who had earned his law degree from Duquesne University, then married well and happily before settling into his rightful place as the third generation of Dixon executive management at AVM.

Rather than compete with that glittering record, Peter seemed to have decided to coast through life on his charm and his family's money. He was more concerned with skiing in Europe and partying on various campuses than following in his brother's footsteps, possibly because he knew he couldn't. I sometimes felt that behind Peter's playboy facade he was hiding a sense of failure, and I felt sorry for him.

Despite several months of steady dating, I didn't take my relationship with Peter seriously until the evening when we met at a pub for an after-work drink and he produced a box containing an engagement ring. I felt shocked, flattered, and torn.

It was the largest diamond I had ever seen—at least one carat in a beautiful marquise setting—and I was tempted to take it. But clearly, accepting it meant confronting some questions I wasn't prepared for. Did I really want to continue my relationship with Peter Dixon? Did I love him? Could I love him?

Up until then I had managed to avoid those questions largely because Peter had never pressured me or made any demand on me, even sexually. I think he knew the tremendous emotional stress I had been under because of my feared pregnancy and heartbreak over John's sudden departure from my life. I think Peter thought that through his patience and understanding, he could earn my love.

At that point in my life, I didn't know enough about love to know whether he could or not. Was love defined by the passionate and obsessive way I had felt about John, or by the comfortable, secure feelings I had for Peter? Could there be two kinds of love? And if there were, which kind was the best foundation on which to build a marriage?

As I sat across the booth from Peter, trying to appear more thoughtful than perplexed, those were the thoughts racing through my mind.

"I'd like to think about it," I said in response to the proffered ring, and I flashed my most positive smile.

With that answer, I thought that I was sparing Peter's feelings while buying time to consider how I really felt about him. I'm afraid that Peter thought that I was playing hard to get. He was used to getting what he wanted, including his pick of girls, and my reluctance made me all the more appealing. He pursued me more ardently than ever, and I, flattered, did nothing to discourage him.

Soon I began to believe that the genuine fondness I felt for Peter would eventually grow to love, and I accepted the ring, although still unsure whether I wanted to marry him. But after that, the idea of our getting married took on a momentum of its own, snowballing into plans, carefully engineered by Peter's mother, for an enormous country-club wedding.

Although I had lived in the same town as Peter's family for nearly two years, it wasn't until after my engagement that I came to realize that they were socially a big part of it. Of course, I knew that the Dixons were of comfortable means and that Peter's father and grandfather were respectively president and chairman of the board of the company which employed me. But as a lowly secretary living in a $60-a-month apartment, I had no sense of the power or glamour that the Dixons represented to Jamestown's establishment. Though we shared the same zip code, our lives were worlds apart.

With a winter home in Florida, an island in Canada, a farm in New York, and a pied-à-terre in Chapel Hill, Pittsburgh, the Dixons were the closest thing to jet-setters that middle-sized, middle-class Jamestown had. Despite their far-flung residences, however, Peter's parents retained a firm grip on this modest community. From their sprawling stone-and-brick house overlooking Lake Chautauqua, where they entertained frequently, Lloyd Jr. and his wife, Charlotte, reigned as the leaders who set the style and tone for local business and society. Not only did Lloyd Dixon run the town's leading employer, American Voting Machines, but he ran the local clubs and charities, too. Charlotte Dixon, who was known as Charie, was less visible but no less dominating a force; she ran the family and vigilantly guarded its social image.

In a way, they remind me of Nancy and Ronald Reagan. Lloyd Jr. was handsome, personable, gregarious, and very well liked. Although he had a commanding presence, he seemed completely without arrogance—not that he ever had to remind anyone in Jamestown who he was. We hit it off right away, I think because he admired my spunk. After Peter and I were married, I got to know his father better and I became very fond of him. I believe he came to look upon me as the daughter he never had.

My relationship with Peter's mother was one of mutual tolerance. Charlotte Dixon was a brittle woman who always seemed to be dressed as though she expected a visiting head of state to be dropping by. Her blond hair was always perfectly coiffed and lacquered into place. Her suits and dresses were understated but expensive, and even on the golf course she wore stockings.

I can only imagine that she must have first greeted Peter's news of his engagement to me with as much enthusiasm as Nancy Reagan displayed when she learned that her daughter Patty intended to marry a yoga instructor.

Once Charie realized that Peter had made up his mind to marry beneath him, however, she was too shrewd to risk alienating her son. She told a mutual acquaintance that even though she considered me a farmer's daughter from the sticks, since Peter was intent on marrying me, she was determined to mold me into a socially acceptable addition to the family.

And so I became Charie's newest pet project, a Pygmalion story the likes of which Jamestown had never before seen. She took me shopping and told me how to dress. She escorted me to her hairdresser for a total makeover. She arranged my sitting at the portrait studio for the photo that would accompany the announcement of our engagement in the *Jamestown Post-Journal*. She led me to the "right" store to register for silver, china, and crystal patterns. And after dissuading me from my initial selections, which I could tell she didn't like, she "suggested" several "more appropriate" patterns from which I was permitted to pick.

All this time John never left my mind. I missed him very much and couldn't believe I hadn't heard from him.

Charie mapped out the prenuptial parties and wedding arrangements like General Patton planning a battle. Since her other son had eloped and she had no daughters to marry off, this was her one and only shot at presiding over the kind of bridal extravaganza that socially pretentious women seem to thrive on.

Probably because Charie called in her chits on years of accumulated social debt, Dixon friends hosted a series of engagement parties in honor of Peter and me with a guest list provided by Charie. She determined that we would be married at St. Luke's Episcopal Church, a dignified brownstone gothic structure in the heart of Jamestown. And for our wedding reception afterward, she chose Moonbrook Country Club, where two hundred of the Dixons' closest friends and about a dozen of mine sipped champagne and nibbled hors d'oeuvres selected by Charie.

I went along with Charie at first. While starring in Jamestown's Wedding of the Year may not seem that momentous to some, it was the best that fate had offered me. After it began to dawn on me that I was more of a prop than a star in this production, I was so intimidated by the fact that the Dixons were paying for everything and by Charie's tyranny of good taste that I didn't dare to disagree with her.

I had no frame of reference for selecting the "right" flowers, champagne, invitations, Wedgwood china, or Tiffany silver. And frankly I couldn't have cared less, although I did insist on selecting my own bridal and bridesmaids' gowns. The only reasons I won that round were that Peter, who did not share his mother's social pretentions, supported me, and my mother paid for them.

But while I may have resented Charie running the show, in truth I welcomed all the prenuptial rituals that she had arranged. The pattern selections, the bridal fittings, the engagement-party toasts to the happy couple all seemed to reaffirm that I was doing the right thing by marrying Peter Dixon.

All of that changed the night before the wedding.

It was late evening when Peter dropped me at my apartment following the rehearsal party, a lavish dinner dance to which the Dixons had permitted Peter and me to invite *our* friends. We had all danced and drunk too much, and my head was still spinning. As I crawled into bed, wondering how I would ever make it up in time for the wedding, I heard the old familiar sound of John's Corvette on the street below. At first I thought my mind was playing tricks; then I heard his knock.

He stood in the doorway looking sadder than I had ever seen him. "I've got to talk to you," he said. "I've been trying to reach you on the telephone for days, ever since I heard about the wedding."

I invited him in, and as we sat there together on the same red sofa where ten months before he had ripped out my heart, he pleaded with me not to marry Peter Dixon.

"You don't really love him," he told me.

I told him that he was being ridiculous, that I owed Peter a lot, and I explained how Peter had helped me after *he* had abandoned me. It was the first time I'd told John of my fear that I had been pregnant and my desperation about what to do. Even after all these months, the memory of the episode brought bitter tears to my eyes.

John took me in his arms, and then he started to cry. "Why didn't you tell me? I never knew. If I had, I wouldn't have left you. Don't you know how much you mean to me? I would have married you, of course. I will marry you now."

It was just what I wanted to hear, what I had longed to hear for over a year, but I knew John well enough to realize he was proposing out of a sense of duty. Marriage at this point would have halted his career.

We made love that night with a bittersweet passion that I have still not forgotten, as though we were trying to turn back the clock through sheer physical energy. Afterward, he begged me again not to marry Peter, even though he knew as well as I that there was no turning back.

I fell asleep crying. When I awoke the next morning, John was gone. But he had left the lyrics of a song he had written, scrawled on a piece of paper next to my pillow. I still remember the gist of his words. The song was all about how he'd never fall in love again, that he'd never again go through the pain of love.

The only thing that could possibly have made that night more melodramatic was if we had both drunk poison afterward in Romeo and Juliet style.

Oddly enough, John now also lives in the Palm Beaches and he has been in and out of my life for nineteen years.

I arrived at the church an hour late, looking as if I was on my way to a funeral rather than my wedding. My eyes were red and swollen, my hair was uncombed, and I was dressed in faded old blue jeans which I had carelessly pulled on over my stockings and white satin bridal slippers.

While I had been mustering the resolve to go through with the wedding, the church had been buzzing with whispers speculating on my tardiness and the Dixons' loss of face. Peter's grandfather, Lloyd Sr., had been pacing impatiently in the back of the church, repeatedly growling,

"Let's get this underway." A few of my friends had even been laying odds on whether I'd show at all.

"We thought you'd chickened out," my bridesmaids joked as they quickly helped me into my gown and veil. I gave no hint to how close to the truth they were.

Somehow I managed to get through the wedding ceremony and reception, although I don't remember much about it except for how hard I tried to play the role of the radiantly happy bride. Finally Peter and I boarded the plane for our honeymoon flight to Hawaii. I was so exhausted from the effort and the night before that I ended up sleeping throughout the flight and my first night as Mrs. Peter Dixon.

It wasn't until the second night of my honeymoon that I collided with the full impact of what I had committed myself to: a lifetime of sex with a man for whom I felt absolutely no passionate feelings. None. I mean, here I was in maybe the most sensuous place in the whole world—an island paradise caressed by ocean breezes and the scent of frangipani—and I might as well have been in the parking lot of the Super Duper in Cassadaga.

Not that Peter wasn't considerate, tender, and enthusiastic—because he was. The problem was clearly me. In my mind, the whole procedure of making love seemed like just that, a procedure.

The next morning, in tears, I phoned my mother, with whom I had never before had a frank sexual discussion. I told her that I just hated sex and I wanted to come home. There, there, she soothed me, women often felt that way about sex at first. But I would get over it as I came to realize that having children and sex was my duty. Her advice made me cry even more.

Luckily, that afternoon I discovered daiquiris. The poolside bar of the hotel where we were staying served every fruit-flavored daiquiri imaginable, and I tried them all—by the blenderful. I spent the rest of my honeymoon at Kona Village in a daiquiri-induced daze.

My mother was right. In time I grew used to the sex.

So that Peter could continue his career as a professional

undergraduate, we moved to Florida a few weeks before the semester began at Florida Atlantic University. Peter chose the school not only because it was near his parents' winter home but because the Gold Coast climate suited his ideas of serious scholarship. Of course, I had no objections to leaving western New York. In truth, looking back, I'm ashamed to say that escaping Cassadaga was probably an underlying motive in my decision to marry Peter.

Until we found a place of our own, we stayed at the Dixons' house in Lost Tree Village, a country-club community, where I was introduced to the palmy life, parrot-green pants, and people who consider placing a call to their broker an honest day's work.

I was completely seduced by it all.

The Dixons' Florida house seemed even more luxurious than the beautiful home they kept in Jamestown. I felt as though I had stepped into the cover photograph of *House Beautiful* magazine. Everything was perfect—perfectly co-ordinated, perfectly arranged, perfectly neat. Even the closets in the master bedroom were organized down to the last shoe. I had never seen anything like it.

Preserving this state of perfection became a sacred trust for me. Despite the daily ministrations of the Dixons' maid, I, who had always hated housework, became obsessed with tidying up any trace of human occupation. Understandably, Peter thought I had flipped.

After a few months we set up housekeeping in our brand-new two-bedroom, two-bathroom mobile home, and my zeal for housekeeping gave way to my thirst for higher education. I enrolled at Palm Beach Junior College, a dream come true for which I was—and still am—grateful to Lloyd Dixon. I signed up for the full course load, studied hard, and earned A's and B's, eager to repay the Dixons' generosity by pleasing them.

It wasn't until much later that I came to see that I had fallen into the same pattern of trying to please the Dixons as their sons had. I also came to appreciate the psychic toll that their generosity exacted. Whenever Peter's parents entertained at Lost Tree, which usually meant wining and dining various government election officials in hopes of selling them voting machines, Peter and I were automatically included. Because Peter's parents always entertained lavishly and because the prospective clients were associated with politics and therefore seemed vaguely glamorous, I enjoyed the evenings—at first. But when it came to discussing the voter turnout in Venezuela's presidential sweepstakes, or handicapping the Beaver County sewer commission elections, my boredom threshold was very low. I did my best to prevent those evenings from becoming mired in boring shop talk, knowing that was why Peter's parents invited us, but it was an uphill battle.

Another sore point with me was Peter's cavalier attitude about his school—the very attitude that had attracted me to him in the first place.

Probably because of my nagging, Peter's class attendance record seemed to improve, even as our marriage was falling apart. So I was rather stunned when, the week before finals, I received a phone call from his chemistry professor, who wanted to know why Peter had been absent from class for over a week.

I didn't know what to make of Peter's absences. I knew that he had been leaving the house every morning with his chemistry books, because I made sure that he did. But I can't say that discovering his deceit took me completely by surprise. I knew that Peter occasionally had trouble with the truth.

I remembered the night we had been out to dinner with another couple when Peter had talked of his Vietnam War experience and how he had smuggled military food to starving Vietnamese children. It had been a very long and touching story. The only problem was that Peter had spent his entire military service in Florida at Eglin Air Force Base.

In the car on the way home that night I asked him why he had told the others he had been in Vietnam when he hadn't been. With a sadly earnest look on his face, he said, "Yeah, but I always *wanted* to be there."

On the evening of the professor's phone call, I was cooking spaghetti with Ragú sauce when Peter arrived home. He laid his books down on the kitchen counter and proceeded to tell me in excruciating detail about the difficult chemistry test he had just finished, while I began preparing the plates of spaghetti.

There had been five students, including himself, he said, who had stayed until the bitter end of the allotted three hours—which was why he was so late getting home. He talked of how he had checked and rechecked his work to ensure getting the best grade possible. I continued ladling the thick red sauce onto the plates. But when I asked him the names of the other four students and he effortlessly recalled them, I completely lost it. I picked up one of the full plates and dumped it on him.

"Don't you tell me you've been at school," I raged at him. "Your chemistry professor called today looking for you! It's finals, for chrissakes, and you haven't been in class for weeks. You're going to fail everything!"

Peter just stood there with this forlorn look on his face, sauce and strands of spaghetti dripping from him. "Well," he said, "I know that's where I should have been."

Totally exasperated, I grabbed my purse and left.

You could say that as far as I was concerned, that was the beginning of the end for us, although for Peter the moment of truth had apparently come much earlier. By the time I realized just what kind of extracurricular chemistry Peter *had* been working on for the past weeks, the marriage was already over.

During a visit from my mother and brother, Keith, a few days after the spaghetti episode, we all went out to the dog track in Miami one night, where we met up with one of my best girlfriends from Cassadaga. Beata Jo, a beautiful girl with a terrific figure, had been a bridesmaid in my wedding and had recently moved to Miami with her husband. I won $150 on a $2 bet and was happily divvying up my winnings with my mother and Keith when I noticed that Peter and Beata Jo were more interested in each other than in my good fortune. They were sitting across the clubhouse table from each other, their eyes locked in a visual vise. I thought: Oh, shit. My best friend. Tell me this isn't true.

Then they began passing their programs back and forth to each other, huddling with their heads bowed as though comparing their picks. Except that Peter wasn't leaving the table to place any bets. After several minutes of this, I couldn't stand it anymore. I reached across the table and grabbed Beata Jo's program just as she was passing it to Peter. Scrawled across the top was the message "Meet me same place 1:00 on Monday."

I flew into a rage. I jumped up, knocking my chair back with a loud crash that resounded throughout the clubhouse, and shouted at Beata Jo, whose betrayal upset me more than Peter's, "You're sleeping with my husband! I thought you were my best friend!"

The entire dining room was staring at me as I ran out.

Days later, after Peter and I had separated and I had cooled off somewhat, I tried, really tried, to be fair about Peter and Beata Jo. I knew that I didn't really have the right kind of love for Peter, that I was far more hurt by Beata Jo's disloyalty than by his.

The more I thought about it, the more I realized that there was only one choice. This marriage had been wrong from the start. It was time to leave it behind us.

{Four}

Peter Dixon moved out a few days later.

My discovery of the jeweler's receipts, the little tokens of Peter's affection for Beata Jo, convinced me that I was the victim in this marital mishap. Never mind that I wasn't in love with Peter; he was my husband and I had really tried to be a good wife to him. In the job of marriage, I had done my best—taking care of him, his things and his needs—*all* his needs, or so I had thought.

So why did I feel like such a failure? Why was it that the prospect of being divorced, even at age twenty-one, didn't feel like being single?

I learned the answer to that a few weeks later when I discovered that I was pregnant—this time really pregnant. There was no question that Peter Dixon was the father and there was no question that I could not possibly have this baby. Not that this indisputable fact or having faced an abortion before made the decision any easier. I felt an overwhelming grief for what might have been but never was.

When I thought I was pregnant the first time, I was a terrified teenager who feared the shame of becoming an unloved and unwed mother, the reaction of my parents, and even the physical process of bearing a baby. My decision then to have an abortion was not so much a choice as an act of fear.

This time, my decision was based on what I thought was the best interests for all involved. The marriage was over, I couldn't support a baby by myself, and Peter was in love with another woman.

I thought I had the choice, until I asked my doctor about the abortion. Because my divorce was not yet final and therefore I was technically still married, he refused to perform one without my husband's consent. I did not want to tell Peter, much less ask his permission—partly because I felt that this was my decision, since it was my body, and partly because I was having enough trouble facing the cruel irony of ending my relationship with him just the way I had begun it: in need of an abortion. So I decided to have the abortion at a clinic in Miami that my doctor recommended.

I felt fine going into the clinic. I even felt fine during the forty-five-minute compulsory counseling session in which the social worker explains the procedure step by step and tries to help you determine whether you are really sure you want to go through with the abortion.

But once I entered the examining room, climbed up on the table, and put my feet in those stirrups, I was overcome by a terrible sense of confusion, like waking up from a bad dream only to find out you aren't dreaming and this is really happening to you. All of a sudden I felt a tightness in my chest, and I began hyperventilating. The room seemed to be spinning and closing in on me all at once. I felt as though I was about to black out when the doctor entered the room.

He was a young Hispanic doctor with a calm, comforting manner and the softest hands, which he placed on mine to reassure me. Instead, his kind gesture only prompted me to burst into tears. I sobbed so hard I couldn't speak. He told me he didn't think I was ready to go through with the procedure, that perhaps it would be better if I waited a day or two and carefully reconsidered my decision. Even as I was sobbing, I kept telling him that I was fine. Now that I was here, I wanted to go through with it.

The next thing I remember was being given a local anesthesia and this sudden, awful vacuum sound, which, in my mind, drowned out the voice of the doctor, who was explaining each step of the procedure. Then, just as suddenly, the sound stopped and it was over.

I was still crying when they wheeled me into a large recovery room with about twenty other women. Seeing all those other women upset me even more. Until then, my decision had seemed a tragic one, but nonetheless a private and very personal one. Now I felt as though I were in the midst of a cattle call, just another callous statistic in the latest popular trend.

I felt cheapened and guilty, as if I had lost my sense of innocence about sex forever, now that I had experienced the tragic consequences of it. I have never gotten over this experience.

My innocence about sex wasn't the only thing I lost in the aftermath of my split with Peter Dixon, however. When the Dixons' monthly allowance checks stopped and I had to figure out a way to pay the rent, I also lost the naïveté about what was required to live the good life in Lake Worth. Peter and I had decided to split the profit from the sale of the trailer, which took two years to sell. In the meantime, I lived there with my brother Keith, whom I talked into moving, so we could split living expenses. Florida's Gold Coast is not an easy place for young women seeking legitimate employment other than waiting on tables or serving as companions to the ailing and elderly—even those women equipped with a two-year degree from such an august institution as Palm Beach Junior College.

After scouring the want ads, I finally seized on one of the few jobs that seemed to have some promise: selling life insurance. Mustering my most earnest career-girl demeanor, I strode into the West Palm Beach office of Gulf Life

Insurance and was hired on the spot as an insurance sales trainee.

I was assigned to work with the office's sales ace, an upbeat, likable young go-getter named Randy Hopkins, whose seemingly easygoing manner was contradicted by his chain-smoking Marlboro cigarettes. Working with Randy mostly meant driving around in his beat-up Cutlass and making sales calls on clients or prospective clients in between stops for lunch or a beer. It seemed a pleasant enough way to make money. Randy, who was only a few years older than I, made selling insurance look easy, and I quickly became convinced that I could be just as successful at it.

I decided to learn everything I needed to know about selling insurance, and Gulf Life was only too happy to oblige. The company sent me to sales training seminars in St. Augustine, where I was pumped full of go-go-go enthusiasm and dreams of fat commission checks. I also took classes which discussed the finer points of making blind sales calls, soft-pedaling the hard sell, and closing the deal. My confidence and enthusiasm were further bolstered by a number of carefully primed referrals that Randy and my boss handed me—so that by the time I showed up to close the deals, the clients practically had pen in hand ready to sign on the dotted line.

My moment of reckoning in the insurance business came about two months after my introduction, when I called on my first big sales prospect—a young dentist and his wife who were neighbors of the Dixons in Lost Tree Village. During my marriage, Peter and I had seen this couple frequently for dinner and I considered them friends, as well as top contenders for Gulf Life cradle-to-grave coverage. Besides assisting them with their personal insurance needs, I was hoping to sell him a group policy to cover his dental practice and perhaps even garner a few of his employees as clients. In my mind, this was going to be the deal of the century.

When I knocked on the dentist's door that evening, I

was nervous. My boss, Mr. Barry, a gentle bear of a man who reminds me of the television character Lou Grant, accompanied me just to make sure I didn't omit anything crucial from my presentation. The couple graciously ushered us in for a poolside drink, and after a few minutes of small talk, I launched into the sales spiel that I had memorized. I was about halfway through my pitch when all of a sudden I could see their faces start to tighten in a look of disbelief. It was the kind of look that you know means you have committed a major blunder of some kind. But what? I had no idea what I had done or said to trigger this reaction. And I thought, Oh God, they don't want to hear this.

But by then I was halfway through my prepared speech, and I couldn't stop if I wanted to keep my job. So I just plowed through to the end, exactly as I had learned at the seminars, winding up with why Gulf Life was the insurance plan for them.

The dentist jumped to his feet just as I finished.

"I thought you were a personal friend of ours," he said, glaring down at me. "How could you use our friendship to come over and try to sell us something?"

It was one of those times when you want to die many deaths if it means just getting out of there—fast. I was so humiliated I could hardly speak. I mumbled some sort of apology, how I thought he understood my visit was to discuss insurance. But the dentist wasn't hearing any of it. He briskly showed us to the door and virtually threw me and Mr. Barry out of the house.

"It's all part of selling insurance," my boss said on the drive back to the office. "It's happened to me many times. You just have to keep a stiff upper lip and not be upset by it. And you did a fine job of handling it, right down to the wire."

As Mr. Barry spoke, I sat there nodding my head in agreement, trying to appear unrattled by the whole experience. But as soon as he got out of the car, I burst into tears. I felt just devastated, totally crushed. To me it was a deeply personal rejection. Not only had I ruined the friendship, but I felt that somehow I had degraded myself in the process, although I didn't understand how or why. Just what was this inviolate distinction between friendship and business, anyway? With Randy, the line between friends and clients seemed to always overlap. For me, though, it seemed that the rules had suddenly changed. It seemed then that the rules were *always* changing for me.

The rejection had such a crushing effect on me that it destroyed any notion I had had that I was cut out for a career selling insurance. I managed to hang on to my job over the next few months by beseeching every relative I could think of to change his insurance policy over to Gulf Life. Fortunately, a few obliged. But I knew in my heart that I was never going to try to sell anyone anything ever again.

It was becoming apparent that whatever destiny had in mind for me could not be found in the actuarial tables of Gulf Life. I somehow began drifting into a relationship with Randy. At a time when I needed someone to fill in the blank space in my life, Randy was conveniently there. Like Peter, he was a gregarious, good-time guy who seemed to see life as one big fraternity party, when he wasn't hustling life insurance. And like Peter, Randy was an inch or two shorter than I, which somehow further underscored his safe-haven status in the stormy sea my life seemed to be turning into. Randy made it easy for me not to think beyond what was on that night's agenda for fun. Soon I was spending nights at Randy's house in Palm Beach, where he had lived all his life as an heir to the Listerine fortune—a fortune that had mostly been lost when he was younger.

We dated on and off for three or four months.

It was Randy who introduced me to Herbert "Peter" Pulitzer. We were on our way home from work one evening when Randy said he had to stop by a friend's house in Palm

Beach to get him to sign some papers. So we drove over to the north end of the island and turned into a driveway so densely overhung with trees it was nearly hidden. The driveway led to a small cypress-shingled house, still under construction, which was framed by banyan and palm trees in a junglelike setting.

Randy walked right in, and I followed him into a large open kitchen and living room with an A-frame ceiling and a wall of glass that overlooked more jungle and a swimming pool. Beyond the pool I could see Lake Worth.

Standing in the center of the room leaning over the countertop grill were two of the thinnest, tannest, most beautiful people I had ever seen. They looked like models for one of those Puerto Rican rum ads—you know, sophisticated but understated in their faded blue jeans. Randy introduced them to me as Susie and Peter.

Susie tossed her mane of long brown hair, arched her eyebrows as if to say *"Who* are *you?"* and gave me a cool hello. I felt as if I had just stepped off the bus from Cassadaga on my way to a Miami Beach convention of Future Farm Girls of America. It didn't help that I was wearing white patent-leather shoes and a pantsuit with red and green strawberries printed all over it.

Peter, or Herbert, as I took to calling him, preferring his given name, was slightly more gracious and seemed amused to meet me. I was struck by how much older he was than she, since I had never before met a couple with such an obvious age gap. She seemed about my age, although much, much more sophisticated. Too old for her, I thought. Yet, apart from the telltale silver tinges in his sandy brown hair, he could have passed for someone twenty years younger. He possessed a rawboned, rugged handsomeness that reminded me of the actor Lee Marvin. His eyes were a piercing blue-green.

I didn't think anything more about Susie and Peter, though, until a few weeks later when Randy asked me to go to a Christmas party at Herbert's house. That's when I first learned that Herbert had some connection to newspaper publishing and the Pulitzer prize. But of much more immediate importance, I also learned that Herbert was a very important client to Randy. Not only did Herbert own a boat, a plane, and cars and houses that needed insuring, but he also owned several hotels and a restaurant in Palm Beach that required coverage. Wanting to be sure to fit in this time, for Randy's sake as much as mine, I skipped the strawberries and wore blue jeans.

The party was one of the most mixed groups of people I had ever seen, not at all like the carefully orchestrated, homogeneous parties hosted by the Dixons and their country-club friends. Some, like me, wore jeans and appeared to be my age; others were older and dressed in formal evening clothes. Still others looked as if they might be on their way to a brawl in some redneck bar. I couldn't imagine what these people had in common other than their invitations.

When Herbert greeted us that night he was once again wearing his trademark faded blue jeans. His shirt sleeves were rolled up above the elbow, and I noticed for the first time the tattoo of a panther on his right forearm. The image that he projected, which I eventually came to realize was one that he cultivated assiduously, contrasted sharply with the haberdashery look that everyone in Palm Beach seemed to favor. Years later, when I introduced Herbert to a friend of mine, the friend was shocked to discover that this was Herbert Pulitzer. The friend had seen Herbert around town and had assumed he was a construction worker.

Herbert flashed one of his arresting smiles at me, revealing perfectly aligned white teeth. I was surprised that he remembered me and even more surprised by his attention during the evening, when he kept coming over to talk to me. Still, I didn't feel that he was pursuing me, for I was struck by how much he seemed to be in love with Susie, who was never far from his side for very long. Rather, I felt that Herbert was simply a very charming host who was trying to make me feel welcome and at ease because he figured that I didn't know anyone else there except Randy. His attentiveness was his way of letting me know that he thought I was interesting and fun and that he didn't care where I came from or how I'd gotten there. Judging from the collection of others there that night, he wasn't terribly interested in where they had come from or how they had gotten there either.

After that night, Randy and I began seeing a lot more of Herbert and Susie. We became part of the constant traveling coterie that seemed to surround Herbert everywhere he went—hunting on his ranch in central Florida, fishing on his boat in the Bahamas, partying at his house in Palm Beach. Herbert was always in charge and everyone else just went along, thrilled to be part of his inner circle and eager to please him and say the right thing. It was as though they were all hoping that through their association with him some of the glamour of his name and money would rub off on them.

I had never seen a man command so much power over people so subtly. Looking back now, the only thing I could compare it to was the way the hangers-on at the Playboy mansion defer to Hugh Hefner, whom I didn't meet until many years later.

To be a friend to Herbert Pulitzer was to serve him. People would literally kneel at his feet while he sat in his favorite rocking chair, smoking an after-dinner Monte Cruz cigar. Not that he was a tyrant. He had a way of making happy servants of his friends. They willingly assumed their subservient roles, fetching him his rum and sodas, catering to his ego, deferring to his opinions.

I once overheard a man say during one of Herbert's parties, "I'd never vote Republican in a million years." A few minutes later across the room, Herbert said to the same man, "Well, of course I voted Republican, didn't you?" And the man replied, "Oh, of course."

At the time, I didn't know quite what to make of the scene surrounding Herbert or the way in which he dominated it. I was simply amazed. But in time I became just as eager to be one of the gang as Randy, who seemed to worship Herbert.

Over the months things were not going too well between Randy and me. He was very career-oriented, and we didn't spend much time together. Gradually Herbert and I became better friends, and he started to confide in me about his feelings for Susie. At that point they had been living together for two or three years, and I learned that what I had mistaken for love on his part was really more a case of just having drifted into a comfortable relationship with her, just as I had with Randy.

Herbert told me that Susie wanted to get married, but he didn't. He said that he was concerned about their age difference, but more importantly, he was concerned about her child from a previous marriage. Having had three children, now grown, during his earlier marriage to Lilly, he had no desire to play daddy to Susie's toddler-aged daughter or to allow the child to intrude on his life. So he had rented a small house near his in Palm Beach where the little girl resided with her nanny, while Susie lived with him. I thought it was very strange that Susie would put up with this arrangement, which I considered evidence of just how eager she was to marry him.

In turn, I confided to Herbert my uncertainty about Randy, who like Susie was talking more and more about marriage. I was beginning to get caught up in the undercurrent of Randy's marriage talk just as I had with Peter Dixon. To Randy, getting married seemed the logical next step, like moving up on the chart of Gulf Life sales leaders. As for me, it wasn't as though I had anything better in mind. My own life seemed rather vacant at that moment, and there was no question that my career in insurance had run its course. Just exactly where was I supposed to go from here, if not down the aisle?

However, it wasn't until the night that Randy hosted a twenty-third-birthday party for me at his apartment, complete with the surprise gift of an engagement ring, that I knew I had to call a halt to his notion of marrying me. Susie, who seemed to be promoting our engagement, had tipped me off to Randy's surprise minutes before I began opening the gifts.

Fortunately, everyone else was engrossed in the party and Randy was the only person watching as I opened the box, feigned surprise, and then quickly closed it and hurried on to the next gift. I wanted to pretend that the ring had never happened, that things between Randy and me would just go back to the way they had been before—easygoing good times, with no commitments.

Randy did not mention the ring during the rest of the party. After everyone had left, he asked me if I hadn't liked my gift. I told him that the problem wasn't the ring; the problem was that I just wasn't ready to get married again. He asked me if there was somebody else. Sadly, I said no, but I knew that didn't make him feel any less rejected.

Although we never discussed it again, the ring seemed to hang over our relationship like a pall after that night. We continued to date and to sleep together, but it seemed more out of habit than affection. We quarreled more than we had fun. The only evenings we seemed to enjoy together were those we spent with Susie and Herbert. Or perhaps I was the only one who enjoyed them, for more and more I was beginning to feel attracted to Herbert. And I sensed that he was attracted to me.

I had first felt the sparks flying between us a few weeks before my birthday party when the four of us spent a week skiing together in Aspen. Susie wasn't very enthusiastic about most sports, especially one as demanding as skiing. Although this was the first time I had ever skied west of the Alleghenies, I had grown up with the sport and considered myself a pretty good skier. I could tell that Herbert, who was relatively new to skiing, was really impressed. He was always asking me for pointers and seemed to marvel at my ability and stamina. While the others couldn't wait to get back to the lodge to sip hot drinks, I had to be dragged off the slopes.

Even when we weren't skiing, I noticed that Herbert had a way of turning up at my side. He would take my hand, or playfully grab the waist of my jeans, letting his fingers linger on my skin. I sensed that Susie and Randy were picking up on it, too.

But Herbert had never said anything to indicate that he considered me more than a friend, nor did he make any overtures. On the contrary, he had told Susie he was planning to return to Kenya, for an extended visit. Susie wanted to get married and live there permanently.

She had fallen in love with Kenya when they had vacationed there, and I think she figured that getting Herbert back there, away from Palm Beach and all the female distractions, was her best shot at getting him to marry her. But as their departure date drew nearer, Herbert used business commitments as an excuse for his staying in Florida a little longer. He told Susie to go on ahead of him, that he would join her as soon as possible. But he had already confided in me that he had no intention of going to Africa.

About a week before she was scheduled to leave, the four of us were having dinner at Maurice's, a popular Palm Beach pasta parlor down the road from Herbert's house, when the conversation turned to sex. We had all been drinking wine and were feeling pretty relaxed, or at least I was, when the subject of favorite sex techniques came up. Someone suggested that we each describe what we liked best about making love.

Herbert spoke first, saying that he liked sex best with the lights on. After much thought on her part and coaxing by the rest of us, Susie went next. Trying to sound like Miss Prim, she said she liked sex best with the lights off in the missionary position. I immediately burst into incredulous laughter. Never mind that Susie was probably telling the truth, I couldn't believe her lack of imagination. This, I thought to myself, was the woman with whom Herbert Pulitzer had been sleeping for the past two years?

Partly as a reaction to Susie's demure answer, partly because of the Italian wine, I decided to be bold. When they all asked me what I liked best about sex, I blurted out, "Oral sex."

Herbert burst into laughter. Randy was clearly flabbergasted. Susie was enraged. She jumped up from the table, demanded to know how I could say such a disgraceful thing in front of her boyfriend, and stomped out of the restaurant with Randy close on her heels.

Herbert and I sat there laughing together for several minutes. Then, as he reached into his pocket to pay the bill, he turned to me and said, "Look, break up with Randy, because I would like to go out with you."

Three days later, Herbert threw a going-away party for Susie at his café, Doherty's, a hip Palm Beach restaurant and watering hole. The party was just starting to get rolling and I was sitting at the bar talking to someone when out of the corner of my eye I caught a glimpse of Herbert and Randy engrossed in what seemed to be a very heated conversation. Randy's face was getting redder and redder. A few minutes later I felt someone yank my hair. As I turned around I heard Randy say, "We're leaving." Next thing I knew, Randy, over my protests, was dragging me out of the restaurant.

"You've been screwing Peter Pulitzer, you bitch," he shouted at me once we were outside.

I was stunned by his accusation, which I realized must have had something to do with the conversation I had witnessed inside. When I denied it, he refused to believe me.

"Don't you tell me any of your lies," he shot back. "Peter just told me that he intends to start taking you out and that you want him to. But I don't buy that. You two have been carrying on for months."

I realized then that no matter how many times or how many ways I denied it, Randy was never going to believe that I had not been sleeping all along with Herbert behind his back. What's more, I couldn't deny that I did want to start going out with Herbert.

During the tense, silent drive home, my thoughts ricocheted between my anger at Herbert—how dare he make his grandstand announcement to Randy without even telling me first, when it was my place to tell Randy anyway? —and the realization that my life was coming unraveled again. My brother Keith was leaving for Cassadaga to get married. I was trying to sell the trailer and was spending more time at Randy's. I knew there was no way that Randy and I were going to patch it up this time, and I frankly didn't want to. But I was also acutely aware that I suddenly had no place to live if the trailer was sold; I was too broke to make a rental deposit on an apartment.

I couldn't help being reminded that this relationship was ending just as catastrophically as my marriage to Peter Dixon, only this time I was the one accused of cheating and I was the one who had to leave.

The next morning I phoned Herbert. I wanted to know why he had messed up my life by so honorably announcing to Randy his intentions to date me without bothering to tell me first.

"Because Randy asked me point-blank, and I couldn't lie," Herbert replied matter-of-factly.

Then I explained to him that it was going to be rather tough for him to begin dating me, since I was leaving for Cassadaga on the next plane, having no other place to live at the moment.

"Look, I'm about to leave to drive Susie to the Miami airport," he said. "After that I have some business to take care of at my hotel in Miami Beach. Why don't you come by there around eight o'clock and we can talk about it? You can always get a flight from Miami."

When I arrived at Herbert's penthouse suite in the Howard Johnson's in Miami Beach, I wasn't quite sure what to expect. We were both so nervous, we ended up spending most of the night talking. It was nearly one in the morning when Herbert suggested that we had better get to bed— which was my feeling exactly. The only problem was how to get undressed and into bed with all the lights still on.

Remembering how incredibly thin and beautiful Susie was, I suddenly felt like the Goodyear Blimp. I didn't want him to see me, because I was worried that I wouldn't measure up.

But once he gently pulled me down on the bed and we started kissing, my inhibitions seemed to evaporate, as though his passion transformed me into a more beautiful version of myself.

Years later, at our divorce trial, one of the most painful moments came when Herbert testified about this night. He said that we had *not* made love, that we had merely spent the night together, platonically, in his hotel room. Since Herbert so convincingly won the case, the judge clearly believed Herbert's side of this particular story. But it was a painful thing to hear him say, because I remember that night so differently. I remember responding so powerfully to his attraction to me. After the weeks of mental foreplay, the physical release was overwhelming for me. And I certainly believed it was for him, too. It reminded me of how sharks quiver when they're about to attack. He slowly started kissing me all over my body—and he was fantastic. I knew he had remembered that this was my favorite thing about sex and wanted to please me as much as I wanted to please him.

Later that night, he asked me, "What are you thinking about?"

I wasn't sure how to answer him. I wondered, Does he want to know how he compares? Am I supposed to tell him how terrific he is? The fact is, I wasn't thinking about him at all. I had been fantasizing, which I always do during sex—and always have done.

I have seven basic fantasies that I have come to rely on in order to reach orgasm. I can't reveal what they are. Somehow that would remove the fantasy element and eliminate their effectiveness. Sorry.

But I wasn't at all sure that Herbert wanted to hear all that, and I was worried that telling him might blow our relationship before it had begun. So I asked him, "What do you mean?"

"I just really want to know what you were thinking."

"Well, don't ever ask me unless you really want to know," I told him. "Because I fantasize about seventy-five percent of the time that I'm making love. It's nothing against the person I'm with. It's just the way my mind works with my body."

"So what were you fantasizing about?"

"O. J. Simpson."

He started to laugh. "I can't believe you're telling me this. No other girl would ever admit to a man that she had not been thinking of him. . . . So why O. J. Simpson?"

"Well, I'm a Buffalo Bills fan. I've never been with a black man. And he's very good-looking."

Oddly enough, my admission really cemented our relationship. I think he respected my honesty and openness, and I respected his ability to accept my fantasies and not view them as some slight to his male ego. After that I always felt, and I think Herbert did too, that there were no taboos or secrets between us when it came to sex. Whatever we wanted, whatever we thought, whatever sexual experiences we had had, we could be uninhibited and frank in discussing them. And we were.

❦[*Five*]❧

Herbert grew up mainly in Palm Beach, where his socialite parents settled during the Depression. It was the time when the island was prized by the rich for its separation from the troubles of the rest of the world as much as for its tropical climate. And it was a time when the self-made industrialists and financial robber barons used their inherited new money to buy entree into old-money society.

And so it was that Herbert, the grandson of Joseph Pulitzer, who was an immigrant Hungarian Jew before he became a legendary turn-of-the-century newspaper tycoon, came to be born into a gilded life of old school ties, Social Register friends, and third-generation money—a leap up the social ladder that was helped by an Episcopal Church christening.

But for all the fortune and connections that went with the Pulitzer name, the one thing Pulitzers seemed to lack was a wealth of love. In an ironic way, this was as much the legacy of Herbert's grandfather as the publishing empire he bequeathed. And the better I came to know Herbert, the more I came to believe that the long shadow cast by the grandfather he never knew was the key to understanding Herbert's private insecurities, fears, and idiosyncrasies. He was in many ways proof of the Biblical caveat that the sins of the fathers will be visited on the following generations.

Although Joseph Pulitzer is remembered by history for his many public generosities—including endowing the Pulitzer prize, American journalism's most coveted award—his generosity did not extend to his dealings with and regard for people, including his own children. He was an autocratic, demanding businessman and father; his almost neurotic need to control obscured his devotion to his children and ended up dividing them as well as, ultimately, his heirs.

He viewed his two older sons, Joseph II and Ralph, as disappointments and treated them like employees. Both went to work early in the family newspapers, starting at the bottom, climbing through management ranks, but never rising to the level of their imperious father's expectations. Ralph, the oldest and meekest, worked principally for the now-defunct *New York World*, the great crusading, sensational champion of the underdog through which old man Pulitzer flexed his powerful editorial and political muscle and built his mighty reputation. Strong-willed Joseph II, banished to the hinterlands after a fracas with his father at the dinner table, toiled mainly for the more profitable but less exciting *St. Louis Post-Dispatch*.

Joseph Pulitzer's pride and joy was his youngest son, who was Herbert's father and namesake. On him he lavished inordinate attention in the irrational belief that the boy, whom he never lived to see reach manhood, had the abilities to someday take over the publishing dynasty.

Like a young prince and heir apparent, Herbert's father was groomed to be a gentleman and a statesman by a succession of private tutors handpicked by his ailing, isolated father. In midlife, Joseph Pulitzer was stricken by blindness and a nervous malady that drove him to self-pitying depressions and made his hearing so acute that the clink of a spoon at dinner would cause him to explode. "Fleeing his nerves," he traveled constantly, usually on his sumptuous 269-foot yacht, *Liberty*, and without his wife and children.

No aspect of Herbert Sr.'s aristocratic upbringing and education was overlooked by his father, whose abiding interest in this son was, according to one biographer, "evidence of his loneliness, his great need to pour love on someone, particularly someone not yet guilty of mature ideas that countered his own."

When Joseph Pulitzer died, alone except for the six male secretaries who attended him on his yacht, Herbert's father was just fourteen years old. He had never worked in the family newspapers and had yet even to demonstrate an interest in following his grown brothers' footsteps. Nevertheless, Joseph Pulitzer willed to Herbert Sr. 60 percent of the income from the newspaper company stock which he had placed in trust. Ralph and Joseph received 20 percent and 10 percent respectively. The remaining 10 percent was to be divided among Pulitzer's newspaper executives. Although Joseph Pulitzer also had two daughters, his will stipulated that only male offspring could inherit company stock. The daughters received trust funds, because he feared fortune hunters might marry them to gain control of the publishing stock.

Instead of reflecting Joseph Pulitzer's ideals of hard work and devotion—albeit domineering devotion—to family, the will forced distrust, dissension, and disappointment on his descendants by giving controlling interest to the unproven, pampered youngest son. Secure in the knowledge that he would never have to work a day in his life, Herbert's father not surprisingly chose mostly not to.

Herbert rarely spoke to me of his late father, except to say that he barely knew him. Nevertheless, he was clear in his assessment of the man. He considered him "a rich bum" who had loved only possessions and had squandered a fortune.

Herbert Sr. graduated from Harvard in 1919, and from then until 1930 he collected nearly $6 million in income from the Pulitzer estate, fashioning for himself an indulgent life of idle wealth and a swashbuckling bon vivant image.

He spent most of his time abroad. He took up flying in France. He traveled through the famine areas of Russia, reporting to the *World* on the work of American relief programs there. He took up big-game hunting in Africa and bought himself a shooting lodge in Scotland. In 1926 at a private ceremony in Paris, he married Herbert's mother, Gladys Munn Amory, a divorcée and well-known tennis player from a prominent Boston family. She had inherited, four years earlier, a one-fifth share in the $3 million fortune of her mother.

Herbert's parents moved to Palm Beach in 1930, the year he was born, and set up housekeeping on the oceanfront estate that stretched to the Lake Worth side of the island. With the move, his father began a long interest in deep-sea fishing in the Carribean and a very short, reluctant interest in the family business enterprises.

Undoubtedly spurred by the *New York World*'s steady losses coupled with the paper's $1,970,000 deficit for the year in 1930, Herbert Sr. assumed the post of president of the *World*. He stayed just long enough to lend a continental air to the newspaper offices with his perfumed cigarettes, longish hair, and full-cut double-breasted coats, and to gain a reputation as an aloof, uninterested owner more concerned with profits than preserving Joseph Pulitzer's memory and most prized newspaper.

In 1931, Herbert Sr. presided over the sale of the *World*, which was merged and eventually killed by the new owners. Ironically, this was the principal management initiative of the man groomed to head the Pulitzer publishing dynasty, and it was executed in contradiction to his father's will. Joseph Pulitzer's stated dying wish had been to "enjoin upon my sons and my descendants the duty of preserving, perfecting and perpetuating the *World* newspaper, to the maintenance and publishing of which I have striven to create and conduct it as a public institution, from motives higher than mere gain. . . ."

Sadly, the weight of this decision fell most heavily on the shoulders of Ralph, the least-praised and most-censured son, who had been in charge of the paper up until Herbert Sr. stepped in. Ralph suffered a nervous breakdown.

The sale of the *World* shifted leadership of the family enterprise to St. Louis, where the *Post-Dispatch* prospered under the hardworking Joseph II. Back in Palm Beach, Herbert Sr. resumed his devotion to social diversion, luxurious living, and travel. In between touring Europe and shooting in Scotland, the senior Herbert Pulitzers entertained frequently and lavishly in Palm Beach. They were often mentioned in the society pages for hosting the Duke and Duchess of Windsor. But perhaps the most important measure of social success for Herbert's parents was their acceptance into the exclusive Bath & Tennis Club and the Everglades Club, whose membership openly shunned Jews, but apparently not Episcopalians decended from Hungarian Jews.

When Herbert was eight years old, his mother died of tuberculosis. Even more tragic than her death, I always felt, was Herbert's lack of any significant cherished memories of her—at least he had none that he ever shared with me. He couldn't even remember the last time he saw his mother. Of course, this may have been because her illness was long and her disease contagious, requiring extended separations from her family as she sought treatment in various private sanatoriums in Europe and later in California. But the impression that Herbert gave was that his Irish nanny, a devoted woman, had played a far more constant and nurturing role in his young life than his mother ever had.

The year after Gladys Pulitzer's death in 1938, World War II erupted in Europe and Herbert's father went off to England to serve with the Royal Air Force. Over the next six years, the only time Herbert saw him was during a brief period when his father was assigned to Nassau as an attaché to his friend the Duke of Windsor, who was then governor of the Bahamas. From then on, Herbert and his younger sister, Gladys, were looked after by their teenage half sister, Gracie, and their nanny. Gracie would be the only member of the Pulitzer family who ever welcomed me into her home. As a child, the only "relatives" Herbert knew were those of his nanny, who used to take the Pulitzer children along on visits to her working-class family in New England. Their cousins in St. Louis were virtual strangers. The only time I ever met Joseph was in the lobby of the Ritz Hotel in Paris. Herbert and he simply shook hands and said a polite hello.

At the age of twelve, Herbert was sent off to St. Mark's in Massachusetts, where his father and uncles had prepped for Harvard. He was far from what little family he knew— his sisters and the servants—and it was a lonely time. He treasured the letters from his nanny, which were his only contact with home. He told me that his father came to visit him once during his six years at St. Mark's and that he wouldn't have recognized him except for the eyepatch he wore then.

I remember thinking how matter-of-fact Herbert was in telling me this, as though he had long ago come to terms with whatever painful emotions must have been connected to his remote father.

Although Harvard had always been the Pulitzer men's college of choice, Herbert enrolled at Stanford for one desultory year and transferred to the University of Virginia for a second before dropping out. Figuring that he was about to be drafted into the Korean War, he returned to Palm Beach during the summer of 1950 and went to work as a roofer because he needed the money to support himself. Rising taxes and the cost of maintaining a mansion and the staff to run it were straining his father's trust-fund income. It was only after the butler took him aside to tell him of all the creditors clamoring to be paid that Herbert learned just how hard pressed their finances were. He told me that his father could not even afford to send Herbert back to college after

Herbert was turned down for military service because of a bum knee.

Though available funds at the time were limited, the opportunities were not. One of the advantages of growing up with the right people in Palm Beach is the ease with which family connections can be converted into venture capital, or a line of credit. It also helped that Herbert had his grandfather's instincts for turning a profit.

With a few thousand dollars borrowed from one of his sisters and the help of the family butler, Herbert opened a small but successful wine and liquor store. Since Herbert was still a minor and therefore could not legally operate such a business, the butler served as front man for the enterprise while Herbert made the deliveries. About the same time, a friend who owned a ranch in central Florida with a small orange grove offered Herbert the proceeds of the fruit in exchange for Herbert's tending the orchard.

In 1951, when Herbert turned twenty-one, he received a $110,000 inheritance from his grandfather's estate. He invested the money mainly in Florida farmland and an orange grove of his own. He soon sold some of that land at a handsome profit to make way for the construction of I-95. That launched him as a small but shrewd real estate developer, a path he has continued to follow in his business investments up to the present.

Herbert has always shunned the image of a capitalist or speculator, however. He prefers to cast himself as a hard-working rancher who rolls up his shirt sleeves and digs fence posts right along with the hired hands, or as a self-made small businessman trying to eke out a living from marginal profits. Like those shrewd Southerners who sometimes employ the good-old-boy guise to conceal steel-trap minds, Herbert has learned to use his workingman image to his advantage in putting together deals and managing his blue-collar employees.

When he was twenty-two, Herbert eloped with Lilly McKim, whose socially prominent mother never did approve of their marriage, no matter how famous the Pulitzer name. Lilly's mother was married to Ogden Phipps, the third generation of a family that has been called the "beef-steak" of the Palm Beach social menu. The Phippses, whose fortune originated with Pittsburgh's Bessemer Steel, also owned the real estate company Bessemer Properties, once the largest landowner in Florida and probably still the largest in Palm Beach. Although Ogden Phipps, one of the last of the gentlemen sportsmen, often hunted at Herbert's ranch, Herbert told me that Mrs. Phipps never did permit him to set foot in any of her homes.

In apparent contrast to her mother, Lilly has always stood out as one of the most unpretentious people in Palm Beach. After attending the proper schools—Chapin, Farmington, and Finch—she detoured from the debutante track to work as a visiting nurse's aide in Appalachia and as a volunteer at Manhattan's Bellevue Hospital.

She was just twenty when she married Herbert, who was one of Palm Beach's most handsome, eligible catches. Not only was he well on his way to becoming a million-aire, but his rugged rancher image contrasted favorably with the manicured preppiness of most Palm Beach men. He cut a wide swath through the cotillion crowd and even briefly dated Grace Kelly and Jacqueline Bouvier, who, of course, later married another Palm Beach bachelor, Jack Kennedy.

But Herbert was smitten by Lilly's down-to-earth personality and extraordinary, almost Polynesian beauty. She was the first real love of his life and in that sense perhaps his greatest love. And despite her mother's disapproval, their marriage seemed the perfect match, blessed as it was with youth, romance, ambition, and a young couple's enthusiasm for the joys of raising a family.

Their first years together were fruitful in more ways than one. She plunged into motherhood, bearing three babies in less than three years—Peter was born sixteen months after his parents married, Minnie twenty-one months after Peter, and Liza twelve months after Minnie. Herbert, meanwhile, plunged into citrus growing.

In 1957, five years after Herbert's marriage, his father died in a Paris hospital from kidney and heart disease. Under the terms of his grandfather's will, Herbert inherited his father's Pulitzer publishing stock. Believing that he could earn a better annual return than the $50,000 the stock was earning, Herbert sold his shares to other family members in St. Louis because he was barred by the will from selling the stock on the open market. After taxes, he ended up with about $1.5 million, which he invested in more citrus groves and a waterfront parcel of land in Miami Beach. He got the land rezoned and built his first hotel, a Howard Johnson's.

While Herbert traveled between his widely scattered businesses, Lilly remained on the citrus farm with the babies. It was a hard time for her, who, after all, had no experience as a farm wife, or even as a housewife. Stuck in the middle of nowhere, cut off from her friends and family in New York and Palm Beach, she began to feel more and more isolated and depressed, to the point where she was hospitalized.

When she was released after several months, Lilly's doctors advised that she needed to move back to town and find an outlet outside the house in which to channel her energy. So they moved to Palm Beach, where Lilly opened a small fruit and juice stand. In between selling gift boxes of fruit and delivering them door to door to the town's butlers, Lilly hand-squeezed gallons of juice herself, a messy, mindless task that she managed to turn into an inspiration.

In an attempt to come up with a comfortable "uniform" in which to work, she selected some color-splashed fabric, because it wouldn't show the juice stains, and found a Scandinavian seamstress who stitched it together on directions from Lilly into a sleeveless, beltless dress. After several prototypes, slits were added on the sides and a bow at the top, and the ultimate garment in which to squeeze oranges was born. When patrons of the juice stand began to ask where she had purchased her dress, the enterprising

Lilly installed a rack of her designs in the juice stand. Soon the dresses, which she dubbed shifts but her patrons christened "Lillys," were selling better than the fruit.

When Jacqueline Kennedy was photographed wearing a Lilly around Palm Beach in the early 1960s, the shifts quickly became a national fashion trend. That, in turn, spawned Lilly Pulitzer, Inc., a multimillion-dollar resort and sportswear line with thirty-three retail boutiques in its heyday.

When Lilly's fashion business blossomed, Herbert added a namesake of his own—the Hotel Pulitzer in Amsterdam. After meeting a KLM airlines executive at a Palm Beach party and learning from him of the need for more hotels in the Dutch capital, Herbert persuaded KLM, Heineken Brewery, and the city of Amsterdam to join him in developing the first new hotel there in two hundred years.

Although the hotel was opened in 1971, the building itself is a charming rabbit warren of interconnected seventeenth-century canal houses. It was one of Amsterdam's largest historic renovations ever. In contrast with the Howard Johnson's, which is middlebrow, uniform, and family-oriented, the Hotel Pulitzer is a luxury hotel in the Old World tradition. For that reason, as much as its name, it is probably Herbert's proudest business achievement.

Herbert's success in Amsterdam opened the door to other hotel ventures with KLM in Indonesia, and he began spending more time on the road than in Palm Beach. His already strained marriage to Lilly ended during a furlough home when he was greeted on the airport tarmac by a summons server bearing divorce papers. After years of marriage, they reached a quiet out-of-court settlement. Herbert later told me that Lilly "got everything"—their sprawling Victorian home on Lake Worth, custody of their children (Peter, nearly twelve, Minnie, ten, and Liza, nine), and public sympathy. Herbert would later end up doing to me what Lilly had done to him.

They had a very strained relationship for years after their divorce. Within a short time, Lilly wed one of Herbert's best friends, Enrique Rousseau, an exiled Cuban aristocrat who managed Herbert's Howard Johnson's. It was a peculiarly Palm Beach insiders' marriage, since Rousseau had been residing for some time in the guest room of the house Lilly had been sharing with Herbert.

"He just moved his clothes down one floor to the master bedroom," Herbert told me, as though men married their best friends' wives every day.

By the time Herbert and I met, he had been a bachelor for six years with a well-deserved reputation as a playboy with a raffish charm, which of course only made him all the more in demand with society hostesses.

There is a saying about Palm Beach that no single man with a tuxedo ever needs to buy himself a dinner. Thanks to his carefully cultivated image as a self-made international entrepreneur, Herbert was able to dine out more than most. He was as comfortable squiring socialites to stuffy fund-raising galas as he was throwing raucous bashes at his restaurant, Doherty's, where the champagne rock-and-roll crowd like to party after hours.

But beneath this successful, hip, self-assured veneer, Herbert was a bundle of insecurities and vanities, not the least of which had to do with rapidly approaching middle age. He drifted into hanging out with women who were more groupies than debutantes. And as he grew older, they became younger and more impressionable. But he drew the line at jail bait, always an ambiguous line as sexual boundaries go in Palm Beach, where there has never been a shortage of old sharks hungry for young flesh.

Still, Herbert often dated twenty-year-olds who were contemporaries and friends of his children. At one point he had even dated a girl whom his son, Peter, had dated.

Learning of this years later from "Shaver"—Peter's nickname—gave me one of my first glimpses into the peculiar rivalry that seemed to govern Herbert's relationship with his son. Of Herbert's three children, Shaver was the only one for whom I felt any real connection or affection. He was a sweet, sensitive, and totally uncompetitive young man who always struck me as being eager for a nod or word of approval from his father, which Herbert rarely provided.

I remember one fishing trip, after Herbert and I were married, when Shaver caught what appeared to be a record marlin off Walker's Key in the Bahamas. It took three men to pull the fish, which weighed in at over 676 pounds, onto the boat. Shaver was so thrilled that his face literally glowed with pride in his accomplishment—until Herbert snuffed it out.

"That's a nice fish," Herbert said, as Shaver was posing for a photo with his catch. Shaver beamed. But Herbert couldn't let the compliment stand. To the mate—but certainly loud enough for everyone to hear, especially on a small boat—he said, "Hey, remember that one I caught last year? It was bigger than this." Shaver was crestfallen.

There were many times after that incident when in smaller but no less effective ways Herbert managed to steal Shaver's moment of glory by upstaging him. And each time, you could almost see Shaver's ego deflate.

Herbert told me that he was disappointed that Shaver didn't have more ambition. Throughout our marriage, Shaver drifted in and out of our lives. He had some inherited money but he also worked, sometimes waiting on tables or tending bar at Doherty's or crewing on his father's boat for the summer. But he was the kind of guy who would work for a while and then suddenly go kayaking, disappearing for months on end. That kind of carefree attitude really bothered Herbert. But since Herbert hadn't been around much during his kids' childhood and adolescence, I wondered what he had done to encourage them in their ambitions or to provide any direction.

Once when we were discussing our childhoods, Shaver recalled, without any hint of being judgmental, that he had grown up mainly in the charge of servants, eating all his meals with them, because his parents were involved with either their businesses or their social lives. I was struck at the time by how sadly similar to Herbert's childhood Shaver's had been.

Whatever the reasons, Herbert's middle child, Minnie, suffered most from a lack of direction. During my years with Herbert, she was often in drug counseling programs to overcome a dependency on heroin. Herbert's attitude toward Minnie was tough disapproval to the point of having nothing to do with her, even at Christmas. I felt so bad for her that I went out and bought her a present and signed Herbert's name to it. When I delivered it to her, I found her living in a tiny house with aluminum foil taped over the windows to block out the light. She looked like walking death.

Herbert never talked about Minnie except to tell me he had taken her out of his will at one time. I never sensed that he felt any responsibility or sense of failure as a parent for Minnie's problem with drugs, which she eventually overcame, any more than he did for Shaver's lack of ambition.

Despite his genuine concern for Minnie's health and his inclusion of Shaver in hunting and fishing trips and parties, there was an emotional distance between them that even Herbert picked up on, but seemed incapable of understanding.

He used to tell me that he wished that he and Shaver were closer, that he didn't understand why they were not. When I delicately tried to give him advice—pointing out the manner in which he seemed to compete with Shaver rather than giving him his due, for example—Herbert had no appreciation for what I was talking about. It was like trying to describe red to someone who was color-blind. He just didn't get it. As much as he craved affection, attention, and reassurance from others—and he did, far more than most—he simply didn't understand how to give it himself. Having grown up virtually without either parent, he felt the need to take, but lacked the know-how to give.

Because Herbert withheld so much, it was impossible to

ever really know him, or to relate to him on any level but a superficial one—something it took me years to realize. To people who worked for him or casually socialized with him, he was a great guy—a fair employer, a generous host, an unpretentious man. The problem was that most of us want more for a husband or a father. With Herbert, you never got it. His definition of love was feeling emotionally close without getting emotionally involved.

Herbert's relationship with his younger daughter, Liza, was in some ways the exception. There was a bond between them that simply didn't exist with the others, perhaps because she lavished affection and adoration on him.

Liza was Daddy's spoiled little girl who never grew up. At parties, and even in restaurants, she would sometimes sit on his lap, smother him with kisses, wrap her arms around him, and hang on his every word. It seemed to me inappropriate behavior, especially later when she was a married woman with children of her own. But I could see that Liza's physical effusiveness endeared her to Herbert. She was his "Baby" and he was her "Dadz," a romantic idol that no other men, including probably her husbands, could begin to measure up to.

And yet for all the gushing displays of affection, Herbert's relationship with Liza seemed to lack a day-to-day involvement in the grown-up aspects of her life—apart from seeing her at parties and providing her with an allowance. When Herbert and I were married, Liza had one son whom she rarely brought to our house. Herbert also never spoke of his grandson. I guess playing the grandfather role just didn't fit into Herbert's self-image.

{ Six }

I had loved my first night with Herbert. I was very infatuated and prayed he felt the same way. I certainly hoped it hadn't been a one-night stand.

But when I left for Cassadaga the next morning, I wasn't sure if I would ever see Herbert Pulitzer again.

My mother, who is always quick to give advice, believes she knows best, and favors the practical approach, kept telling me that the last thing I needed was another man in my life. What I needed, she argued, was a place to live and a job. She was still trying to convince me when, near the end of the second week of my visit home, Herbert phoned.

"I want you to come back tomorrow," he said. "I'm in the Bahamas calling you from the boat. I'll fly my plane in and meet you at customs at the West Palm Beach airport around five o'clock."

Thank God he wanted to see me again. I was so excited I could hardly contain myself. I used my last $200, the money I told my mother I needed for a rental deposit, to purchase the one-way ticket from Buffalo. I was a bundle of nervous anticipation and apprehension standing there waiting with my little suitcase in hand when Herbert showed up at the airport. He charged into the customs area in his typical let's-get-this-show-on-the-road manner, pausing just long enough to give me a warm welcome hug.

The hug allayed my uneasiness about just how I would fit in with the entourage I knew would be there waiting for us at Chub Cay. In the Bahamas, Herbert always had a group of fifteen or twenty people staying with him, many of whom I had met when I was dating Randy and Herbert was dating Susie. Now that the partners had changed, I wasn't sure what the others' reaction would be, or for that matter what Herbert's intentions were. Was I simply being invited along as one of the crowd?

The flight down in Herbert's twin-engine Bonanza, a six-seater that he had painted with a green and red Gucci stripe around the center, took about an hour. We spent most of the time discussing how the fishing had been, with Herbert animatedly recounting the past two weeks fish by fish.

Though it has not much in the way of tourist attractions, Chub Cay is Herbert's summertime haunt. Every year since I have known him, he has spent May through September in the Bahamas, starting at Chub Cay because the tiny island adjoins one of the best fishing and diving reefs down there.

During every trip that I have made there with him, the daily agenda, scheduled by Herbert down to the minute, has always revolved around fishing. There was no time for dawdling, delays, or impromptu digressions.

Typically, the day began at six-thirty when Herbert, already awake, dressed, and impatient to get started, would bang on everyone's door, calling us to rise and shine. After gulping breakfast, he would then climb into the forty-two-foot fishing boat, the *Tiger*, and turn the key in the ignition. The shrill warning bell before the boat's engine kicked in was the final call for any guests who hadn't made it up for breakfast and didn't want to be left behind on the big boat with nothing to do for the rest of the day but count the swells. I soon became practiced at getting fully dressed and on board in the seconds it took for the engine to warm up.

Once the fishing boat left the big boat, there was no turning back, which, of course, meant that everyone on board was a captive of Herbert's itinerary. We trolled when he said troll. We fished when he said fish. We paused for lunch at the designated time and place, which on a lucky day meant a deserted little island and a chance to stretch our legs and maybe search for shells. And we went scuba diving when Herbert decided it was time for a break from fishing.

Newcomers to the group sometimes had trouble keeping up with Herbert's pace, particularly during the diving expeditions. They might be stung by the fire coral, pummeled by the surf, or caught up in the tide. Or if there were sharks in the water, they might panic. Tough luck. Herbert has very little patience for anybody else. Lagging behind and holding up everyone else was the equivalent of mutiny. You could forget about ever being invited back.

When we arrived from the airport, Herbert's entourage were clustered in the kitchen of Herbert's rented houseboat, waiting. I was conscious of entering a scene that was charged with hostility toward me. A few, I knew, were Randy's friends, which made me feel awkward as I stood there with my suitcase, wondering where I was supposed to put it. In one of the guest rooms? In Herbert's room? In the cottage that he had also rented just beyond the dock?

Finally, Herbert took my bag and carried it upstairs to his room, giving me the first unmistakable indication of where I was sleeping, if not exactly where I stood. I felt thrilled and happy, but far from reassured. We were making the leap from friends, who had known each other for nearly two years, to lovers—without ever having been on a formal date.

Night fishing was not my idea of a fun first date, especially since I used to get seasick back then. But I understood that it was up to me to get with the program. And I was so eager to please him that I quickly stepped in to fill the role I had seen Susie playing so well. I took my place at his side as I was expected to do. We stood in the tower of the swaying small boat during rough seas, and I ended up throwing up in a bucket—but I still fetched him his rum and sodas, and I fished.

In time, I found Herbert was right. If you stay on a boat long enough, by the end of the summer you're not throwing up anymore.

My slowly emerging confidence in the role I was playing in Herbert's life sputtered to a momentary halt two weeks later when we returned to Palm Beach and he announced, "Tomorrow we're going to look for an apartment for you to live in."

This embarrassed me, because I had no money, but I didn't know what to say. When I awoke the next morning, Herbert had, in typical fashion, already taken charge of the apartment search. Scouring the rentals in the morning paper as he sipped his coffee by the pool, he had found just the place for me. I dressed quickly and we drove over to a tiny, plain Spanish stucco building on Brazilian Avenue, the closest thing to a low-rent district in Palm Beach. In an ironic twist of fate, years later, immediately following the divorce, I ended up renting an apartment that was catercorner from this one.

The landlady ushered us into a small ground-floor studio with flamingo-pink walls.

"Do you like it?" Herbert asked.

"It's fine," I replied numbly.

"I'll take it by the month," Herbert said.

As it turned out, I never spent a night in the apartment. Day by day, night by night, our relationship that summer naturally evolved into an inseparable one.

In between weekend fishing trips to the Bahamas, we worked side by side staining the cypress siding on his house in Palm Beach. Herbert relishes any opportunity to try his hand at manual labor, particularly if it involves wielding a paintbrush. I doubt that Michelangelo derived more satisfaction from his frescos on the ceiling of the Sistine Chapel than Herbert did from his handiwork in varnishing the bar at Doherty's, his restaurant in Palm Beach. One of the proudest accomplishments of his youth was the

college summer he spent working as a roofer in the broiling
Florida sun.

Coming from a background in which people viewed
such work as a hard-earned livelihood rather than a hobby,
I could never understand why anyone who didn't have to
do it would *want* to. But I went along with it as one of
Herbert's little idiosyncrasies, like the way he allowed his
friends to use his house as a place to crash and party. In
truth, though, I was much less enamored of his bachelor
friends than of his penchant for paintbrushes, probably because I sensed that his friends were not especially enamored of me.

When you have a live-in relationship with a man, it's
very difficult to know what—if any—role you're supposed to play in the bachelor household. Was I supposed to
make my bed in the morning? I was brought up to believe
that good houseguests make their own beds, and so I did,
until the maid, Goode, took me aside and said, "Listen,
honey, that's my job." Did the maid's seeming willingness
to take directions from me mean that I should give them?

And what right to privacy did I have as a live-in girlfriend? Did I have to put up with the first mate and his
girlfriend sharing the two-bedroom house with us? How
much longer did I have to be a good sport about the dirty
dishes and sheets left by his friends on the weekends that
we were gone?

Increasingly, Herbert's wild, messy friends were becoming a sore point with me. Perhaps this was partly because I felt myself in competition with them for his time
and attention. It seemed to me we were rarely alone. But I
also recognized that I'm not one who enjoys having a lot of
people constantly hanging around. My slowly simmering
frustration about the Animal House atmosphere of Herbert's life boiled over one night when we returned from a
weekend away to discover the vestiges of what appeared to
be fraternity hell night.

"That's it," I told Herbert. "You're going to have to
choose between them and me." I don't know what sur-

prised me more—my assertiveness in this instance or Herbert's siding with me.

It was a little victory, but it went a long way toward making me feel more like the mistress of the house and the main person in his life. Flushed with confidence, but still groping for a way to demonstrate my emerging domesticity and desire to please Herbert, I hit upon cooking as the answer.

To say that the kitchen was unfamiliar territory to me is like saying the Alps were unfamiliar to Hannibal. Up to now, my capabilities as a cook were limited to Ragú sauce out of the jar and hamburgers. But with a little determination and help from Betty Crocker, I was sure I could master the finer points of gravy, mashed potatoes, stuffed pork chops, pot roast—the sort of stick-to-your-ribs, truck-stop fare that I believed to be the surest route to any man's heart, or as I now know, heart attack. Much later I learned that Herbert was a gourmet cook who preferred grilled fish, veal, and salad recipes from *The New York Times Cook Book*.

After about two weeks of my whipping up calorie upon calorie, I was struck one night by how Herbert's usual lean body now appeared downright skinny.

"Look, Roxie," he said, after admitting that he'd lost ten pounds. "I'm going to ask you a question, and I want you to answer it from the bottom of your heart. If you really want to cook and be a really good cook, then I'll be happy to send you to whatever cooking school you want to attend. Cordon Bleu, you name it. But first I want you to answer this question: Do you absolutely love to cook, or are you cooking to please me? You see, I could send you to cooking schools forever, but unless you really enjoy it, you'll never be good at it."

I felt like such a failure that I started to cry. "I want to cook for you," I said between sobs, "because I want to please you."

"You don't have to cook to please me," he said, putting

his arms around me. "If you really want to please me, let me hire a cook."

From that day on, I relinquished my apron and channeled my domestic urges into tending the houseplants. Within a week of retaining a new cook, Herbert gained back his ten pounds and the plants had never looked better.

Even as our domestic life settled into a daily routine over those first few months together, I was still far from secure in the relationship. Herbert is just not one to easily articulate his feelings. Although I longed to hear him say it, there were no "I love yous" in the beginning.

I was also acutely aware that his relationship with Susie, who was now in Africa, was still unresolved. During our first night back in Palm Beach, Susie had phoned Herbert from Kenya. I overheard Herbert telling her, "That's great. That's wonderful. I'll be there as soon as I can."

With me, however, Herbert flatly denied that he planned to follow her there. According to Herbert, he had made it clear to Susie before she left that Kenya was a nice place to visit but that he had no intention of going there to meet her.

A few days later, a letter arrived from Africa addressed to Herbert. As usual, I placed the letter with the rest of his mail on the hall table, knowing that Herbert would be away overnight on a business trip to Miami. All evening the temptation to open that letter nibbled at my conscience. Eventually, my curiosity won out. As I steamed open the sealed airmail envelope, hating myself for doing it, I rationalized that it was the only way to find out what was really going on. Still, I was stunned to learn that Susie clearly expected Herbert to arrive momentarily.

I just couldn't believe that Herbert was so duplicitous—or perhaps I should say that I didn't want to believe it. So instead, I justified his apparent deceit by telling myself that he really cared for me, but didn't know how to tell her.

Of course, *now* I see that it was all very neatly planned. He had orchestrated Susie's departure from his life as carefully as a day's activities on the boat, salving his conscience and her heart with an extended Kenya vacation for one.

As much as I wanted to confront Herbert about Susie's letter, I didn't dare. When she phoned from Africa a couple of weeks later and Herbert excused himself to take the call in another room, I was in agony.

"Susie, I'm not coming," I heard him say. "I've met someone. . . . It doesn't matter who. . . . You don't need a name. . . ."

That, as far as I know, was the end of Susie. But it was just the beginning of my battle for Herbert's heart. A few days later, he announced that he was going off on vacation with another woman.

I was crushed. My first thought was that I was getting the same brush-off treatment as Susie. But Herbert couldn't have been more nonchalant about the trip. He said that it had all been planned long before I had moved in with him, and he seemed to regard it as casually as a previously accepted dinner engagement. I later learned that the woman was well acquainted with many in Herbert's circle of friends. Like them, she had grown up in Palm Beach, had attended the right boarding schools and belonged to the same clubs. In short, she fit in with them better than I did.

I tried to appear as cool about his vacation as Herbert was. I really had no choice but to accept it. After all, we had no agreement between us whatsoever. Even though we had not spent one night apart in nearly three months, he had not invited me to formally move in with him. We never discussed any long-range living arrangement, much less any emotional commitment to each other. And I was too intimidated to raise the issue.

During the week that Herbert was away, I continued to stay in the house in Palm Beach, as he suggested. He phoned twice to tell me he missed me. And when he returned to Palm Beach, we picked up our relationship where we had left off, or so it seemed at first.

But a few days after he was back, I sensed that something was troubling him. He seemed indifferent, brooding, less passionate in bed. I finally worked up the nerve to ask him what was wrong.

Confirming my worst fears, he told me he wanted to see the woman he took on vacation again. Perhaps, he explained, it was better for him to date women closer to his age, rather than the young women to whom he had gravitated after his divorce from Lilly.

I was devastated, mainly because I didn't believe age was the issue at all. In my mind, social background and fitting in—dating a typical Palm Beach girl—was the issue. But I swallowed hard rather than let my wounded pride and aching heart show. Crying, I knew, wasn't going to get me anywhere.

Instead, I calmly told him that I thought he was making a mistake. "I don't think you two are each other's type at all," I said. "You'll never be happy with a typical Palm Beach girl because you're not a typical Palm Beach boy."

We agreed that I should return to Cassadaga until Herbert sorted out his confusion. On the drive to the airport, I was determined to be the picture of cheeriness, optimism, and pluck. The last impression I wanted to leave him with was not one of a sniveling, broken-hearted teenager, even though that was exactly how I felt.

But while I was putting on the best appearance possible, Herbert's sorry expression resembled that of a man on his way to death row. As we parted, *I* was the one reassuring *him* not to worry because everything would turn out for the best.

"Don't look so sad," I said, surprised at my own self-assurance. "I'm going to see you before you know it. You're just not going to be able to live without me."

Back home at my mother's house, however, I became a basket case. "I'm never going to see him again," I sobbed. For days on end, I just lay on the living-room sofa drenched in despair and hoping beyond hope that Herbert would call. The more my mother tried to cheer me up, the more despondent I became.

"Why don't we go shopping in Jamestown and I'll buy you something?" she suggested. "Or out to dinner? Or to a movie?"

But moving off the couch, not to mention driving into town, required more energy than I cared to muster—until the day she told me about the great new psychic who was visiting Lily Dale. If there was ever a time in my life when I needed spiritual guidance, this, I figured, was it. So I tied a blue bandanna over my bedraggled hair, donned dark glasses to conceal my swollen eyes, and headed for the Stump.

During the annual summer camp meetings at Lily Dale, visiting psychics frequently give public readings, holding forth at a podium—the Stump—and conveying spiritual messages to the individuals assembled there. As soon as I took my seat among the others gathered there that day, I sensed that I would be one of those receiving a message. In that moment, like a bolt from the blue sky, the psychic motioned to me, saying, "That girl in the blue bandanna."

I stood, bracing myself for the worst and wishing the earth would swallow me.

"You're all upset over this love affair for nothing," he said. "This man is going to call you very shortly."

Then the psychic went on to say that I would end up marrying a much older, wealthy man, that I'd bear his children, and live in a house with large glass windows overlooking the water. He also cautioned me not to worry about our age difference.

Here was someone whom I had never before met describing details in my life that seemed to come inexplicably from thin air.

My spirits lifted, I went home and washed my hair. The next day, Herbert phoned.

Chalk one up for the psychic.

"I'm having a terrible time," he said. "I miss you and

I'm never going to leave you again. Please fly back to-night."

When Herbert met me at the West Palm Beach airport, his manner was very different from our last friendly but hardly passionate reunion. This time when he put his arms around me, I *really* felt he had missed me. I sensed that he cared for me much more than before I had left. And much to my surprise, so apparently did his new girlfriend.

"Here, this is from her," he said, handing me a little gift box. Under the circumstances, I thought it strange that she would give me a gift. But then Herbert's well-bred Palm Beach friends never ceased to perplex me with their little rituals of social behavior. Inside the box was a bottle of perfume and a card: "It's only fair that the best girl should win. . . . I'm happy for you."

I was too flabbergasted at the time to know what to make of this acknowledged "victory," much less how I managed to win it. But looking back, I realize that the reason I had "won" was that I was so different from most of the other women Herbert had known and dated through-out his life. I wasn't sophisticated, or socially ambitious. I wasn't worried about chipping my nails or messing my hair. And above all, I wasn't making any demands. I was totally and completely happy to allow my life to revolve around Herbert, Herbert's interests, and making Herbert happy.

Although I longed for the psychic's entire prediction to come true, I was by no means counting on it. A second marriage for Herbert at this stage in his life seemed at best a very distant possibility. He never mentioned any longer-range plans other than the need to get ready for hunting season now that October was fast approaching. I was com-pletely taken by surprise when he brought up the subject of marriage after returning from a brief business trip to check on his hotel in Amsterdam.

I knew something was up because he phoned me from Europe and told me to hire a limousine from Park Taxi and bring a bottle of Cristal champagne to meet him at the airport in Ft. Lauderdale. "We are going to be busy the next few months," he said, as we sipped our champagne in the rear of the car. He talked about finishing up the new seventy-two-foot boat he had begun building in time for next summer. He discussed the work that needed to be done to prepare his ranch in central Florida for the upcoming hunting season. He talked about the need to begin making arrangements for the large Christmas party he was planning in Palm Beach. Then, almost as an afterthought, he said, "And, of course, we have to get married." At that moment I turned my head, and we were looking directly into each other's eyes.

"Yes," I said, trying to sound as matter-of-fact as Herbert had, even though my heart was pounding so loudly I thought he would hear it, "we'll have to do all of those things."

As impromptu as Herbert's decision to get married seemed at first, in retrospect I came to realize that it was based on longstanding underlying needs, not impulse. Although we never really discussed why he wanted to marry me, I believe that I filled an emotional void in his life, a yearning for something he had never had, or perhaps had never fully appreciated before. I think that he saw in me those bedrock, small-town, all-American values—a sense of family, loyalty, honesty, strength, trust—that had been missing from his childhood and his life. I was his alter ego, the ideal mate for the man he truly saw himself to be. That man was a virile, hardworking, Bronco-driving ordinary guy with a tattoo on his arm who liked to varnish, fish, and hunt. The sophisticated Palm Beach socialite whose entrepreneurial instincts had parlayed inherited millions into much much more was merely a public image thrust upon him by his family name. That image was one he manipulated to serve his business interests and his ego.

At forty-four, having made his mark, Herbert was becoming more settled, more private, more interested in leading a relatively quiet life with a woman at his side whom he could mold into the perfect mate. At twenty-three, with no clear idea of who I was or where I was going, I was a likely candidate. I had fallen completely in love with Herbert and believed I could live happily ever after leading his life and letting him make all the decisions in mine. The only problem, which I don't believe either of us foresaw, was that I was inevitably bound to grow.

Shortly after Herbert decided that we should get married, he announced that we should travel to Cassadaga together to tell my mother the news. I believe Herbert saw this as a smart move in family politics, not just a mere formality. Given the difference in our ages—he was two years older than my mother—I think he felt it was important to reassure her and forestall any concerns she might have about our marriage.

My mother's main worry, which she didn't hesitate to voice as the three of us sat at her kitchen table discussing our plans, was Herbert's attitude about having more children. I knew Herbert believed that the children had played a big role in the downfall of his first marriage. He had repeatedly told me that kids change your life too much, that they come between husband and wife, that they're a lifelong responsibility. He had very strong arguments against them. I, on the other hand, didn't really have strong views about having children. Herbert's opposition to them wasn't an issue with me because I was in love and fulfilled with the immediate present.

To my mother, however, this was a major stumbling block. She sternly insisted, despite repeated kicks from me under the table, that she would not approve our marriage if Herbert denied me the right to have children.

Though advice from my mother was the last thing I wanted from that visit, the more I thought of it, the more I realized that this was another time when she was actually right. Even back then it didn't seem quite fair to me that Herbert should be deciding the question of children for me.

"If you're telling me I can't have children, I can't marry

you," I told him. "I'm only twenty-three and I'm too young to know whether or not I'll ever want to be a mother. I just can't make that promise."

"Well," he said, "I'll make an agreement with you. You can reserve the right to decide whether or not you want to have a child. But just one. And on one condition. You must agree to have a nanny live in so that you will be free to travel with me and we'll never have to spend a night apart."

I agreed. At the time, it sounded very reasonable. I had no inkling of how difficult it would be to honor that agreement once I became a mother, or of how torn I would sometimes feel between him and our children. Looking back, I realize that the time I spent with Mac and Zac was the source of much jealousy on Herbert's part and that he frequently seemed to be competing with them for my attention.

But the problems of becoming a mother proved much easier to cope with than those of becoming a stepmother, at least as far as my relationship with Herbert's nineteen-year-old daughter, Liza, was concerned. From the start, Liza and I got off on the wrong foot. Our relationship sped steadily downhill from there.

We first met one night in Doherty's, shortly after Herbert and I began living together. I was sitting beside him at the bar when I suddenly heard a female voice erupt in an ecstatic squeal: "Dadz!" Next thing I knew, this very attractive brunette was wedging herself between us and hugging Herbert affectionately. Without even acknowledging my presence, much less saying hello, Liza chatted on with Herbert while I just stood there, taken aback by her rudeness. I could tell that her reaction made Herbert uneasy. Nevertheless, though he did introduce us, he didn't reprimand her for her lack of manners, which I felt would have been the natural parental response. But then, over the years, as I observed Herbert's dealings with all of his grown children from his first marriage, I came to realize that he was loath to play the role of father, preferring instead to be regarded by them as a contemporary and friend. However, that night at Doherty's, after Liza had left, Herbert did feel compelled to apologize for her. He explained that she still hadn't accepted his divorce of years before and the resulting fact of his dating other women.

Liza didn't take Herbert's announcement that he planned to remarry any better. Shortly after he set our wedding date for January 12, 1976, he went to Liza's apartment to break the news. Herbert told me later that Liza was "just devastated" and burst into tears. "I don't think she's coming to the wedding," he said, seeming unruffled by Liza's reaction, "but don't let that upset you."

Far from being upset, I was relieved to learn that Liza would not be attending our wedding. Even though it was a quiet family affair at Herbert's house, the fact is I was so worried about making a good impression in my debut as Herbert's wife that my insecurities were raging at an all-time high.

Typically, Herbert handled all the arrangements for the ceremony and party. *He* decided to have his lawyer, Irving Yellen, marry us. *He* decided on a four-o'clock ceremony followed by a champagne-and-lobster buffet. *He* ordered all the floral arrangements from Old Town. *He* made out the guest list, which came to about fifteen people. My mother was going to be my matron of honor and Herbert's son, Shaver, his best man. The only decision left to me was what to wear, and in truth I was so unsure of my taste that I managed to work myself into a dither over that. I must have hit every shopping mall between Miami and Jupiter in pursuit of the perfect dress before finally settling on a plain knee-length beige crepe frock that the sales clerk from Saks assured me would be appropriate.

On the afternoon of the wedding, minutes before the ceremony, I was arranging the flowers above the living-room mantel when Liza breezed into the room. She looked stunning in a pink broad-brimmed hat and matching mid-calf-length dress. My heart sank. In that instant I felt like Sleeping Beauty's mother when the wicked fairy godmother shows up at the christening. I also felt as if I were wearing somebody's hand-me-down high school graduation dress.

"Well," Liza said as she approached me, "I can see I'm the only one here who is prettier than the bride."

Shaver winked at me as if to say, "Don't let her bother you." Yet I don't know which was worse—hearing her say it or knowing she was right.

❧[*Seven*]❧

I can't imagine ever being more in love than I was at the moment when Herbert slipped the simple gold band on my finger, vowing to "love, honor, and respect" me as he shyly looked down at the floor like a schoolboy reciting his lessons.

And I can't imagine ever being more determined to prove myself worthy of someone's love than I was the day I became Herbert's wife. When Herbert took me in his arms, sealing our wedding vows with a kiss, I felt such an overwhelming sense of security and belonging that even today it's hard to put into words—or out of my mind. At that moment, I felt so protected that nothing in the world could ever hurt me. This, I thought, must be what it feels like to be hugged by your father when you're a little girl.

In my mind there was no question—I was the happiest, luckiest girl on earth to have been chosen by him. So convinced was I of this that I would not allow anything or anyone to cast doubt in my mind or spoil my dream come true.

Not Liza, despite her cutting remarks. Not even Herbert—although he came very close to doing so on our honeymoon.

We spent our wedding night in the penthouse suite of Herbert's Howard Johnson's in Miami Beach, where we had first spent the night together nearly a year before. This time my only fantasy during our lovemaking was of Herbert and all the blessings I envisioned lay ahead for us. Afterward, we talked about how lucky we were to have each other and our promising future.

A two-week Caribbean honeymoon began the next day when we arrived at Martinique at the Plantation de la Ritz, a lovely old French colonial manor that has been transformed into an elegant resort. That night we dined by candlelight in the bougainvillea-draped courtyard of the old manor house, a perfect prelude to what I envisioned as a romantic night of lovemaking.

Have you ever so desperately wanted everything to be great that you wouldn't let yourself believe it was not? That you just kept pushing any negative thoughts out of your mind, refusing even to acknowledge them?

Well, that's how I felt that night.

Our lovemaking, throughout much of our marriage, sometimes scared me. It certainly did that night. Because I had never before experienced such intensity, passion or physical abandon, at first it was difficult for me to understand. But I was more than willing to do anything Herbert wanted—mentally or physically. That's how desperate I was to please him. And I knew I did please him. After that first frightening night, I needed to believe that the way we made love was Herbert's physical expression of his love for me, a love which Herbert had never really professed. The morning after, I desperately needed to hear him express it, and I figured that pouring out my heart to him would do the trick.

"I love you," I told him over breakfast. "I'm so happy, I just want you to know how much I love you."

I waited for him to respond. Silence.

"I don't think you really understand," I said, pressing on, "how much in love with you I am."

"Well," he said after a long pause, "I love you as a person. I don't know if I'm *in* love with you. But I'm hoping that it's going to grow to that. And I think you've shown me how to reach that point. I feel that I have the best chance of falling in love with you that I have had with anyone since Lilly."

His words, though not intended to be cruel, cut more deeply than anything he has ever said to me since—even during our most spiteful fights later on. Somehow I managed to conceal my hurt and disappointment.

Brutal frankness was not what I wanted, or needed, to hear that morning. If he couldn't have brought himself to lie, a few words of tenderness or affection would have gone a long way toward reassuring me. Yet I could tell that he had no awareness of the emotional scar he had inflicted. No awareness that my blissfully secure, protected feeling had dissolved into doubt and uncertainty. I felt I was standing on the brink of an emotional abyss.

Once again, I pushed the negative thoughts from my mind. It was my mistake, I told myself, for assuming that the reason he had married me was that he was *already* in love with me. People at this stage in life got married for different reasons, I rationalized. For him, maybe love was something that had to grow over time.

From that day on I vowed to make Herbert Pulitzer love me as much as I loved him. I became totally devoted to that goal, believing that once I had achieved it, I would recapture that lost, fleeting feeling of security. I came to crave that feeling as an addict craves a fix. I believed I had enough love for the two of us.

Once we returned from our honeymoon, Herbert was eager to begin work on his new boat, the *Sea Hunter*. The completed hull, then in a dry dock in St. Augustine, was ready to be varnished and painted, and Herbert wasn't about to let just anyone do it.

Except for a glimpse of the seventeenth-century Spanish fort from which the city takes its name, I didn't see much of St. Augustine's historic sights during those weeks there. We slept in a Howard Johnson's, gulped our meals in fast-food eateries, and worked in the boatyard. Although I varnished right alongside Herbert, for me the fun was helping to select the color scheme and furnishings for the custom interiors.

The *Sea Hunter* was a seventy-three-foot fishing trawler, outfitted like a luxury yacht with a fully equipped galley, spacious lounge area, two guest rooms, three lavatories, and a master stateroom which I decorated with a queen-size brass bed and mirror on the walls. There were additional quarters for the crew of three.

After St. Augustine, the boat moved down the Florida coast for further installations. We followed, driving from port to port, so that Herbert could make sure that each job was performed to his specifications and met with his approval. I only wish he had lavished that much attention on me during those first months of our marriage! I was beginning to think that the boat, not I, was destined to be the real love of his life. Yet despite his preoccupation at the time, I would later look back on those vagabond months as among our happiest together. Especially the month we spent in a tiny rented apartment in Vero Beach. There, because we were totally alone together, I truly felt like a newly married bride.

The *Sea Hunter*'s maiden voyage was a three-month cruise through the Caribbean during the summer of 1976. To ensure that there was never a shortage of hands on deck while showing off his newest toy, Herbert invited his usual gang of admirers—and more—to join the floating party.

With Herbert and his hobbies, guests are never invited along as just company Whether it's hunting or fishing, everyone has his job to do. Hunting requires you to help with stalking the game, loading the slain animal onto the jeep, and butchering the carcass. Fishing requires help shuttling the fish back to the main boat, cleaning them, and setting up the reels.

Like an admiral planning a major naval battle, Herbert mapped out the itinerary weeks in advance, making sure we hit all the best fishing grounds along the way and some of the best scuba-diving spots, too. From Palm Beach we headed for the Tortugas, down the coast of Mexico and South America as far as Colombia. While we were in Spanish Honduras, we met up with my mother, stepfather, and brother Kenny.

In the beginning of our marriage, Herbert was always very gracious about inviting my family to be his guests on the boat, at least twice a year, or at the ranch or at his home in Palm Beach. Before our troubles began and the inevitable battle lines were drawn along blood lines, I think he genuinely enjoyed their company, respected their values, and admired our closeness.

He especially got on with my stepfather. Both enjoy hunting, fishing, and taking charge of situations—although in that respect my stepfather seemed to have met his match in Herbert. The only time I ever saw my stepfather challenge Herbert, although I knew there were many times when he didn't agree with him, was during that first cruise.

A few weeks before joining us, he and Kenny took a scuba-diving certification course in preparation for the trip. The safety procedures of diving, such as checking your air tanks and equipment before entering the water and staying with a buddy, were still very fresh in their minds. Herbert, on the other hand, had been diving since he was a kid, and when it came to diving he tended to still act like one. He was so eager to be the first one in the water that it was a race to keep up with him. There was never any checking equipment with Herbert. As soon as the boat's engine had been turned off, he would pop the regulator into his mouth and he'd be gone. It didn't matter whether you were a new diver or his guest, you were either with him or you were left behind.

I could tell that Herbert's slapdash approach to scuba diving disturbed my stepfather, who is by nature a very patient, methodical man, particularly when safety is involved. But when Herbert's impatience to get going nearly caused an accident involving Kenny, who was then fifteen, my stepfather exploded.

Coming up off a reef in very rough surf, Kenny and a couple of other divers were having trouble making it back to the fishing boat. Herbert, who was safely on board, ordered the captain to start up the engine and circle around to pick up the stragglers. The six-foot swells made it difficult to see the bobbing heads of those still in the water, and the boat almost ran over Kenny.

My mother was nearly hysterical. My father almost strangled Herbert and the captain.

The climax of our supposedly relaxing cruise came a few days later on the island of Roatán when Herbert's moral principles clashed with the native business principles, sparking a tense standoff that ultimately required the intervention of the office of then Secretary of State Henry Kissinger.

It all began when we pulled into Port au Costa on the Mosquito Coast of Honduras for repairs to the *Sea Hunter*'s main generator and after throwing out our lines discovered that there was no machine shop in the seedy, desolate harbor. So without ever touching shore, we sailed on through the night to Roatán. One of the last great pirate ports, rustic Roatán is known to aficionados of funk for its beautiful diving, its lack of telephones, and its indifference to drug smuggling. We learned too late that extorting money from pleasure boats apparently ranks right along with fishing as a local industry.

Minutes after we docked and began taking on water and electric power, the customs officials showed up with the military police and demanded to see our passports. Then they insisted on *keeping* our passports. Relying on the serviceable Spanish spoken by Herbert and one of the crew, we determined that the *Sea Hunter* had been reported by the ever vigilant Port au Costa authorities for failing to clear customs during our previous stop there. Herbert argued that since technically nobody set foot on shore, it wasn't necessary for us to clear customs under international law.

Apparently there were no international lawyers in the group of officials, because they were not convinced.

Next thing we knew, two armed men dressed in mismatched uniforms climbed aboard, stationed themselves at opposite ends of the boat, and began playing with their triggers. A third made himself comfortable in the living room. They told us we were all under arrest. Their leaders had trouble explaining the alleged crime but they were very clear about demanding a $500 fine. When Herbert, who was not about to let anyone intimidate him, refused to pay it, they ordered us not to move the boat.

At first we were permitted to go ashore. Believing our captors would eventually back down if we just waited them out, Herbert suggested that we make the best of this adventure. But after three days of befriending stray goats, exploring the island's dirt roads, and diving on the nearby reefs, we began to grow restless. Because of the trouble with the boat's generator, our radio communication was cut off, along with our air conditioning, and we started to worry that we might be spending Christmas in Roatán, given up for lost. This concern was underscored on the fourth day, when we were informed that the fine was now $3,000 and ordered not to leave the boat.

Perhaps because our guards sensed trouble if my parents failed to arrive home at the designated time, they relented and freed them. As my stepfather was leaving, Herbert secretly handed him a list of names to contact, which included Secretary of State Henry Kissinger and Senator Ted Kennedy, a boyhood friend and Palm Beach neighbor. For the first time in days we felt confident that our little adventure would soon be over. In fact, it was just beginning. That evening Herbert was informed that the ante had been upped to $6,000 and he decided to attempt an Indiana Jones-style escape under cover of darkness.

"You're crazy," I said. "They'll shoot you. And if they don't kill you, they'll claim you were trying to escape arrest and lock you up forever. This is their country and that will be it."

But for Herbert this was an opportunity to prove all his Great White Hunter fantasies that was too good to pass up. His years of experience stalking game in the wilds of central Florida were finally going to be put to the test. Nothing I said was going to dissuade him.

Just before dawn, Herbert stole off the boat and into the darkness. Too scared to move, I lay in bed, listening for the sound of gunfire in the distance and praying that he would make it to the airstrip in Roatán. There he planned to catch a morning flight to Tegucigalpa, the capital of Honduras and the location of the nearest American consulate.

As morning faded into afternoon with still no word from Herbert, I became increasingly desperate. Deciding that I could no longer wait to find out if Herbert was okay, I managed to slip off the boat and into a group of tourists who had gathered on the dock to admire the *Sea Hunter*. I hoped that I could find a radio somewhere to call the States.

One man, with slicked-back hair, wearing an unbuttoned shirt and gold chains, seemed to know his way around. When I introduced myself and explained my predicament, he offered to help by having his pilot fly us in his private plane to the next city. "They have telephones over there," he said with a self-assured wink.

The flight was mercifully brief, but long enough to let me know that my new friend had more on his mind than finding a telephone. He suggested we go to a hotel to place the call. I was in no position to argue, since he spoke fluent Spanish and I barely spoke any. It was nearly dark when we arrived at the town's only hotel, where he informed me apologetically that there was only one room available. Nevertheless, I was eager to get up to the room and place my call, so I went along.

The grappling session began as soon as we entered the room. When I told him I was about to call the offices of Henry Kissinger and Ted Kennedy he backed off long enough for me to dial. After several more attempts—his on the bed and mine on the phone—I reached Herbert's business manager, Enrique, in Palm Beach. Enrique told me that Herbert was safe in Tegucigalpa. He gave me the name of the hotel where Herbert was staying.

I immediately placed a call to the hotel. After several frantic minutes of ringing his room, the operator finally located him. He was relaxing by the pool, sipping a rum and soda.

"How is everything?" he asked nonchalantly. I considered the seedy hotel room, the lecherous Lothario sprawled on the double bed, and my own sweaty, dirt-smudged dishevelment and wondered how to begin to answer.

"Terrific," I replied, collapsing in a heap on the floor. "Just terrific."

I stayed awake in the chair all night listening to the snores coming from the bed.

The next day we returned to Roatán with a representative of the American consulate, who, on order from Washington, demanded that the Honduran officials drop the charges and fines and immediately release the *Sea Hunter* and everyone on board.

The swiftness with which the U.S. State Department stepped in on Herbert's behalf in Roatán provided my first inkling of the connections the name provides. But it was many years later before I began to understand the extent of the personal power that was connected to Herbert Pulitzer.

Although it was obvious that he lived comfortably and beyond the reach of most people, Herbert was far from extravagant or lavish. Despite his boat and airplane, which were justified as tax-deductible business expenses, he eschewed the showy displays of money around which Palm Beach revolves. In a town where Rolls-Royces and Ferraris seem to outnumber taxis, Herbert drove a Ford Bronco, which was leased to one of his hotels. His house, while situated on a prime lakefront parcel of land, was a modest frame two-bedroom structure that seemed to fit Key West more than Palm Beach. And although he always seemed to come up with money for the boat or the plane or the ranch, getting him to part with $50 to buy a toaster oven took months. Persuading him to pay for covering the soiled, worn upholstered furniture in the house took years.

From the first, Herbert was always crying poor to me. When he learned shortly after I moved in with him that I had received a $7,000 check from the sale of the trailer, he asked me if he could have it, saying he needed the money for the boat. I thought he meant he wanted to borrow it because he was short that month, so I signed over the check to him without hesitation. Although I never asked him for the money, I was surprised that he never paid me back until *after* our divorce.

While Herbert lived in a resort that flaunted its reputation as a playground of the idle rich, he cultivated an earnest, hardworking image, albeit with an air of *noblesse oblige*. Published stories in the *Palm Beach Daily News*, known as the Shiny Sheet, and even *Town & Country* gushed about Herbert's entrepreneurial instincts, his "active" schedule, and how he had bootstrapped his way up from the ranks of trust-fund dilettantes to become a successful businessman in the best American tradition. Never mind that he seemed to devote more time to his hobbies than his business interests, or that his household included a cook, housekeeper, handyman, and first mate for the *Sea Hunter*; Herbert seemed to view himself as a man struggling to live within his means, a view that he succeeded in impressing upon me.

Herbert's prudence about money was matched only by his reluctance to talk about it. In seven years of marriage, he never discussed his financial affairs with me. He did, however, once ask my brother Keith's wife, Janice, to type up a statement of what he said was his annual income. This request guaranteed that the information was filtered back to me and my family. I'm not sure whether it was intended to impress us or shock us, since his reported income—

$300,000—barely kept pace with the considerable expenses of his hobbies and household.

The only time we even touched on the subject of his financial matters was when his lawyer, Irving Yellen, tried to get me to sign a prenuptial agreement a few weeks before the wedding.

We went to Yellen's office that day ostensibly to ask him to officiate at our wedding. But we had barely sat down when Yellen said to Herbert, "Even though you haven't brought it up, Herbert, as your lawyer, I really think you should consider a premarital agreement."

I was completely taken aback and insulted by the suggestion. Although I tried to appear unrattled, I was thinking that this was the end of our wedding. There is no way I would have signed such an agreement then or ever. To me it's like betting against yourselves going into the marriage. I believe that if you do that, you're never going to make it. And I really wanted to go into this marriage believing it was going to be forever.

To my great relief, Herbert shrugged off his lawyer's suggestion without hesitation. "I know," he said with a tone of finality that renewed my faith in him. "Thank you for telling me."

From the start of our relationship, my financial dependence on Herbert was complete, as was my insulation from the day-to-day household expenses, which were all handled by him. Since he didn't want me to work so that I could be free to fish, hunt, and travel with him, Herbert began giving me $1,000 a month allowance shortly after I began living with him, and he continued it throughout our marriage. "This way," he explained, "if you want to go shopping or see a movie, you don't have to ask me for the money."

While the gesture was a generous one, I was often hard pressed on a monthly basis to afford the expensive lifestyle that I had married into and felt obliged to measure up to. I became acutely aware that the Palm Beach dress code didn't cover much that was in my wash-and-wear wardrobe. A $200 pair of Gucci loafers, *de rigueur* for just kicking around, or a $300 Louis Vuitton handbag might seem extravagant, but in my insecure mind they were essential to fitting in. Evening clothes for the black-tie events we frequently attended during the winter social season became another new and costly necessity. Although Christmas invariably meant a stunning designer dress from Herbert, purchased at Martha's or one of the other chic Worth Avenue boutiques, these shops were beyond my budget. Purchasing my Christmas presents for Herbert, which I wanted to be as thoughtful as his were to me, meant spending thousands and required months of saving. One year I gave him a $6,000 hunting trip to New Mexico; another year there was one to Alaska, both paid for out of my allowance.

My marriage certainly did not provide me with the blank-check existence that was portrayed during the trial, and that many in Palm Beach seem to enjoy. Keeping up in Palm Beach frequently stretched my allowance to the limit, especially when Herbert was late with my check, which was often. I was never really sure whether Herbert derived some satisfaction from making me ask for the money or was simply experiencing the same cash-flow problems that I was, on a much larger scale, of course.

In truth, becoming Mrs. Herbert Pulitzer lifted my social standing far more than my financial one, as I cruised into my second Palm Beach social season.

When Herbert and I had been simply living together, I had often felt like a social leper. Engraved invitations addressed to Herbert often bore handwritten postscripts instructing him, "Please come alone." Herbert would just laugh and toss them into the wastebasket, but I was too hurt to see the humor and too proud to let my feelings show. Determined not to let it get me down, whenever the occasion—or hostess—permitted, I gritted my teeth and went with him.

I frankly didn't expect that I would ever be truly welcomed by the hostesses of Palm Beach, or that I would eventually strive to be one myself. But once I was Mrs. Pulitzer, it all changed. Within days of returning from our honeymoon, I was being invited to lunch at Café l'Europe, or to play doubles at the exclusive Bath & Tennis Club or Everglades Club, where Herbert was a member. Marriage meant I went from being persona non grata to being acceptable, even sought after.

During my debut in Palm Beach society the previous winter, I had been totally unprepared for the icy reception that I had received as Herbert's latest live-in girlfriend. My illegitimate standing was not helped by the fact that I was a Social Unknown with no established boarding school, club, or family credentials. I didn't even know what the Blue Book was. The only registry in which my family was listed was the Cassadaga phone book.

To show you how naïve I was about all this stuff, I once almost got suspended from the Bath & Tennis Club for bringing a Jewish girl there to hit some tennis balls with me. When I got home, Herbert was waiting to scold me.

"They called from the club," he said. He then told me it wasn't a good idea to bring Jews there. Not only didn't I realize that, I told Herbert, I didn't know my friend was Jewish.

"What's her name?" he wanted to know.

"Rosenthal," I said.

"And that didn't give you a clue?" he asked incredulously.

To tell you the truth, it didn't. I just never paid attention to things like that. I couldn't care less. I still don't care.

I was way too naïve then to understand the importance of social distinctions. In the beginning, when I was introduced to people at cocktail parties and they would ask me where I was from or what my family did, I would forthrightly explain that I was from Cassadaga, that my father had skipped town when I was five years old, and that my mother was a waitress. The conversations invariably ended there. After a barely polite pause, the listener would bolt to the other side of the room and I would be left standing alone.

Dinner parties were even worse, since I had no experience in sustained social repartee and *au courant* conversation. I was usually exiled to a table in Siberia, where I was the captive of dinner partners who talked around me. Herbert, on the other hand, was typically seated at the head table on the opposite side of the room, on the hostess's right, regaling everyone with stories of his fishing and hunting exploits.

I was uncomfortable, and sensing this, Herbert began offhandedly suggesting useful pointers for these parties. He would recommend magazine articles that he had read, saying, "You can always find an interesting topic to discuss at dinner if you're up on what's going on in the world." He also suggested that books on the *New York Times* nonfiction list provided good conversation pieces.

One night while we were reading in bed, he came up with the idea of a word quiz to help me expand my vocabulary. "It will be a great game," he said. "Every night I'll teach you five words and then I'll quiz you on them the next day." The first word he taught me was "anathema"; the second was "pundit," which became my nickname for him.

Tennis and French lessons soon followed. The results were mixed. Although my command and pronunciation of the French language never evolved much past the level of Miss Piggy, my natural athletic ability served me well on the tennis court—and off. Social tennis proved to be the one Palm Beach ritual at which I learned to excel, and tennis elbow was the one type of dinner-party conversation I found to be of almost universal interest. For all its social pretensions, I learned that Palm Beach has justifiably few intellectual ones.

Herbert became my teacher in the rituals and manners of Palm Beach society. He taught me about food—to drink champagne instead of milk, not to drink from the finger bowl, what fork to use, and never to gulp down the sorbet that was served between courses because it was just meant to clean your palate.

I could tell that Herbert was pleased and proud of my Eliza Doolittle transformation and resulting social confidence. For me, that was gratification enough. But in spite of all his refinements of me and me of myself, nothing pleased him more than my unshaved underarms.

Herbert kept telling me how sexy he thought unshaved underarms were, that it reminded him of European women, whom he found especially sexy.

I reminded him that I was taking French, adding in half-joking exasperation, "Isn't that European enough?" But he persisted. And eventually I relented. I certainly didn't want him sniffing around any European women. But I was embarrassed every time I reached for an overhead shot on the court at the Bath & Tennis or showed up for a party wearing a sleeveless dress, where real or imagined eyes were fixed on my hairy underarms.

❧[*Eight*]❧

Because the ranch provided me with my most private time with Herbert, I looked forward to our weekends there. In the hunting blind, we were far from the intrusions of the telephone, the help, and the usual crowd of friends. In the enveloping silence, the stirring of a wild turkey in the palmetto might be the only sound for hours on end. It was just us, the open sky, and the golden stretches of Florida savannah toasting in the autumn sun. We made love there, of course. We made love everywhere you could make love. But in the blind it always seemed like a special union with nature accompanied by a single thought: There was no place I'd rather be.

There was a price to pay for those moments of solitude and serenity, however. Herbert insisted that we be in the blinds before sunrise. At four in the morning in November or December, central Florida feels like Buffalo. Instead of snow on the ground, though, there are chiggers, scorpions, and rattlesnakes. But over the years I learned to get up with a smile on my face.

And I learned to pack extra socks and long johns to wear under my snowsuit, to grit my teeth for the bracing ride in the open jeep, to look for creatures before I sat in the blind.

Although we always referred to it as the ranch, the term

seemed a misnomer. "Ranch," to me, conjures up the image of a sprawling farmhouse surrounded by split-rail fences and pastureland. In fact, the rustic accommodations more resembled a campsite, similar, except for the airstrip for Herbert's plane, to the summer camps around the Finger Lakes near Cassadaga. The main structure was a double-size trailer connected to a large screened-in porch, living room and kitchen combination. I recognize now that as much as the peacefulness of the place, the reason I enjoyed our time there was that the ranch's humble familiarity probably satisfied a subconscious homesickness.

For Herbert, the pride of this modest retreat was the surrounding 24,000 acres of flat Florida scrub land that was well stocked with deer, wild turkey, wild boar, and an occasional uninvited alligator lurking in the pond. Here Herbert was king of all he surveyed. The ranch, more than any other place, was where Herbert Pulitzer wanted to be—in complete control.

Hunting with Herbert was a lesson in territorial imperative that few cared to repeat, although there were usually just enough hangers-on to round out a weekend hunting party. Until his death a few years ago, Bobby Kleiser, a great little old man, was Herbert's regular hunting partner. He owned a small gun and hunting store in West Palm Beach that his son still operates, which in Herbert's mind seemed to qualify this unassuming man as a true aficionado. Years of supplying Herbert with top-of-the-line Weatherby rifles at a favorable price and arranging hunting trips for him all over the world also had earned Kleiser a special distinction. He was one of the few people Herbert would allow to sit in his blind with him. He also helped me with many of Herbert's birthday and Christmas presents.

Typically, Herbert decided which guests were stationed at which of the ten or so blinds that were located throughout the ranch. After going days without sighting so much as a turkey, while Herbert rarely returned empty-handed, newcomers began to get the feeling that they had been purposely placed far from the areas favored by the game. A few laughed behind his back and never returned. But nobody ever complained.

A guest who was lucky enough to be at the ranch soon learned that he could not fire first if he wanted to be invited back. Herbert expected to get off the first shot and bring down the first animal.

For Herbert, the act of slaying an animal was an intensely cathartic experience. He seemed to crave that release as though it were some powerfully addictive drug. An unlucky day in the blind often made him cranky and depressed. He was so accustomed to having his own way that he expected nature to conform too.

When nature didn't, my efforts to soothe his savage heart proved unsuccessful. I would sit on the arm of his chair after dinner, put my arm along his shoulder, and lean my head toward him. But he would recoil from me. I would try to reassure him that tomorrow he was bound to get a deer or at least a boar. But he would snap, "Leave me alone."

It didn't take many of those withering rejections before I gave up trying to change his mood and prayed instead for a change in his luck.

Eventually, I came to attribute Herbert's impatience for the kill to the manner in which we hunted. Since we never stalked game at the ranch, the only real test of the hunter was marksmanship. We would sit in the blind waiting for an animal to approach one of the mechanical feeders or the corn we had laid out on the ground as bait. Once you had the animal locked in the scope of your rifle as it came to feed, the only challenge was to bring it down with one shot before it picked up your scent.

When I hunted with him away from the ranch it was always at an organized hunt—for a certain price, paid in advance, you bought lodging and the opportunity to shoot game on a private "preserve." Of course, there was no assurance that you would bag anything during your stay. But Herbert was not one to leave empty-handed. Complaining that he hadn't come all this way for nothing, he would often pay extra to stay until he had bagged something impressive enough to have mounted on his wall as a souvenir.

It was a very different way of hunting from the one I had learned as a girl from my stepfather. For him, the pursuit of his prey—whether it was a ground squirrel or a deer—and the pleasure of a walk in the woods on a crisp autumn day were as much a part of the experience as actually getting something. He judged a hunter by his cleverness and stealth as much as by his skill with a rifle. From him I learned a sense of resourcefulness, respect for wild life, and a feeling of sorrow over the kill, and we never killed more than we could eat.

The only rule hunting on the ranch seemed to have in common with the rules I had learned as a girl was not wasting what was slaughtered. Herbert was as deadly serious about putting meat on the table and in his freezer as he was about decorating his walls with mounted animal heads. We sometimes had a cook at the ranch who was excellent with wild game, but mostly Herbert would cook and I would prepare the salad and dessert.

What I enjoyed about hunting with Herbert was proving to him that I could drop the animal in one shot. Nevertheless, I was always careful not to shoot too well or too quickly, until after Herbert had bagged his animal. But one weekend during my mother's first visit to the ranch, I was overcome by eagerness to impress her with my marksmanship.

Mom and I were alone in a blind just one down from Herbert's when through my binoculars I spotted two bucks, an eight-pointer and a ten-pointer, approaching us dead on. I whispered to my mother to bend over. Then, slowly, so as not to rustle our camouflage of crackling dry palmetto, I lifted my rifle to my shoulder, braced the barrel on my unsuspecting mother's back, and aimed at the larger stag. The cross hair in the gunsight was straight on with the animal's chest as I pulled the trigger and fired. The shot rang out, felling the ten-pointer and scaring off the smaller deer, not to mention my mom.

Once she had recovered from the momentary shock of the rifle's boom, my mother was excited and proud, as always over any accomplishment of mine. And I was thrilled too—at first. But as I bent over the stag and began slitting the carcass to drain the blood, my dilemma hit me: What if Herbert got a smaller deer? Or worse, what if he got nothing?

"Oh my God," I said to my mother. "If I've gotten the bigger deer it's going to ruin Herbert's night."

Just the thought of Herbert in one of his dark moods, snapping at me, pouting all night, treating me with cold indifference, was so upsetting to me that I would do anything to avoid it. Now here I stood faced with an impending night of stony silence and rejection that I had brought on myself, especially since I really didn't want to kill animals anymore. I was only doing it for Herbert.

My mother gave me a puzzled look. "Don't be silly," she said. "Herbert is forty-five years old. He has hunted all over the world. He hunts every weekend. This is his ranch. He's not going to care that you shot a deer."

"You don't understand," I said. "He's just up the road. It's been at least fifteen minutes since the other deer ran off, and we haven't heard Herbert shoot yet. He's not going to get anything today, and I'm telling you, his night will be ruined."

Though I could tell that she did not believe me, I managed to prevail upon her to at least help me.

"We've got to hide the deer," I said, dragging the dead stag toward the palmetto by one antler while my mother pulled the other. "I'm going to cut some of the branches to hide the deer, and we're not going to tell him I shot. Remember, when he comes back for us, we're not going to tell him that I shot."

By the time Herbert drove up to our blind about an hour later, the deer was well hidden in the brush.

When he asked, "What did you get?" my throat went dry. "I didn't get anything," I lied.

"Well, I heard a shot," he said.

"It must have been poachers," I replied.

Then with a dejected, crestfallen look, he said, "I didn't get anything either."

That night we all commiserated over our mutual bad luck in the field that day and blamed poachers for scaring off the game. My mother remained uncharacteristically quiet throughout. But I joined right in, voicing my outrage at the interlopers, burying myself deeper in the lie.

The next morning when we arrived at the blind, we were greeted by buzzards circling over the spot where the deer carcass lay exposed by the scavengers. Overwhelmed by fear of Herbert's displeasure and shame at my lie, I burst into tears and confessed before Herbert could say anything. "I shot a buck yesterday," I said between sobs. "And I didn't tell you . . . because I thought you'd be angry at me. So I hid it under the palmetto."

"Don't be silly," Herbert said, smiling the condescending smile of a superior to a particularly thickheaded subordinate.

My mother, who had said exactly the same thing the day before, chimed in with "What did I tell you?"

In that moment, I felt like a small child who realizes she is powerless to persuade her parents that her fear of the dark is not unfounded, that there really is a bogeyman lurking in the closet. I did the only thing I could do: I bowed to authority and pretended to believe that there was nothing to fear—that I had just been foolish.

When I learned just after our first wedding anniversary that I was pregnant, I knew better than to expect Herbert to be ecstatic like me. Still, I was hoping that the prospect of becoming a father again would ignite a spark of enthusiasm, if for no other reason than that it testified to his virility.

I waited until he arrived home that night to tell him the news. I had his usual drink, specially imported Matusalem rum and soda, waiting.

"Guess what?" I said as he walked through the door.

"You're pregnant," he replied flatly.

Well, I told myself, shrugging it off, I guess it's not as exciting the fourth time around.

The prospect of becoming a mother at age twenty-seven filled me with enough happy anticipation to override Herbert's indifference. The time now seemed right. I felt that my life was settled, content, secure, and happy beyond anything I might have dreamed. I wanted to share it with a baby, Herbert's baby.

At first Herbert wanted no part of natural childbirth, deciding names, purchasing the layette, or any of the other shared rituals of expectant parents. More out of necessity and the desire to protect his domain from the encroaching nuisances posed by a baby, he decided that the addition to our family warranted an addition to the house. Within days, plans were drawn up for a separate, self-contained nursery wing to accommodate the baby and nanny, and to ensure that neither intruded on his peace and privacy.

But six months into my pregnancy, when I learned that I was going to have twins, Herbert was the first to phone everyone with the news. From that day on, his paternal pride seemed to swell right along with my considerable girth.

He doted on me, coached me through Lamaze class, and on the August Sunday morning when I went into labor a month before my due date, he rushed me to Good Samaritan Hospital.

I started right into hard labor, which lasted for eight hours. The contractions were so close together and so intense that it was impossible for me to think about breathing, timing the contractions, or any of the other Lamaze techniques we had practiced so faithfully. Having Herbert there with me, urging me on and looking like a veteran

Lamaze coach in his scrub suit and surgical cap, was the only thing that got me through it.

I kept begging the doctors for a shot—anything—for the pain, and they kept insisting that they couldn't risk it. The babies, they said, were too premature and undoubtedly too small, since I had gained only twenty-two pounds. Further complicating matters, the first baby, Zac, was breach, and Mac's head was slamming down on top of his. Finally, because the doctors were concerned about the effect on Zac, they gave me a shot of Pitocin to induce the labor.

After half an hour of sheer hell for me and presumably no fun for him either, Zac popped out without so much as a whimper, followed two minutes later by Mac, who was yelling at the top of his tiny lungs. They weighed in respectively at five pounds fourteen ounces and six pounds —a far cry from the underweight preemies the doctors had predicted.

Before I could hold Zac or even get a good look at him, they whisked him away to the intensive care nursery. They told me that they couldn't get Zac to cry and that they were worried about brain damage. He was what they called a "depressed baby." The impact of the words was more wrenching than any contraction. I was still reeling from the news when the nurse placed Mac in my arms. As I held him for the first time, I didn't know whether to be happy or afraid, whether thanking God for one perfect, healthy son was conceding that the other twin was not. This awful emotional ambiguity stayed with me for the next three days as Zac lay in the intensive care nursery in an oxygen tent, his tiny head connected by electrodes to a battery of machines, while Mac snuggled safe and well in my arms.

By the time they brought Zac to me on the third day, his first day of breathing on his own, I had braced myself for the worst. He had lost weight and seemed so much weaker and more vulnerable than his brother. Herbert, who stayed by my side during those uncertain days, even sleeping on a cot in my room at night, never lost hope that Zac would be all right. This was very comforting, and I was grateful to him.

The next day, just before I was scheduled to leave the hospital, we learned that the tests had determined there was absolutely no brain damage. Although Zac had been badly traumatized by the difficult birth, the doctors assured us that he would soon catch up with his brother in weight and stamina, which he did.

It was the first moment since I had been wheeled into the labor room four days earlier that I actually felt a sense of total elation. My ordeal was over, and I was now a very happy new mother. Both my babies were fine. I didn't realize that I was trading one trial for another.

From my first day home with the twins, I unsuspectingly acquired a third child—Herbert. I didn't notice the change in him until a couple of days after the babies and I were home. I was so caught up with the exhaustion of the babies' schedule and the excitement of friends stopping by to see them that I didn't pick up on the fact that Herbert was feeling upstaged. I attributed his lack of interest in feeding or holding his sons to having done it all three times before. Who could blame him, I rationalized, for wanting no part of it this time around. When he grumbled about my getting up in the middle of the night to help the nanny with the feedings, I chalked it up to his general impatience with the disruptions caused by children.

The real reason behind Herbert's indifference toward fatherhood finally became clear to me one evening as he strolled through the door looking happier than I had seen him in days. "Good news," he said. "We're leaving for a dude ranch in Colorado next week."

At first I thought he was joking. The babies were only two weeks old. He must have sensed it, because he hastened to add: "We need to get away and spend some time together. Just the two of us."

After all the times that I had suggested getting away together with no success, his timing now seemed intended as a test more than as a romantic holiday. I remembered my agreement not to let children interfere with my willingness to travel with him. I had never imagined that he would hold me to it just days after giving birth.

But as much as I wanted to stay home with my babies, I felt a duty to Herbert as my husband to keep my promise to him. That September week at the dude ranch turned out to be one of our most romantic trips, since most of our other travels usually revolved around Herbert's business meetings or hobbies. Even the daily horseback rides and hikes, which I had been anticipating with considerable trepidation, proved enjoyable. The Colorado canyons were ablaze with fall colors, and I was mercifully provided with a gentle horse.

I sensed Herbert tenderly reaching out to me in a way he never had before. It was almost as though he was afraid of losing me, and needed to be reassured that he was and would remain the number-one person in my life.

During that week that we were alone together, when I was thousands of miles from my babies, I began to feel the pull of motherhood. Until then, Herbert had been the single focus of my life, but within days of my return home, I sensed the inevitable conflict between my roles as wife and mother, a conflict that was exacerbated by my growing frustration with the overbearing nanny whom Herbert had hired.

Nanny Number One was from the old school that believed any deviation from the Schedule was tantamount to spoiling babies. After more than twenty years of rearing children in some of Palm Beach's most privileged families, she was confident that nobody knew better than she when it came to the care and feeding of infants. Since I had no previous experience with either nannies or babies myself, I felt reassured by her glowing recommendations and considerable experience—at first.

But it soon became clear that my maternal instincts clashed with her professional efficiency. If I picked up the babies just to cuddle or play with them, she made me feel that I was an intruder in the nursery. If I suggested that she should have the bottles ready and waiting before they awoke, rather than having them crying with hunger while she prepared their next feeding, she acted as though my suggestion was presumptuous. Still, I felt too insecure in my own judgment, as I think she sensed, to insist that she do things my way. I had trouble giving orders to an older person. As a matter of fact, I even had to sneak into the nursery each day to watch Mac and Zac sleeping.

I knew better than to try to discuss my problems with the nanny with Herbert. He wanted no part of babies or the problems connected with them. When he came home, he wanted them out of sight and out of mind. It was all I could do just to get him to hold them for a few minutes each day in the naïve hope of fostering some fatherly bonding.

After two months, my frustration with the nanny exploded one afternoon when she came home unexpectedly and "caught" me holding Mac and Zac to show them to my friend Chris Seaton. "This is their nap time," she said, leaving no doubt from the tone of her voice that her statement was intended as a rebuke to me.

As far as I was concerned, it was the last straw for her. "These are *my* children," I told her, my voice rising with anger. "Don't you ever tell me again when I can and cannot pick up my children."

My obvious hostility toward her stemmed from the fact that I resented her because I wanted to be taking care of my own babies. But it didn't seem to daunt her. "Mrs. Pulitzer, you seem to think you know so much about babies," she said acidly, "when in fact you know nothing."

"I know one thing," I said. "I want you out. Pack your things now."

Whatever momentary satisfaction I derived from telling her off and firing her turned quickly to panic when I realized that I was now, in fact, completely in charge of two infants without any prospects for help on the horizon. Handling Mac and Zac would be the easy part; handling Herbert I wasn't so sure about.

When he arrived home that night, the babies were fuss-ing uncontrollably and I was frantically scurrying between their bassinettes, trying everything I could to calm them.

I couldn't have invented a homecoming that would be better calculated to irritate Herbert. The look on his face confirmed that.

"Where is the nanny?" he demanded.

Swallowing hard, I told him, "I fired her."

"You fired her?" The words rolled off his tongue slowly, so as to drive home the seriousness of my breach of his authority. "Well, now it's all up to you," he said, shaking his finger at me. "*You* find a nanny. But *you* find her before we leave for Amsterdam in ten days."

I did find a nanny. In fact, I found *two* nannies—which came back to haunt me at the divorce trial.

I hired a terrific young girl named Robin. She had no real professional experience, but I was tired of the professionals. And besides, Robin was great with the boys. The only problem was that Robin wasn't used to the demanding schedule of a real nanny, six or even seven days a week. Feeling a little sorry for her, I frequently used to give her an extra night or two—or an extra day or two—off, so she could spend more time with her boyfriend.

Around this time, my cousin Sandy—Sandra Andreasen—came to stay with us for a few weeks. She loved Mac and Zac, and she also became very friendly with Robin. The weeks turned into months and, in effect, Sandy became the second nanny. I thought it was the perfect setup. They each worked three and a half days a week, and they really fit into our life-style much better than a stuffy, professional Palm Beach nanny. They were fun to have around. And I saved us money. The two girls cost us a total of $125 per week, plus room and board. The professional nanny got $275 per week.

As torn as I felt between Herbert and the children, as demanding as he could sometimes be of my time and attention, I was flattered by his jealousy. More than any words of endearment or expensive gifts, this unspoken need for reassurance must be the proof that I needed of his love. I knew, even if he didn't fully appreciate it, how much he depended on me. I was very conscious of the role that I played in his life. My job was to provide the peace and contentment that he was always saying he needed more of. I was his port in the storm. I was the one who was there for him, from morning till night, rejoicing in his smallest successes, sympathizing with his smallest setbacks and problems, building up his confidence, accepting him and his actions no matter how selfish or spoiled, fulfilling his desires no matter how difficult or demanding.

In the sense of providing emotional sustenance and strength, I was a mother with my husband as much as with my children. When I put my arms around him, I know that Herbert felt as secure and loved as Mac and Zac did when I hugged them. I could actually see it in Herbert's face. After a few hours with me, he looked rejuvenated, relaxed, with a sincerely happy smile on his face. At this time in our life together, I knew that I was giving him something that was important, something that I sensed he had never had before in his life—a closeness, an unqualified acceptance, a complete understanding.

And in giving it, I regained that sense of being protected and of belonging that I had first experienced so briefly on our wedding day. For the first time in my life, I felt truly *connected* to someone, as if there were an invisible emotional cord binding us. It was a total mental and physical upliftment.

At times when we were together, I felt that we almost gave off a glow. We were very strong as a couple, and I was always so proud to be with him. People used to say to us, "You two look so happy. I wish my marriage could be like yours."

And yet, as secure and needed and beloved as I believed myself to be, I was acutely aware that my security depended on keeping Herbert happy and content, in making sure the sex was good and that everything went his way. Each day was a new test of pleasing Herbert and keeping the hassles at bay.

It was also a test of keeping other women at bay. Hardly a day passed without some former girlfriend phoning, some new acquaintance sidling up to him at a cocktail party or at the bar at Doherty's, or anywhere. Maintaining my place in his life meant maintaining my place at his side, which is another reason why I was eager to travel with him.

But the one threat I felt helpless to overcome was Liza's relationship with her father. At the trial, I later testified that "Liza told me she was always going to be number one in his life"—although Liza testified that she never said any such thing. But the way I distinctly remember it, during a party a few months after Herbert and I were married, Liza turned to me when we were briefly alone in the bathroom and said: "I feel sorry for you, Rox. It's so obvious how much you love Dadz and how he's number one in your life. But you'll never be number one in his. You're always going to have to settle for number two, because if I weren't his daughter, he would have married me."

I was, of course, completely flabbergasted. I just stood there too dumbstruck to utter a word, much less a comeback, as Liza flashed me a mocking smile and walked away.

Was Liza's exulting just the idle boast of a foolish, spoiled, confused young woman? Or was she a rival declaring her supreme confidence in a victory already won?

I told myself that we were inevitably locked in the same subliminal rivalry for Herbert's affection and attention as he was with Mac and Zac for mine. But I was never completely able to convince myself. When I looked at Liza, I didn't think *stepdaughter*, I thought *threat*.

❦ [*Nine*] ❧

Long before I met Jacquie Kimberly, during the summer of 1976, I had heard about her. The Kimberlys were one of Palm Beach's most talked-about couples, a dubious distinction which I later learned they carefully cultivated. Their forty-four-year age difference, his and her Ferraris, and extravagant life-style stood out even in a town devoted to flaunting wealth and May-December marriages.

That summer, rumors swirled *around* the Kimberlys, fueled when Jim sued Jacquie for divorce in 1975 and then dropped the case ten months later after they agreed to stay together.

Although Jacquie, a former receptionist who was then twenty-five, and Jim, the sixty-nine-year-old playboy grandson of the founder of the Kimberly-Clark paper products fortune, had reconciled, they had a long way to go in convincing Palm Beach that theirs was a marriage made in heaven and destined to continue happily ever after.

Probably to allay suspicions that their marriage was shaky, Jim staged a glittering formal birthday dinner party for Jacquie in June 1976, complete with society photographers, at their chateau-style mansion on El Vedado Lane. Jim was one of Herbert's closest friends, and Herbert was anxious to introduce me. When he brought Jacquie over to meet me, she intimidated me a little. Although she spoke in a breathy, girlish voice and exuded a sense of wide-eyed vulnerability that was underscored by her tiny ninety-pound frame, her sophistication and poise belied her youth.

When she called to invite me to lunch the next day, I was surprised and flattered, since it was the first such invitation I had received in Palm Beach. But I was even more startled to find that despite her perfect coiffure and her couturier fashions, Jacquie was self-effacing, irreverent, and a lot of fun.

She was already seated at her usual table in the orchid-filled front room of the very chic Petite Marmite when I arrived for lunch. Her opening remark immediately put me at ease and made me realize we had more in common than our ages.

"Well, did they roll out the red carpet for you in Palm Beach like they did for me?" she asked with a sarcastic laugh.

Over the next couple of hours, our friendship was forged by shared stories of the snubs we had suffered as Palm Beach parvenues and by a $100 bottle of Dom Pérignon champagne, which became our regular lunchtime drink.

"I like you a lot and I want to be your friend," she said at the end of lunch. "But I just want to warn you about something. Being my friend means that you're going to end up with a reputation."

I assured her that the risk seemed a small one to take for the sake of friendship.

That was the only time Jacquie ever raised the subject. I figured that her bringing it up was her way of letting me know that she wasn't bothered by the gossip about her and perhaps to test whether I was.

For all her worldliness and sophistication, I think deep down Jacquie was as eager as I for a close friend and confidante her own age with whom she could just be herself. And that was really the essence of our relationship. We were like two high school kids together, consulting on the telephone over what I would wear to parties, sitting around the swimming pool eating potato chips, drinking Cokes, and gossiping, or listening to blaring rock music in her enormous dressing room.

I was awed and fascinated by her. I loved going through her room-size closets, which contained hundreds of designer dresses and gowns and accessories all carefully zippered in plastic and arranged in color-coordinated order. I could listen for hours to her talk about her travels all over the world. And when it came to men, Jacquie had *many* admirers.

While the attraction between Jacquie and Jim was puzzling to many, I always felt that the similarity in their personalities more than made up for the difference in their ages. I have never met two people who possessed a greater sense of publicity or practiced a greater degree of conspicuous consumption. "Living well is the best revenge" was their credo. They did everything—entertaining, traveling, dressing, choosing their hobbies—with a flashy flourish that frequently bordered on excess. They were the couple Herbert and I saw the most during our marriage.

When the four of us were in London, staying at the same hotel, Jacquie and Jim brought twenty-one pieces of Louis Vuitton luggage, including two steamer trunks. Jim hired a convoy of Daimlers just to carry their bags from the airport to the hotel. Herbert and I each brought two carry-ons.

Jacquie's steamer trunks, I discovered while watching her unpack, were full of boxes of Kleenex and rolls of Kimberly-Clark toilet tissue.

"Jim won't use anyone else's toilet tissue," she explained, with no indication she found this the least bit eccentric.

Jacquie deserves a lot of credit for my becoming a "Palm Beach girl." She had me flying to New York for haircuts at the trendy salon of Clive Summers on Fifth Avenue; she taught me to have a manicurist and hairdresser from Domani come to the house before a party; she directed me to Georgette Klinger's for facials, to Elizabeth Arden's for massages.

As Herbert had indicated, Jacquie was an excellent hostess. She taught me to have my invitations printed at Cordially Yours, to use *only* Frank Dale as a caterer, and how to arrange my table settings for parties. When I ran out of anything—silver, china, table linen—Jacquie would send her maid over with the anything.

Despite the image of fabulous wealth—or more than likely because of it—Jim Kimberly's fortune was rapidly diminishing.

Over the years, he had been forced to sell his country estate on Maryland's Eastern Shore; his fleet of yachts, except for a thirty-two-foot motorboat; his prized home, El Vedado; and his lakefront house. The house was purchased by Jordan's King Hussein, a close friend, who generously permitted the Kimberlys to use it when he was away.

Notwithstanding his dwindling inherited fortune and notoriety as a playboy, Jim preferred to think of himself as a retired executive. He kept an office and staff in the Poinciana Plaza, a sort of world headquarters for Kimberly Enterprises, where seven wall clocks marked the time in cities from Nairobi to Honolulu to Palm Beach. But the only investment I ever heard him discuss was his venture into marketing National Football League team medallions for use as bumper stickers, paperweights, and wall plaques. I never quite understood the NFL-Nairobi connection. When I asked Jacquie what Jim did at the office, she told me that he mainly made lunch dates.

Nevertheless, Jim professed a firm belief in the work ethic. "Working was always number one; it always has been with me," he frequently insisted. His idea of work, however, didn't exactly require rolling up his shirt sleeves. He headed the Palm Beach chapter of Chevaliers du Tastevin, a wine-tasting society. He served as Commissioner of the Port of Palm Beach, an obscure $2,400-a-year elected post which he spent $10,000 campaigning for. He acted as the honorary consul of Jordan, a position that carried more prestige than power.

Besides the right to a special foreign consul license plate for his Ferrari, the Jordanian "job" gave him the opportunity to play the role of self-appointed spokesman for King Hussein, whenever the king was in Palm Beach. I always thought that it was this role that Jim savored most. Thanks to him, Hussein's vacations in Palm Beach made daily front-page news in the local papers, particularly during a 1977 visit when the monarch was reported to be romancing a twenty-three-year-old Disney World tour guide named Honey Rex, three months after his wife, Queen Alia, had died in a helicopter crash. Jim was kept busy for days volunteering denials of the alleged romance as "nothing more than the media's attempt to make something out of nothing."

Jacquie and Jim were also always in the news—constantly being quoted, photographed, and interviewed. With his striking silver hair and silk ascots, Jim's flamboyance was legendary and prompted some to dub him Gentleman Jim and the Grey Fox. He reveled in the latter moniker. He christened his Maryland estate Grey Fox Farm. He kept his yachts, *Grey Fox*, *Sly Fox*, and *Kit Fox*, tied up at the Fox Dock behind the Fox's Lair.

But I always thought that the most egregious example of Jim's flamboyance was the small gold hoop that he wore in his right earlobe, long before such adornments were common among men, as they are today. When asked about the earring, which naturally drew stares and questions from curious acquaintances, he often merely said his reason for wearing it was a private matter, which of course only intrigued people even more.

For Jim, privacy and publicity were not mutually exclusive. However, I once read a story about Jim's earring in the *Palm Beach Daily News*. According to the story, the earring was a talisman awarded to Jim and four of his fishing buddies by a Bahamian juju mama to ward off evil spirits. The men made a pact among themselves that anyone who removed his gold ring had to pay the others $1,000.

Jacquie shared Jim's love of publicity. Both their lives were chronicled in meticulously kept scrapbooks and diaries containing newsclips about Jacquie's love of sky diving, the travails of hosting King Hussein and having to endure having a hundred Secret Service men hanging around their house, and Jim's various exploits in sport fishing and sports-car racing.

Jim and Jacquie loved to entertain lavishly. Not only did they have monarchs such as King Hussein and King Juan Carlos of Spain, but also many Hollywood figures such as Sammy Davis, Jr., and Wayne Newton.

Although Jacquie's size-four wardrobe rivaled that of Imelda Marcos, she shopped for clothes as regularly as most people shop for groceries. She was always stopping off at some chic Worth Avenue boutique after lunch and rarely left a store without charging something. Her taste was top-dollar: Yves St. Laurent, Valentino, Hermès. An impulse purchase could be anything from a $200 belt to a $10,000 evening gown, and she was always urging me to follow suit. "Come on, Roxie, buy it," she would tempt me. "You're Mrs. Pulitzer. You can charge it."

Her free spending of Jim's money always made me nervous. Except for my allowance, I never felt comfortable spending Herbert's money and never had the opportunity to. But Jacquie seemed to feel that the prenuptial agreement she had signed before marrying Jim, which limited her to $18,000 a year in alimony for each year of marriage, justified her exorbitance.

"There's no guarantee that I would get any alimony," she told me. "Jim's other two wives didn't get a dime." She said that her clothes and her car were her only possessions, since everything else was in Jim's name.

Even though she seemed to spend the most when she and Jim were fighting, Jacquie always managed to get away with her prodigal purchases. But one afternoon when she rang up several thousand dollars on two Valentino gowns, I was sure she had exceeded the limit. That was the last time I underestimated the power of Jacquie's considerable charm, however, and I came to see that she had refined wrapping Jim around her finger to a regular ritual. That evening, in preparation for his homecoming, I watched as she prepared all his favorite hors d'oeuvres, setting them out on little silver trays, mixed a tall pitcher of martinis, and donned the more alluring of the two new dresses to model it for Jim. The other gown she hung from the living-room chandelier. Bewitchingly beautiful in her gown, Jacquie greeted him when he walked in that night with a spellbinding look of adoration that clearly left him enchanted. And that was *before* Jim got into the martinis. I was so nervous I couldn't wait to leave; however, the next day Jacquie told me that Jim had loved the dresses and that he had agreed to let her keep them both.

Jim was not always so easygoing. He is the typical Leo. His suspicions of Jacquie frequently turned into jealous rages. She told me that one night when he woke up and she was gone, he came looking for her with one of the loaded Magnums that he kept in his bedroom. In their own divorce trial in early 1986, Jacquie testified that this was the reason she was divorcing him. Jim flatly denied the allegations.

Jacquie lived life on the edge, and I think that her untamed recklessness was the very quality that Jim loved most about her. Her full-tilt approach to life was certainly one of the traits that I most prized in her as a friend.

But she also had a melancholy side that she kept hidden behind a gay facade. Jacquie just wasn't one to easily open up to people.

Although I felt I probably knew her better than anyone, she rarely confided much about herself even to me. She rarely spoke of her family, or her childhood, for example. Her background was sketchy. She told me that she grew up in Europe, where her father was an investment counselor, and that she never received a high school diploma because she was tutored at home by her parents.

Over the years, I pieced together bits of Jacquie's past.

She was born Roberta Jacqueline Tresize, in Pasadena, California. When Jacquie was sixteen and was working as a part-time receptionist at an art gallery on Worth Avenue, she met Jim, sixty, and began dating him. Beginning when she was seventeen, they lived together on and off during the two years before their marriage in 1969.

Jacquie never discussed with me all of her reasons for marrying Jim Kimberly, but I always sensed that she understood what she was doing in bartering her youth and beauty for a shot at fame and fortune. I also believe she had a genuine affection and a strong love for Jim, in her own way, as much as any teenage wife is capable of loving a husband old enough to be her grandfather. More than a mate, she was an adoring, starry-eyed keeper of the flickering flame of Jim Kimberly's aging virility. She was always fluffing up his ego, telling people while he listened how exciting Jim was. He was a great hunter, a trailblazer in sports-car racing before the professionals took over, a swashbuckling eligible man about Palm Beach.

Jim also loved Jacquie very much. He was very generous and very protective of her. I was impressed by the way he treated her and the respect he showed for her in public.

Jim was always very thoughtful and gracious with me, too. He would often make me my favorite dessert: blueberries in creme caramel. And once he even hired a private plane to take me to Tampa to see a girlfriend for the afternoon; he stocked it with Perrier-Jouët rosé champagne and beluga caviar.

No doubt in the beginning it must have seemed very glamorous to Jacquie to be chatelaine of Jim's mansions, dressing up in the latest Paris fashions, dashing from sky-diving lessons to jet-set parties. But relinquishing one's youth is a terrible price to pay for the privileges of wealth. In time I think Jacquie came to feel cheated and imprisoned by her life and marriage.

Jacquie's moment of truth came when she became friendly with one of her sky-diving instructors, a friendship that ended before I met her. When it ended, Jacquie confided to me years later, she was devastated and went into a deep depression. She showed me several letters and poems that she had written at the time, all about death and dying, a side of Jacquie I had never seen. I remember phrases about the "black engulfing" her and being able to be free "from the pain of this earth."

Jim became worried about Jacquie's friendship with the instructor. His concern increased after one of the servants found a valid airline ticket issued to Jacquie's instructor in Jacquie's car and told Jim's secretary about it. That sparked an inquisition of the rest of the household. Jim filed for divorce. Jacquie fought it and denied under oath that she had been intimate with the instructor. Eventually, Jim relented and dropped the case.

The harsh reality of the divorce, the prospect of losing Jim and her way of life had to be a sobering one for Jacquie. In the end, he was all she really had. And he cared for her in his own way, enough anyway to forgive her and take her back.

This time, instead of bartering her youth and beauty, I believe she may have lost a bit of her soul. And I came to believe that her seemingly carefree, reckless adventurousness really was propelled by a desperate need to fill an emotional void. In her darkest moments, she told me that she felt that her life was meaningless and empty.

There were times when she would lock herself in her dressing room for days. Jim would call and ask me to come over and try to get her to come out, because nobody even knew if she was alive in there. There were times when she wouldn't eat for days on end and her weight would slip dangerously to the point of emaciation.

She was never going to have any children. When Jim died, she'd be left all alone with only a fraction of the wealth she was used to.

What was there to look forward to?

With Jacquie, there was only one thing: adventure.

{[Ten]}

When it comes to being hip or on the cutting edge of social trends, I've always considered myself hopelessly out of step. While the rest of my generation was marching against the Vietnam War, I was marching down the aisle. I always felt that romance was a far greater turn-on than alcohol or drugs and that nothing elevated mind and spirit more than being in love.

So when I was first offered cocaine at Palm Beach parties during the Christmas holiday season of 1978, I wasn't particularly eager to try it. I thought cocaine was dangerous and very similar to heroin.

Then, during a party at our house, everybody seemed to be streaming in and out of my bathroom.

"You've got to try this," someone urged me, holding up a little brown bottle of cocaine with a tiny silver spoon dangling from it.

"No thanks," I replied, explaining that I was already feeling light-headed enough from champagne.

"It's not like that," one guest insisted. "It will sober you up." I was hesitant and went to fetch Herbert.

Someone else poured a dab of white powder onto the little spoon and showed us how to snort it. I took one sniff and felt . . . absolutely nothing.

"Didn't you like it? Wasn't it great?" another guest asked.

"Well, not really," I said, wondering what all the fuss was about.

The others urged Herbert and me to go dancing with them, but we were tired and stayed home.

At the trial, by the way, both Herbert and Liza testified that Herbert did not use cocaine this night. Liza testified that Herbert was in bed while all this was going on. I testified that they both were present—and I stand by my story.

I didn't think anything more about the experience until a few weeks later when we went skiing in Aspen, where there seemed to be as much snow indoors as on the slopes and I suddenly found myself confronted by a form of etiquette not covered in my Emily Post book: the elaborate ritual of social tooting.

The night of my twenty-eighth birthday, Herbert threw a lovely dinner party for me at one of Aspen's most elegant restaurants. A few couples whom we knew from Palm Beach were there, as well as some of their friends. The champagne was flowing and we were all ordering dessert when a waiter appeared at the table with a tea-service-size silver tray.

On the tray, laid out like icing on a cake to spell "Happy Birthday Rox," were maybe fifty lines of cocaine—a gift, I learned later, from one of the guests.

As everyone began singing "Happy Birthday," all I could think was: My God! What am I supposed to do with this? It was like seeing a finger bowl for the first time and wondering whether or not to drink it. Was the whole tray supposed to be for me, or was I supposed to pass it? Where was the little spoon? And what were those two little silver straws on the tray supposed to be for?

I didn't have a clue where to start or how, and I was too embarrassed to ask. So I stood up from the table and excused myself to go to the bathroom. Everyone laughed, I guess because they thought I intended to take the whole tray into the bathroom for myself. I laughed along, knowing that I was ignorant enough about cocaine etiquette to almost do it.

Fortunately, several people went ahead without me, while I peeked through a crack in the ladies'-room door. I saw someone pick up one of the silver straws, hold it to his nostril, and do one line. Then he changed hands and nostrils and did another line. Then he passed the tray.

Once I understood that that was how you did it, I breezed back to the table and snorted my first line . . . and my second. By the time we left the restaurant, the tray had been passed four or five times.

But it wasn't until an hour or so later, after we had moved on to a local disco called the Paragon, that I felt the effects of cocaine. Although I had been drinking champagne all night, which normally makes me woozy after a couple of glasses, I was clear-headed, very awake, and very up. I realized that it had to be the cocaine.

Over the next month in Aspen, at night we attended a lot of parties thrown by George Hamilton, Obie Obolensky, and other Aspen regulars. Every day I was busy teaching Mac and Zac how to ski.

During that month I also helped teach Herbert to ski. Although he testified at the trial that he only used the drug once during this period, I recall that we actually tried cocaine several more times, and each time I found it had the same effect. Suddenly, at the point in the evening where I would normally be ready to go home and crash, I felt this rush, as if I had just had eight hours of sleep and could dance and party all night. I liked the idea that with cocaine I could stay up until three or four in the morning and still be lucid, wide-awake, and in what I thought was control.

Nevertheless, I was still concerned that there might be some downside to the drug that I hadn't yet experienced or heard about. I had always equated drugs with addiction. And I'm enough of a health freak to be uncomfortable with putting any harmful substances into my body, which is why I never tried psychedelics or speed, and don't even like to take aspirin.

So after I returned to Palm Beach, I started asking around about the possible dangers of cocaine, which was turning up at more and more parties and even in restaurants and night spots. People would stand at the bar and snort lines in front of everyone. Butlers would serve silver trays of the stuff garnished with marijuana. Social tooting was a new way of showing off how hip and avant-garde you were. Everyone was doing it, and you had to go out of your way to avoid the stuff. Cocaine had replaced Dom Pérignon as the new status symbol for everyone from trust-fund babies to doctors, lawyers, bankers, realtors.

Some said it was an aphrodisiac—but frankly, it never had that effect on me. Making love was not what I wanted to do when I was high. I just wanted to talk and dance and party. Others said it was just another form of speed, only without the edginess usually associated with uppers. All in all, the party line on the party drug in those days was that cocaine was no more dangerous than alcohol or marijuana.

In fact, the only side effect I had noticed was a welcome one. It made me lose weight. During a night out with cocaine, I could skip my dinner without regret.

When the Palm Beach party season began to wind down, as it always does in March, and fishing season began, so did our use of cocaine. We never did cocaine on the boat or at the ranch. It just wasn't a part of our private life—that revolved around Herbert's hobbies and business trips to his hotels. And for the most part, we lived a private life. The Palm Beach night life was never the all-consuming preoccupation for us that it is for so many there, or that it was portrayed to be for us during the trial.

Cocaine, for both of us, was something we identified with going out on the Palm Beach social scene. And eventually, it became just as indispensable to a night of partying as donning evening clothes. And that's when the problems started. There were parties, and then there were parties.

For all the glamour and opulence associated with Palm Beach soirées, they are typically stuffy, boring affairs that are far more work than fun, which is why all the aging, jewel-encrusted society matrons you see photographed at these events are always smiling through clenched teeth. I used to think that if it weren't for the champagne and the caviar and culinary concoctions, nobody would even bother to attend them, until I realized I was usually the only one eating.

But then I came to understand that the purpose of these parties is not relaxation or even enjoyment, but garnering mentions and preferably photos in the Shiny Sheet and the society pages. These elaborate social affairs are really opportunities for the rich and powerful to promote themselves under the guise of philanthropic fund-raising and/or business entertainment—and to thus become even richer and more powerful. In the end, those lavish, tax-deductible social productions with their endless courses accompanied by vintage wines and served by bevies of black-tied waiters probably cost their rich hosts less than your Saturday-night suburban dinner party.

Occasionally, to lighten up the evening for Herbert, I would unobtrusively flash my gown at him and be rewarded with a secret smile.

Even the chic little dinners for "just a few of our close friends" have very little warmth and intimacy. Palm Beach hosts and hostesses don't fling the doors open to their Addison Mizner mansions and ersatz Roman villas just for the hell of it, or even to be neighborly. They do it to show off their important art collections, their faux marbre walls, their antique furnishings, their new French chef.

Take, for example, the late Patrick Lannon, the former chairman of the board of ITT, who was probably the best-known collector of museum-quality contemporary art in Palm Beach. His collection and the striking contemporary oceanfront home he had built to house it had been featured in numerous fashionable shelter magazines, the ultimate tribute of recognition. Nevertheless, every time I was there for dinner, Lannon would lead his guests on yet another tour of his collection, never tiring of discussing in detail the history of each piece and how he had acquired it, while stomachs growled and eyes shifted hungrily in anticipation of dinner.

Because Patrick was a kind man and genuinely passionate about art, his guests dutifully permitted him those long curatorial cocktail sessions.

One night, he took me aside for a detour *tour à deux* to a room containing his private collection of pornography. Mounted on the red walls like works of art were leather dominatrix outfits complete with whips, special love chains and handcuffs, erotic paintings and sculptures, what appeared to be an authentic medieval chastity belt—you name it.

I didn't know what to make of it all, especially since Patrick was then in his seventies. Groping for the polite response to this honorary tour, I feigned obliging interest, as he, ever the connoisseur, explained the origins and special appeal of each piece, never hinting that his interest was anything but scholarly.

Some of the longest dinners I ever sat through were at the home of Guilford and Jane Dudley. Not because the Dudleys weren't gracious or accomplished hosts. On the contrary, this politically well-connected couple probably knew more about entertaining in fine style than anyone, since Guilford had served as ambassador to Denmark under Richard Nixon. The reason I came to dread their dinners was that, whether inadvertently or intentionally, I was always seated next to Alfred Bloomingdale, the aging multimillionaire founder of Diners Club and longtime contributor to Ronald Reagan's campaigns.

Bloomingdale, you may recall, scandalized the Reagan White House a few years back when his young ex-mistress, Vicky Morgan, threatened to reveal sadomasochistic videotapes of, among other things, her riding him pony-style.

The times I sat next to him at dinner the poor old dear was practically catatonic. He sat there propped up in his chair like a mummy before nodding off in his soup. The kinky sex habits were hard to imagine.

Eventually, I came to feel that the more coveted the

invitation, the more boring the evening. And though I don't mean to blame others for my drug abuse, more and more those glamorous Palm Beach nights with such sparklers as Alfred Bloomingdale created a need for some diversion to get me through to the dessert course. After a couple of hours of lighthearted conversation on the latest junk-bond issues or heated speculation about who would be named to replace so-and-so on the board of such-and-such or yet another mellow rendition of a Beatles tune by the Neal Smith Band, I was ready to hit the ladies' room, puh-lease!

I had no inkling that cocaine was already weaving its subtle web into our lives. If there ever was a danger signal deep in my heart, I did not heed it. I was letting myself be lured ever so unwittingly onto a path that would eventually lead only to destruction and would contribute to shattering my marriage and carefree happiness forever. I saw no signs, heard no secret alarm bells, so I just let the good times roll. The judge, in his Final Judgment, decided that "for a time, the husband turned to cocaine, as a crutch, to give him the stamina to keep pace with his younger, energetic wife." Well, as the younger, energetic wife, as near as I could tell Herbert seemed to enjoy the drug as much as I did, and in my mind, this made everything just fine. I always trusted his judgment in all the things we did together.

Little did I know then that one of cocaine's most hidden and deadly effects is that the users of this drug remain blind to its ever-increasing hold on them.

Judging from the activity in the bathrooms during many of those deadly dull Palm Beach social extravaganzas, a lot of others shared my boredom threshold. Fueled by cocaine and a nagging feeling that the real fun was somehow eluding us, a kind of post-party party crowd evolved of reckless revelers who were hell-bent on high times. Following an evening at some swank Palm Beach soirée, people would climb into their Ferraris and Porsches, snort Colombian crude, and zoom off to whatever disco joint happened to be in at the moment: West Palm's Marrakesh, Fort Lauderdale's Studio 51. Then it was on to the home of whoever had the largest stash of drugs in the larder. By the dawn's early light, they would stagger home and into bed—some with their original partners, some with different ones.

In truth, for me, the after-hours life became fun and quite regular, just as getting high became a kind of escape. I was twenty-nine, and the five years of marriage in which I had trailed along like an eager-to-please puppy were beginning to take their toll. I felt inescapably mired in a life over which I had no control.

In so many subtle but no less effective ways, ways that I didn't even realize at the time, Herbert governed me, my every move and decision, and continued to interfere with my relationship with Mac and Zac. I was now beginning to make more and more excuses to Herbert to stay home so I could have more time with the children.

If Herbert came home from the boat or the gym for lunch, as he did most days unless he was out of town or had an appointment, he expected me to be there to have lunch with him by the pool. And he didn't want Mac and Zac running around on their scooters or splashing in the pool during lunch. This was his inviolate time for peace and quiet. I learned to make sure that the kids were either napping or riding their three-wheelers on the Lake Trail when Herbert came home for lunch. I wanted to please him, yet at the same time I resented him for always making the children eat their meals alone in another part of the house. I would sit with them to keep them company but wouldn't eat until later with Herbert.

At one o'clock, after lunch, Herbert and I would go take a "nap." This was his favorite time. This, I knew, was what he expected, and I did it unquestioningly.

When we were at the ranch or on the boat, it was always a struggle to get him to include the boys. And when he did, he was always testing to see how long I would stay in the blind or out fishing before I would insist on going back to check on Mac and Zac. If Herbert had his way, we would leave before the children awoke and be back just as they were going to bed. Eventually, after repeated urgings, I got him to agree to interrupt his day of hunting or fishing to go in for lunch with Mac and Zac. But each time Herbert made me feel that I was cheating him out of potentially his biggest fish or his best shot. As generous as he was in some ways, he had a knack of attaching emotional guilt and psychic strings to his concessions to me and I was beginning to resent it.

At this point, Herbert started staying out hunting or fishing without me. So it was just the two children and myself. We would make sand castles, look for butterfly shells, walk in the woods looking for flowers. Mac and Zac were such gentle, easy children—so trusting and adoring—so lucky to have each other. They had their own language as twins. They always had lots of smiles and hugs.

My friendship with Jacquie became another test with Herbert. He had decided that she was a bad influence. In spite of his initial encouragement to see Jacquie, he started insisting that I was spending too much time with her, time that I should have been spending with him. I came to wonder whether it was Jacquie's influence or Herbert's fear of losing control over me that was the reason for his disapproval of our friendship.

Still, I loved Herbert Pulitzer. My whole identity was dependent on being his wife. My whole sense of emotional security was dependent on making myself indispensable to him. I was obsessed with the man, with pleasing him, with understanding him, with reassuring him. But instead of feeling fulfilled, I was beginning to feel emotionally drained and confined. Even worse, I felt powerless to take control of my life in any significant way, so I chose instead to ignore and repress my frustration.

My thoughts at this period of my life were centered

more around Herbert than my spiritual growth. And there were more than enough distractions in my comfortable existence to divert my attention from purposeful ponderings and to lull me into complacency and irresolution. In the end, my lack of purpose would be my path to destruction.

Without even realizing it, I was becoming a Palm Beach girl. I was completely caught up in the privileges of being a well-kept wife, even as I was feeling trapped in my role.

My transformation was so complete that during one of our annual trips to the Golden Door health spa outside of La Costa, workplace of the indolent rich, I even managed to convince Barbra Streisand that I was just another "rich spoiled brat."

When I walked into my aerobics class there and discovered Barbra Streisand sweating just like everyone else, I couldn't believe it. I mean, Barbra Streisand! The Voice. My all-time most favorite recording star. One of the most powerful and talented women in Hollywood. I had always wanted to meet her.

I tried not to stare, while at the same time trying to lock eyes with her, which I hoped would lead to the chance to strike up a conversation. But as far as Barbra was concerned, I was part of the woodwork, along with the other four women in the group. She didn't even so much as glance my way or anyone else's, much less smile at me.

I was no more successful at getting her attention during the volleyball class that followed. I guess I must have seemed pretty obnoxious, because when we finally ended up side by side during water ballet later that afternoon, Barbra turned to me with a patronizing look and said: "I want you to tell me your first impression of me and I'm going to tell you mine of you."

I couldn't believe what came out of my mouth. "I think you're a stuck-up Hollywood snob who thinks she's too good to talk to anyone."

"Well," she replied in an icy voice, "I think you're a rich Palm Beach bitch."

"For your information," I told her, "I happen to be a

poor Cassadaga, New York, bitch. And before now I was one of your biggest fans."

For some reason, trading insults with Barbra was the critical ice breaker. After that, we really hit it off! She sent a handwritten invitation asking Herbert and me to join her for dinner at her table with her entourage—Jon Peters, the hairdresser-turned-producer who was her boyfriend then, and record producer Charles Coppelman and his wife, Bunny. Although I never expected to hear from Barbra again after I had returned to Palm Beach, she continued to stay in touch, calling now and then just to say hello and writing letters. I had the feeling that Barbra Streisand didn't strike up many impromptu friendships, that in a sense she was emblematic of the ennui that seemed to go hand in hand with having too much. I came to suspect that fame, like money, took all the spontaneity out of life. For some reason, it always seemed that the very people whom you would expect to be having the most fun were actually having the least.

The predilection to party till dawn wasn't any more unique to Palm Beach than cocaine. In those days, it seemed that wherever people gathered with too much money and too much time on their hands, the nights always seemed to take on an inexorable momentum of their own, like a downhill racer on a slalom course of white powder.

One minute it was two in the morning and you were dancing in a nightclub with a group of friends. The next minute it was six in the morning and you were realizing that you had been sharing intimacies with a bunch of strangers. During those unaccounted-for hours in between, you had been moving through another dimension, a kind of cocaine-induced Twilight Zone. The details were fuzzy, but you knew you had been there because you could still hear Rod Serling's theme song throbbing in your head.

Following an evening at Manhattan's Studio 54 disco, which used to be one of the most popular "in" night spots,

Herbert and I ended up partying in the exclusive apartment of a friend of a friend. In his penthouse overlooking the East River, we were greeted with fishbowls full of cocaine that were set out on the coffee tables like hors d'oeuvres. Although the scene was like so many others with the usual ingredients—aging champagne hippies, yuppies, Penthouse Pets, and a sprinkling of escapees from the bowels of the underground—there was an unusually debauched flavor to the mixture. Several extremely young-looking women seemed to be having trouble keeping their clothes on. When I slipped upstairs in search of a bathroom, I discovered why. On the second floor was a huge Jacuzzi that was overflowing with people. The king-size bed in the master bedroom was covered with naked bodies.

Preferring to leave the herpes research to others, I certainly didn't want to be caught up in this party's activities.

At the trial, Herbert would ultimately portray me as the instigator of our *ménage à trois* with Jacquie Kimberly. But, in fact, for over a year, Herbert had been trying to persuade me to join him in a sexual threesome with another woman, and I had been stalling him. Although I had never before refused him anything in our marriage and consider myself to be sexually open-minded, this request was different. I felt threatened by the prospect of Herbert being with another woman and totally turned off by the prospect of making love with one myself. But I strongly sensed the danger in flatly refusing him. I felt it would be like extending an open invitation to him to try it without me. I didn't want him to do that, so instead I kept putting him off.

Herbert first began to suggest the *ménage à trois* during one of our frequent trips to the red-light district of Amsterdam. After a long day of business meetings at the Hotel Pulitzer with those dour Dutch bankers and corporate executives who sat on the board of directors, we would often slip off for a quiet dinner at the Osterbar for baby shrimps and a bottle of Pouilly-Fuissé. After dinner we would walk the canals, then stop at one of the many nightclubs there that specialize in live sex shows.

Unlike those of most cities, Amsterdam's red-light district is more like Las Vegas than skid row, and attracts a solidly middle-class clientele that is a mixture of tourists and businessmen—at least it did before everyone started worrying about getting AIDS. One night, for example, I struck up a conversation with an older, very proper-looking British couple who were sharing the table next to us with their equally proper-looking daughter and son-in-law. They were all out on the town to celebrate the parents' fiftieth wedding anniversary.

But unlike Vegas floor shows, where scantily clad show girls parade around in lavishly decorated sets, Amsterdam's shows typically feature couples, threesomes, groups, you name it, performing live sex acts that are set to music, while British mums and pinstriped bankers sip vermouth and politely applaud.

Frankly, I always found these shows to be more bizarre and amusing than erotic. But afterward Herbert couldn't stop discussing a performance, or speculating on what it would be like to work on stage as an exhibitionist. Did I think fucking in front of an audience would be a turn-on? And what did I think about the physical attributes of a particular man or woman performer? Did he or she turn me on?

One night, after he had taken me to see an all-woman show, he started asking me very pointed questions about whether women's bodies turned me on. What kinds of women, he wanted to know, did I find beautiful? Did I ever imagine myself making love with a woman? *Could* I imagine it?

In truth, I had never before been exposed to or thought about having a sexual experience with a woman and had no interest in contemplating or pursuing one. The idea just didn't turn me on. But Herbert persisted. Always willing to please him, I told him that, yes, I would consider a *ménage à trois,* even as I wondered how I was going to get out of it.

A few months later, during a trip to Paris, Herbert

brought the subject up again after an evening at Le Crazy Horse, a fashionable cabaret that is famous for its beautiful nude show girls. All night and the next morning he kept on about the girls, wanting to know which ones I thought were the prettiest, what I thought it would be like to be with one. Then later that afternoon when I returned to our hotel suite, Herbert told me in great detail about the beautiful Eurasian girl who had given him a massage at the salon next door to the hotel. He suggested we have her come to the room that night to give us both a massage.

She was waiting for us at the back entrance of the Ritz, on rue Cambon, when we returned from dinner. Herbert was right—she was gorgeous, with almond eyes, olive skin, and long black hair down to her waist. Dressed in a plain white blouse and dark skirt and carrying a small cosmetics case, she looked more like a secretary than an outcall massage girl. Nevertheless, Herbert was so nervous about the three of us being seen together in the lobby of the Ritz that he practically pushed us into the elevator.

Up in the room, we ordered champagne and Herbert and I undressed. Very businesslike, she proceeded to go to work, opening the cosmetics case containing all the various emollients and asking us which we preferred. She started with Herbert. While she massaged him, sensuously stroking every inch of his body back and front, I sat on the edge of the bed chatting with her. She told me that she was nineteen years old and a native of Thailand, and had been living in Paris with an American couple for two years. I thought it was an intriguing living arrangement, but I didn't want to ask just how it worked.

Eventually it was my turn. I was nervous and apprehensive. I could see that Herbert was very aroused and I wasn't sure what to expect. I lay down on the bed while he sat on the edge. She began gently massaging my neck and shoulders with almond oil, slowly working down to the inside of my thighs. Gradually, I felt the tension in my body give way to a warm relaxed feeling, a heaviness in my limbs, as though I were sinking into a billowy cloud.

Herbert slid down onto the bed next to me, and we began making love while she massaged both of us. It was a very sensual experience. But apart from the massage, she did not join in or remove her clothes.

In his deposition, Herbert was asked if he'd ever brought a masseuse to our room at the Ritz. Herbert's answer was, "Yes, she wanted a massage." *She* was, of course, *me*.

The next question was, "Did anything ever happen other than massage going on there involving you?"

HERBERT: "You mean what kind of massage?"
LAWYER'S QUESTION: "Involving you with any of these massage girls."
HERBERT: "No."

The lawyers never pursued this line of questioning—and, as a result, nothing more was brought up at the trial.

But that night in Paris went a long way toward easing my apprehensions about three-way sex, if not exactly fostering my enthusiasm for it. I was not put off by the masseuse's presence, nor was I particularly uncomfortable with it. And after that, what had begun as simply a subject of fascination and discussion for Herbert, became a regular topic of conversation and eventually an ultimatum for me.

A few weeks after Paris, while we were having a drink outside before dinner, at the Brazilian Court, Herbert asked whether I had been thinking any more about doing a threesome. Since this had been a recurring question in our lives for weeks—months—I replied, yes, I had been thinking about it a lot.

"Well, Roxy," he said, "make up your mind. Are we going to do this or not?"

I was scared to death. But I knew from the insistent tone in his voice that there would be no more stalling. So it fell to me to figure out who to get to join us. Should I bring in a stranger whom we might never see again so that there would be no emotional tie? But what if he fell in love with her and they started meeting on the side afterward? Should I bring in a friend—someone we both knew? Or was that potentially too emotionally damaging to all of us? And what if she went home and told her boyfriend or husband or anyone and it got all over town?

For days, I agonized over how to handle it before finally deciding what should have been obvious to me from the beginning. There was only one woman whom I trusted enough to ask.

That woman was Jacquie Kimberly.

I trusted Jacquie not only because she was my best friend, but because I knew she totally disdained Herbert. So much so that I had given up asking her advice about Herbert. Every time I brought up some new problem with him, she would tell me, with obvious disgust, "He's such an asshole. Why don't you just tell him to go to hell?"

There seemed to be no question that Jacquie was not going to enjoy doing anything with Herbert, much less anything sexual. Nevertheless, she did owe me a lot of favors for all the times I had helped her out of predicaments by covering for her.

I decided to call in all my chits. I invited her for drinks. We met at an appropriately named bar, Taboo, where we settled into the back booth with a bottle of Jacquie's favorite champagne and her telephone. But I was so nervous that after two hours and one and a half bottles of Dom Pérignon, I was stone sober and still trying to work up the courage to ask her. Finally, I took a deep breath and just blurted it out.

"Jacquie," I said, "I have something to ask you. And you're going to think I'm nuts. But I really need a favor from you. And if you say no, fine. But you're going to have to help me with this.

"Herbert wants to do a threesome in bed. He's going to do it with two strangers if I won't do it with him."

"Oh, all men want to do that. They love it," Jacquie said. "They think it's a big deal."

"Yes, but I really don't want to be left out. It's just too

risky. He could fall for either one of them, and I don't want to take that chance. Will you do it for me?"

Jacquie burst into laughter and just kept laughing and laughing.

"Look, I know it's ridiculous," I said. "But who else can I go to? At least I know that you're not going to run off with him."

The idea of her running off with Herbert threw her into another fit of laughter. "No question that you can count on me not running off with him," she said, wiping tears of mirth from her eyes. "Herbert's not my type. But for you, Roxy, sure, I'll do it."

[*Eleven*]

From the beginning of our marriage, Herbert taught me this understanding about sex: There would be no cheating as long as each partner was game for whatever the other wanted to try. I went along with him willingly. In my mind, whatever we did together somehow always had the stamp of approval.

I *wanted* to be the one to fulfill his deepest sexual desires. To me, that's one of the most important roles a wife can play in a marriage—certainly more important than cooking and cleaning. And up to then, except for our honeymoon night, acting out Herbert's fantasies had been fun for me, too.

It was a kick for me to dress up in provocative outfits and perform a strip tease. Each Christmas we would stuff each other's oversized stocking with X-rated movies and magazines and funny paraphernalia—love potions, creams, silver lamé jock straps, vibrators, Frederick's of Hollywood lingerie.

It was all a game. Harmless, private, provocative—and, above all, fun.

As uninhibited as I was, however, I drew the line at participating in a threesome or group sex. To me, involving others in our most intimate moments just seemed an invasion of privacy. Our bedroom was one of the few places where Herbert and I could be alone together. I wanted to keep it that way. And the last thing I wanted to do was open the bedroom door to another woman or couple. I certainly had no desire for another man. I was very content sexually, more than I had ever thought possible.

Involving Jacquie, at least, made it seem like less of an invasion, since I had already shared some of my most intimate secrets with her.

Herbert was surprised when I told him that Jacquie had agreed to be the other girl, but I could tell he was very intrigued. I knew that he found Jacquie attractive and that he had no idea what she really thought of him.

Finding a place for our escapade was the second hurdle. We couldn't do it at our house with the kids running in and out. We couldn't do it at Jacquie's and risk sparking the suspicions of the servants or Jim. Herbert, ever the hotelier, suggested renting a room at a motel just outside of town in South Palm Beach. So that Jacquie would not be missed by Jim, we agreed to meet in the afternoon.

The day of our rendezvous, Jacquie and I went out to lunch at the Flame and got bombed on two bottles of champagne. We were flying even before we climbed into my Porsche and tore off down South Ocean Boulevard to the appointed Holiday Inn on the ocean, where Herbert had registered in his name. Nevertheless, entering the hotel room to find Herbert waiting for us was one of the most sobering experiences of my life. A small voice inside questioned the advisability of proceeding any further. But as usual, particularly lately, I ignored it. I was listening to my heart instead of my head.

We were all nervous and self-conscious. Nobody wanted to be the first to suggest anything. Herbert was as bad as I was. He kept chattering on about his boat and all the work that needed to be done, as we sat in opposite corners of the room drinking one of the bottles of Clicquot that Herbert had brought along. It crossed my mind that after all this talking and planning, the whole thing was going to turn out to be a flop because we were all too embarrassed to do anything. I knew *I* certainly would not be the one to make the first move.

Cocaine eased my tension considerably.

The rush from the coke was exhilarating. I knew this moment was going to be major in my life. I could feel the heaviness of it.

Next thing I knew, Jacquie slowly began unbuttoning my blouse and slid it off my shoulders.

Then she unbuttoned her blouse. Herbert sat there fully dressed, watching. Nobody said a word.

Jacquie gently pushed me back onto the bed and began caressing and kissing me. At first I was nervous because I didn't know what to do. Even though I told myself to relax, that this was my best friend, my heart was pounding and I had a million thoughts racing through my mind. It was impossible to relax. She was kissing me on the breasts, letting her hands wander, tracing the curves of my body with her fingers. But I was too tense to be turned on. It seemed to be going on for a very long time, and I kept wondering what Herbert was thinking. Even though my eyes were shut, I could feel him watching. I didn't want to look at him, to see his expression.

Herbert was undressed now. His hands began to move over my body, and I felt a little wave of relaxation roll over me. He was familiar and soothing. He began kissing me all over. I remember thinking that Jacquie was watching, but I was too caught up in the act to feel self-conscious. Jacquie began to gently caress Herbert. Then I rolled over on top of Herbert and we made love.

Afterward, while we were all dressing, we laughed and joked about how it hadn't been such a bad experience, and which one of us had been the most nervous. But no one, including Herbert, admitted to actually enjoying it. Then Herbert left in his Bronco and I left with Jacquie.

My only feeling at that point was a sense of relief that this escapade was over and I wouldn't have Herbert badgering me about it anymore. It had been a long year of trying to avoid it.

When I arrived home, Herbert was waiting impatiently. I could tell by his smile that he was very pleased with me. He couldn't stop talking about that afternoon—step by step. How did I think it had gone? Would I have made the first move? What did Jacquie think? And on and on.

Once I saw how delighted Herbert was, I began to think that I actually had enjoyed it. I had expected to come out of it feeling cheap and dirty, but I didn't at all. Seeing that nobody had been hurt or upset by it, the whole thing seemed okay. I knew I had just made him happier than I had ever seen him.

The next day Herbert brought me twenty-five white roses, the only time I can remember him ever doing that, with a note saying, "I will always love you."

I must add here that at the trial and to the press during the trial, Jacquie repeatedly denied ever participating in our *ménage à trois*. (It was about the only thing Herbert *didn't* deny; it may have been the only thing we agreed on!) Part of Jacquie's reasoning may have been simple phraseology. She was asked at the trial about our lesbianism. She denied that—and properly so. Neither one of us considered what we did lesbianism. We considered it exactly what it was—a *ménage à trois*. I'm certain that part of her reason for the denial was loyalty to me and part was also a normal desire to avoid very unpleasant publicity. Look, I also denied it to the press. In the strict sense of the word, yes, I lied. But at the time I felt more as if I were protecting my privacy and my very life. I believe Jacquie must have had some of the same emotional desire to protect herself. I can't fault her for it at all.

Over the next few weeks, after our daily three-mile jog on the Lake Trail, Herbert and I would often sit on the dock talking while Mac and Zac played tag on the grass.

During these chats, the threesome with Jacquie would

frequently come up as a topic of conversation. Herbert loved reliving it. I was very proud of the way I had handled the whole problem, and I was sure it was over and done with. But to my dismay, Herbert started casually asking me when it would happen again. Here I was, right back where I had started! Following the same pattern as previously, I hemmed and hawed and prayed he would forget about it.

In October, Herbert and I attended the wedding of my cousin Sandy, the one who had come to Palm Beach to work for us as a nanny. She had met and fallen in love with the brother of my friend Inger. A flaxen-haired Scandinavian beauty who had been a successful New York model, Inger was married to Harry Loy Anderson, Jr., a member of one of Palm Beach's most prominent and powerful families.

Inger and Harry Loy hosted a small but elegant wedding and reception for family and a few close friends. Afterward, a group of us went out for dinner and then on to a nightclub to do some dancing. Herbert and I snorted a few lines of cocaine in the car. Although everyone else was ready to call it a night at closing time, Jacquie and Herbert and I were still up for partying. Herbert suggested we go back to our house for champagne. Jacquie followed in her Dino and headed for our home. But rather than wake the sleeping household, which included my parents, who were in town for the wedding, Herbert suggested we go down to the boat, which was docked behind the house.

From the moment we stepped onto the boat, I think we all knew where we were headed, however reluctant I was to admit it. We uncorked a bottle of champagne, which proved to be the end of any lingering inhibitions. Suddenly we were all in bed, naked, touching, entwined, for what seemed like hours.

Through my haze, I was intensely aware of Herbert. I wanted to please him more than ever. I felt I was totally relinquishing my body and mind for him, and he would love me forever for this.

And then it seemed the spell was broken. Once again we were separate, naked.

"Bring on the champagne," Jacquie said, raising her glass high in a gesture of levity that seemed somehow amusing. We all laughed, and I stumbled into the bathroom to freshen up.

Minutes later, when I returned to the bedroom, I found Herbert making love to Jacquie. I was stunned. The sense of shock and betrayal was like a dagger being plunged into my heart. I couldn't get my breath, and I just stood there, dazed, watching them greedily going at it as though they were devouring each other's bodies, still unable to believe what I was witnessing.

Because Jacquie's involvement had originally been at my suggestion and as a favor to me for Herbert, he was the culpable one in my mind. After all, the whole idea of a threesome was his in the first place. And throughout all our discussions about engaging in three-way sex, Herbert had repeatedly promised me that this would never happen. Making love with another woman wasn't the point at all, he assured me. He only wanted to watch *me* make love to her and then for him and me to make love. And never, never before had it even crossed my mind that Herbert would fuck Jacquie.

This wasn't part of the plan. I wondered how, where, at what point the situation had taken this turn. And I heard a little voice inside answer: Wise up, Roxanne. You made your bed when you agreed to get into this act in the first place. There was no one to blame but myself. I knew the voice was right.

Numbed by this realization, I just sat there passively, trying to act as though nothing were wrong. When Herbert lazily rolled off Jacquie onto the mattress, I scoured his blank face for some sign of guilt, even sheepishness, as he lay there limply on his back. Nothing.

The first rays of morning light were beginning to filter through the drawn curtains over the portholes.

"Oh my God!" Jacquie exclaimed. "What in the hell am

I going to tell Jim?" She threw on her green satin Chanel suit, dressing faster than I had ever seen her, raced out the door, hardly saying goodbye, and ran down the Lake Trail to her car, which was parked in Ogden Phipps's driveway.

Herbert quickly donned his rumpled tuxedo, and I slipped into my disheveled halter-topped evening dress. I knew that the kids and therefore my mother would soon be up, and I wanted to sneak into the house before anyone saw us and began asking questions.

We tiptoed through the garden, past the pool, toward the rear entrance of the house. Slowly, so as not to make a sound, I pulled back the sliding glass door which opened into the kitchen and stopped dead in my tracks. Sitting there in the kitchen, her eyebrow arched in that suspicious look I remembered so well from my errant youth, was my mother. In that damning moment, I felt as though she could read my mind, and there was no use lying because she knew everything. So instead I tried to avoid the subject of just exactly where I had been.

"Gee, Mom, up already?" I said, trying to sound nonchalant, as if Herbert and I always came off the Lake Trail at this hour in black-tie attire.

"Well," she said, pausing for effect, "I haven't been able to sleep all night. It's none of my business where you two have been, but Jacquie is missing, and Jim Kimberly has been in and out of here looking for her. He's worried and furious." For the first time, I put myself in Jim's shoes. What would he think of his best friend, Herbert, being with his wife and me? I worried about how he could handle something like this at his age.

I felt myself gasp, and I shot Herbert an accusing look as he slinked out of the room, leaving me to maneuver through the minefield that our kitchen had suddenly become. I had no idea what my mother or Jim Kimberly already knew or suspected. Thank God Jacquie had parked her car down the street from our house just in case Jim drove by. Presumably, nobody else knew that Jacquie had been with us all night.

"Jacquie?" I asked, shrugging my shoulders as if to say I had no idea where she might be.

This seemed to satisfy my mother. Relieved and wanting to avoid more questions, I excused myself to shower and change for the day.

Instead of the usual lingering signs of a wasted night—rivet guns hammering inside my head, tidal waves cresting in my stomach—my regained soberness was focused on the image of Herbert and Jacquie together. The morning hours had done nothing to dull my sense of betrayal.

A little later, while having lunch with Herbert by the pool, I could no longer contain my feelings about the night before. More hurt than angry, I wanted to hear what he had to say for himself. Finally, it became obvious that Herbert, contrary to his previous habit of detail-by-detail discussions, was not going to bring up the night before.

"I'm pretty upset about your making love to Jacquie," I told him. "You promised me that it would never happen."

A sincerely penitent look crossed his face. "I couldn't help it," he said apologetically. "I know I said it would never happen. I know we agreed to it. But I was drunk and high and turned on. It just happened."

I listened, saying nothing. Herbert had spoiled my gift to him. There was really nothing more to say. I knew that the whole thing had gone wrong somehow and that nothing like this could ever happen again.

I once read, long after this, that those who betray others, whether within a marriage or in life, are the ones who fear betrayal most. They know in their own guilty hearts what they are capable of and they jealously assume that everyone else shares their capacity for treachery.

It was certainly true in Herbert's case. However much he enjoyed our three-way escapade, he never suggested that we do another one, probably because he knew I wouldn't go for it. Instead, his sexual fantasizing took another turn. Over the next few months, he became obsessed with the idea that Jacquie and I were secretly carrying on as lovers and leaving him out.

I was never really sure whether he was jealous of the imagined love affair or angry at being excluded. Whatever, he was absolutely determined to believe it. Herbert's earlier concerns before the threesome that Jacquie was a bad influence on me became an absolute insistence that she was.

He began badgering me about the time I spent with her. Every lunch with Jacquie potentially became the subject of an inquisition from Herbert and an argument. At one point, he even forbade me to see her, an order that I ignored, as he knew I would. He began phoning me at restaurants and timing my lunches.

Although I didn't realize it then, I'm sure that our increasing use of cocaine inflamed Herbert's paranoia as it did all the other long-repressed smoldering grievances and insecurities that seemed to be suddenly flaring into major confrontations all too frequently during that late fall of 1980.

For me, part of the ritual of getting ready to go out was going into the bedroom safe, where the cocaine was kept. I sometimes rolled seven or eight little cigarette-paper pouches of coke that Herbert could tuck into the inside of his cheek, because snorting bothered his allergies.

Cocaine seemed to make the fun times more fun. With cocaine, all those initial reservations and inhibitions I had about fitting in seemed to fade, along with the hour.

And while I was at times aware that the drug also had the effect of making us both irritable and especially suspicious—by the end of the night, for example, any strange noise could be someone breaking into the house, any strange car following too closely could be the police—the next morning my brain couldn't recall the paranoia. All I would remember was the fun of the high. This is the big danger of cocaine. Even the increasing trouble I was having sleeping was outweighed by the obvious benefit of my weight loss. At last I was finally becoming a bona fide Palm Beach girl—too rich and too thin. My normal weight of 122 plunged to 109, and I felt that I had never looked better. Foolishly I hadn't yet made up my mind that cocaine was the problem, or even part of the problem.

As far as I was concerned, the problem was Herbert's need for control over me and our marriage, and my refusal to continue to give in to him. And there was another problem: Liza.

More and more my own threatened feelings about Liza were turning into jealous rages with Herbert. I found it increasingly impossible to put up with her.

I testified at the trial—testimony which, while he was on the stand, Herbert flatly denied—that Liza and Herbert "would lie on the bed together drinking champagne, she would sit on his lap and be kissing him and hugging him for hours."

But even more than this odd behavior, it was her attitude that really bothered me.

Once I came home and found Liza trying on my clothes. She turned to me and said very confidently, "You will never win this war, Roxanne."

It truly scared me and I thought, What if she is right?

I honestly don't think I was being paranoid about Liza. Back in 1979, when she married Bob Leidy, a really nice guy in his middle forties, Herbert and I went to the wedding. We were sitting at a table with a group of friends when Liza came over to sit on Herbert's lap. She had obviously had a lot to drink.

"Dadz, I know I got married tonight," she said, loudly enough for the whole table to hear, "but you know I wouldn't have gotten married if I could have married you. But since you're my father, I had to marry someone."

I sensed that people were staring, and I felt embarrassed for her, for Herbert, for me. But he seemed unmindful of the scene she was making, or the uncomfortable silence that hung over the group after Liza had blithely walked away. Then Inger, who was sitting at our table, spoke up.

"Why don't you do something about this situation with your daughter?" she said to Herbert. "It looks ridiculous. You're making a fool of Bob and Roxanne."

I was stunned by her audacity. But Herbert responded nonchalantly. "She's my blood," he answered.

"Well, that's no excuse," Inger said. "She's not acting like a daughter, she's acting like a girlfriend."

Herbert just sat there impassively, saying nothing more. I didn't dare say a word, even though I secretly felt a measure of vindication for my complaints to Herbert about Liza.

I became more adamant and contentious than ever about Liza. I even foolishly demanded that he stop seeing her unless I was present, which made about as much sense as his insistence that I stop seeing Jacquie.

Despite the storm brewing between Herbert and me, my times with Mac and Zac remained as special as ever for me. I always found great joy and peace in their company as well as a childish sense of fun that invariably left me refreshed and happy again.

Every day my cares would disappear temporarily as I tended to their needs or romped with them.

They had grown into two beautiful blond boys with my blue eyes and a definite Pulitzer look. I was always surprised that none of my friends and sometimes even the nannies couldn't tell them apart.

Whatever the aftermaths of late party nights, I was always eager to wake up to their warm, welcoming little faces for breakfast. And later, after the morning nursery-school classes were over, I would look forward to the games we would play in the pool or at the parks.

Often on the way back and forth to school we pretended we were being followed by the Hell's Angels, and every motorcycle in sight would provoke squeals and laughter.

At this time, I came to know a tall, slender, beautiful girl, Lorraine Odasso, who seemed to follow very much the same daytime routines with her two small children as I did with mine. I had met her before at cocktail parties, and on another occasion in the company of Jimmy Buffet, the country rock singer whom I knew from Aspen.

Lorraine, along with looks and charm, was born with a silver spoon firmly lodged in her mouth.

A member on her mother's side of two glamorous Palm Beach old-guard families, the Phippses and the Guests, she was also the daughter of a French count who had been a renowned aviator and war hero.

Lorraine lived a fairy-tale childhood in a beautiful Louis XIII pink chateau surrounded by moats and gardens and hundreds of acres of property outside Paris. She traveled frequently to London, New York, and Palm Beach to visit family members.

Given this background and her own natural elegance, Lorraine might have turned out a phoney jet-setter, but as I grew to know her better, I found that, to the contrary, she had been raised to value her privacy and guard it ferociously.

One afternoon at a children's birthday party, I was amused to see Lorraine race off and whisk her own two children away from the offending lens of a society photographer, even as other mothers were trying unobtrusively to shove their own little darlings in that very direction.

However, two years later, when my reputation had hit rock bottom and all my Palm Beach friends were deserting me like rats fleeing a sinking ship, publicity-shy as she is, Lorraine was the *only* one to stand up for me at the trial as a character witness.

Herbert and I seemed to be going around in downwardly spiraling circles. When we weren't arguing about Liza, we were arguing about Jacquie. When we weren't arguing about Jacquie, we were arguing about including the children on our trips, and when we weren't arguing about them, we were arguing about cocaine.

I think we both recognized that in the ups and downs of marriage, our relationship was in a tailspin and neither of us was able to pull out of it. We had no idea how to handle all these crises, because our communication was so poor. It was becoming a battle of wills. At Herbert's suggestion, we began seeing a marriage counselor. I approached the whole experience in good faith. My main reason for seeing him was Liza, because I couldn't cope with the competition anymore. But after two short hour sessions, it became apparent that we were getting nowhere so we stopped seeing him. However, unbeknownst to me—at least until I learned it at the trial—Herbert went back to see him nine months later.

Over the summer, while we were in the Bahamas on the boat and far removed from the various provoking influences of Palm Beach, everything seemed to be fine again. On the surface at least, we were getting along. But once we returned to Palm Beach for the party season in the late fall and winter and were back on the regular track, all the old unsettled emotions began erupting again.

Herbert began to blame the cocaine as well as Jacquie for our problems. I blamed his inability to handle my having any outside life or friends apart from him, and his exclusion of the children. But as tense as our marriage was at times, I had no idea just how much our marriage had already been jeopardized until the day Herbert took me to see another one of his lawyers, Chuck Nugent.

I assumed that my visit with Herbert to the lawyer's office was to discuss some of Herbert's business. I was totally taken by surprise when Nugent handed me a document at the top of which was typed "Postmarital Agreement."

"Herbert wants you to sign this," he said, while Herbert sat there expressionless, saying nothing.

I was confused and didn't know what to make of the situation, or exactly what it was that I was being asked to sign. I had never before heard of a postmarital agreement. I proceeded to read the paper, which outlined several provisions. The only one I recall vividly now discussed the custody of Mac and Zac. He gave me full custody of the children. The agreement said the kids and I "shall have the right to remain in the Husband's home for a six (6) month period following the signing of this agreement. Thereafter, the wife shall, with the aid of the Husband, find a suitable place for herself and the parties' children." He also agreed to give us $3,000 a month in support and to pay for the children's medical and school expenses. It struck me as a fair agreement. One that I could have signed gladly had I not thought that I still loved Herbert Pulitzer and that our quarrels would just fade away with a little effort on both sides.

I was seeing the words on paper but not really comprehending them. None of this was really registering in my brain. The only thing that did register was the fact that if we ever got divorced, this agreement would likely become effective as the final settlement. This was the first time that the subject of divorce had ever come up between Herbert and me. I felt as though my heart had stopped cold. All I could think of was that I didn't want to get divorced. I couldn't believe that Herbert was contemplating a divorce. How long had this been going on in his mind?

When I had finished reading, I looked over to Herbert's face, which gave no hint of emotion. "I would like you to sign it today," he said calmly.

I turned to Chuck, whom I had come to regard as an honest, forthright man, after many meetings with him. "Can you advise me, as an attorney?" I asked him. "Should I sign it?" He looked at me, then at Herbert. I could tell that he felt uncomfortable. "In my honest opinion," he replied, "I would suggest that you hire a lawyer and have him look at it."

Herbert glared at him as he grabbed the document from the desk. Then he turned to me and said, "Let's go, Roxie."

That was the last I saw or heard of Chuck Nugent. But it was only the beginning of Herbert's plot to divorce me.

It is a shock to me now that I never saw all this coming. I was so obsessed with Herbert that I convinced myself that a divorce would never happen as long as we both worked harder at preserving our marriage.

I didn't want to sign anything rashly, in the heat of an argument, that could lead to a possible and immediate divorce.

Had I not been so blind and naïve that afternoon, I believe Mac and Zac would still be living with me today. It never occurred to me that Herbert would soon use them as a legal tool to get his way. I trusted him, and I just couldn't imagine him ever wanting to hurt us. I lost my children that day because I couldn't face reality. I blame myself for my lack of insight, but one just doesn't hear what one is not ready for. The knowledge can only come when the consciousness is ready—and mine obviously wasn't.

❦ *Twelve* ❦

Christmas had always been a special time for our family. Herbert and I were both like our own little kids, playing Christmas carols, decorating the tree and the house, and really getting into the holiday spirit. It was also the time of year that I associated with the happiest periods of my life. Our wedding had been in January, and I had discovered that I was pregnant just before Christmas.

But Christmas 1980 was far from jolly. The postmarital agreement hung like a pall over our entire holiday. It seemed as though every other day Herbert had a new reason for me to sign it. He kept after me about it in the same way that he had pestered me before about the threesome. He told me my signing it would make him feel more secure, because he was worried that I might leave him for a younger man someday. He told me it was a way for me to protect myself in case *he* ran off with someone else—not that he was planning to, of course. He tried to make it a test of my love, telling me that if I really loved him, I would sign it. And finally, he tried to persuade me that the whole thing was really no big deal, so why didn't I just go ahead and sign it?

I knew, though, that it was a big deal. I tried to make light of the subject every time Herbert brought it up in order to avoid an argument or provoke any more of his anger. But I couldn't help wondering, Why this, Why now?

The postmarital agreement wasn't the only point of contention, however. Herbert had decided that cocaine was the root of our problems and a corrupting influence in our lives. I thought this was a bit extreme and told him so. But his mind was made up. Typically, *he* decided that *we* would no longer use it. I, of course, rebelled at yet another command. I was not taking orders very well anymore. That sparked more arguments. One night he went into the bedroom safe where we kept our stash of coke and drug paraphernalia, packed it all up, and stormed out of the house, saying he was going to throw it away.

Less than two weeks later on New Year's Eve, Herbert turned around and produced a packet containing several grams of coke "to celebrate," he said. I didn't understand why it was suddenly okay to use coke again.

At the trial, Herbert testified that he never used cocaine after this January of 1981. I testified that we both used it into 1981, "not very much, though." In essence, this was the end of our cocaine use.

It wasn't until a few weeks later that I began to believe that the impetus for the postmarital agreement might have something to do with Herbert's jealousy. While celebrating our anniversary at the opening of a play at the Royal Poinciana playhouse, Herbert turned to me as we were dancing, with the saddest look I had ever seen in his eyes.

"Promise me you'll never leave me," he said. "Please tell me you'll never leave me."

"Of course I'll never leave you," I reassured him. I meant it with all my heart. I was stunned that he could think that I would ever leave him. However, it occurred to me that Herbert had been showing signs of insecurity about his age lately.

The very next day, however, Herbert's plea for the promise of my fidelity turned to an accusing rage implying that I had been less than faithful by having lunch with another man. As soon as I walked in the door that evening, he began yelling at me that Susie Asquith, who was then our nanny, had just finished telling him that I had had lunch with her boyfriend, Brian Richards, weeks before Christmas.

"Are you crazy?" I said. "I had lunch with Brian because we were shopping for Christmas presents for Susie."

"You're a liar," he said. "If you didn't have something to hide, you would have told me."

I simply didn't understand why Herbert was making such a big thing of this. Brian was at our house on a daily basis for the year he dated Susie. The four of us had often double-dated. Brian was a lot of fun. I knew that Herbert liked him, too. We had once all dressed up for a Halloween party at the Yacht Club, and we very often all went dancing together.

Brian and I often danced together and I enjoyed his company, but I couldn't believe that Herbert saw him as any kind of threat or competition. He wasn't especially handsome. He was just a nice guy who worked at the Yacht Club. Susie was a short, rather heavyset girl who was insecure about her appearance, and I sensed that Susie saw me as a rival for Brian's attention during his visits to the house. As Herbert was ranting and raving, I stormed down the hall into Susie's room and screamed at her, "How dare you tell my husband stories about me? It's not your place to interfere with your employers' private lives. You're fired. Pack your bags now."

When I walked back into the living room, Herbert was standing there waving the postmarital agreement at me.

"Either you sign this agreement right now," he said, the veins in his forehead pulsing with anger, "or I will take the children from you. With my power, my money, and my name, I'm going to bury you."

"I'm not going to sign it," I said. "I'm not signing it because you'll add your signature to mine right now and we'll be divorced."

"Fine," he said acidly. "I'm moving out." And with that he headed for the bedroom and he packed his bags.

A few minutes later, my cousin Sandy, who had been living with us for three years and helping with the boys, appeared in the living room with *her* packed bags. I suddenly felt *I* should be packing my bags too! Where was everyone going?

Sandy had brought Susie Asquith down from Cassadaga some months earlier and was her best friend. Sandy was very angry that I had fired Susie. Unbeknownst to me, Herbert took advantage of this situation and had Sandy make—the very next day—an incriminating tape about me that was used by Herbert's lawyers in the big trial. At the trial, Sandy testified that Herbert told her I wouldn't allow her to see Mac and Zac ever again. He also told her that if she made the tape, he would never ever use it in court; he said it was strictly a scare tactic to try to patch up his marriage. In her anger, Sandy fell for it, and she didn't find out until later that I had never said anything of the sort about Mac and Zac.

That night, Herbert moved onto the boat, which was docked just in back of the house. Over the next couple of weeks, as we continued to see each other during the day when he would pick up his mail or drop off his laundry for the maid, I believed that he would eventually cool off and come to his senses. Then one evening, I answered a knock at the door to find the sheriff on my front step serving me with what I thought were divorce papers. I was so upset I didn't even read them before signing the receipt. My knees went weak. As soon as I closed the door, I broke into tears. I ran to my bedroom and locked myself in the walk-in closet, where I curled up on the floor and just sobbed and sobbed. I remained there for hours, hoping, I suppose, to shut out reality. I didn't want to let Mac and Zac see me.

When her efforts failed to get me to come out, Annie, the kindly old black woman who worked as our maid, phoned Jacquie. Jacquie kicked the door of the closet open and started yelling at me, as she stood over me with a glass of vodka and grapefruit juice in her hand. "Come on out of there, you asshole," she said. "What are you doing?"

"Herbert has filed for divorce," I said.

"It's not the end of the world," she said. "You're better off without him anyway. Where are the papers?"

I handed her the crumpled, tear-soaked document I still had clutched, unread, in my hand.

As Jacquie proceeded to read the papers, I saw the smirk on her face go slack and her brow become furrowed.

Looking up from the last page with an uncharacteristically serious expression, she said, "Roxie, he's not only suing you for divorce, he's suing you for child custody."

"That can't be," I said, snatching the papers from her hand and beginning to read them for the first time. "There must be some mistake." I lunged out of the closet, grabbed the phone, and began dialing Herbert's number on the boat. "He's just angry," I told her as the number rang, "and he probably did it in the heat of anger. He doesn't really mean it. It has to be a mistake."

I let the phone ring and ring.

"You've got to get a lawyer," Jacquie said, shaking her head. "I'm going to arrange an appointment for tomorrow."

The next morning, Jacquie showed up, dressed, as usual, as though she were on her way to a White House luncheon. Still wearing yesterday's blue jeans and T-shirt, I hadn't even been able to function enough to brush my teeth or comb my hair, much less get dressed. I had been sitting next to the kitchen phone all morning trying to phone Herbert and waiting for him to call me.

"The appointment is for an hour from now," she said. "Come on, Roxie, get going."

"I can't until I've talked to Herbert," I said. "I haven't been able to reach him yet."

"Look, just go talk to the lawyer," she said, grabbing me by the arm and handing me a pair of sneakers that were lying on the floor. "That's all you have to do."

We had no sooner pulled into the parking lot of the lawyer's office in West Palm, than Herbert's Bronco roared up behind us, its brakes screeching. Herbert jumped out of the truck and ran over to my side of the car, throwing open the door. How he knew where I was I'll never know, unless the maid overheard Jacquie and me talking.

"Get in the Bronco, Roxie," he demanded. "You're not going to see any lawyer. I'm taking you to a therapist. You're not going to get involved with all these lawyers."

I climbed out of the car and started to go with Herbert, who had me by the arm. Jacquie began pulling me by the other arm. "Roxanne, we have an appointment," she insisted. "We're late."

"You take your goddam hands off of her or I'll kill you," Herbert screamed at her. For a moment I thought he was going to hit her. "You're killing her. You're taking her away from me and you're killing her. She has a drug problem and she's not well."

Despite all our previous disagreements over cocaine, this was the first time I had ever heard Herbert describe me as having a "drug problem," and I was a bit taken aback by the deviant sound of it. After several moments of their wrangling over me, I spoke up.

"You filed for divorce, Herbert," I said, desperate to hear his explanation. "I got the papers yesterday."

"Just ignore them," he said.

"No, I can't ignore them," I said. "If this is what you want, I've got to go up and talk to this lawyer now that I'm here. You're suing me for Mac and Zac."

Jacquie and I walked toward the building with Herbert trailing behind into the lobby, up in the elevator, insisting the whole time that I was going with him while Jacquie kept telling me I was going with her. At the door of the lawyer's office, he grabbed my arm again. I relented and went with him, leaving Jacquie standing at the door, shaking her head in dismay. Herbert turned to me and said, "I would never take the children away from you, Roxie. It's just part of the standard divorce papers."

Herbert and I drove in silence back across the bridge to Brazilian Avenue. He stopped in front of a little garage apartment. He told me we were going in to see Ed McCabe, a drug and alcohol counselor who was going to help us work out our problems. Although I had never before heard of McCabe and didn't know it at the time, he was virtually the town's group-therapy guru. Several people in our circle of friends were seeing him.

Herbert introduced us, and just as we sat down on the sofa together, the phone rang. McCabe handed me the receiver. On the other end of the line was Jacquie's lawyer, Joe Farish.

"Jacquie is sitting here with me now," he said. "I know I've never met you. But I just want to tell you, do not say anything to this counselor today. You're involved in a very volatile situation, and you don't know how it's going to turn out. So don't say anything, because it may hurt you later."

I thanked him for his advice and hung up. But, of course, I was more confused than ever now. I looked at Herbert, sitting next to me, and I looked across the room to McCabe for some clue as to how to proceed. I knew I didn't want a divorce, and it seemed at this point the only hope I had of avoiding one was to go along with Herbert and ignore Farish's warning. Ed McCabe seemed like my last, best hope. So I stayed.

We went through the session. McCabe started out by telling me that he had already had several sessions with Herbert and that now he wanted to hear what I thought went wrong with the marriage. I let loose with everything: Liza's strange affection for her father, Herbert's domineering ways, cocaine, the threesome, Herbert's jealousy of Jacquie, and on and on. McCabe appeared sympathetic, reassuring. Afterward, I felt a great sense of relief, of being unburdened. I really liked Ed from the first five minutes. He did not bow down to Herbert as everybody else did. He told us that we were both guilty of a lot of wrongs.

At the conclusion of the hour-long session, McCabe told us we should come back and try to work this out. I felt that he was sincere and on no one's side.

Herbert and I drove home and made love, and I don't think I've ever tried harder to please him. I wanted so desperately for him to say he would come back, that he loved me, that he wanted to start over and put the past behind us.

But instead, he told me, "If you're really serious about this counseling and do it with me, then I'll move back in a few weeks. Right now and for the next few weeks, I have certain commitments and invitations I've accepted that I have to keep."

I was very hurt. I knew he was being seen around town with other women. Still, I had no alternative but to accept his conditions for reconciliation.

The next morning, Jacquie showed up at the house.

"You're going with me to see Joe Farish," she said. "Now."

More to appease Jacquie than because I felt the need for a divorce lawyer at this point, I went with her. On the drive over to his office in West Palm, she told me all about Farish and how he had represented her aborted divorce from Jim. To underscore his reputation, she also told me that Farish had represented Mary Alice Firestone in her divorce from tire tycoon Russell J., one of the bloodiest battles in the annals of matrimonial law—up to then, of course.

"He's a sharp, tough lawyer," she said, "and you're going to need one, Roxie. This is Palm Beach, and Herbert's lawyer is Ronnie Sales—we know *his* reputation of going for the jugular."

As soon as I met Farish, I was struck by how little he looked sitting at his huge desk.

He spoke with a good-old-boy Southern drawl, and on the floor next to his desk stood maybe sixteen expensive leather briefcases—from Gucci to Mark Cross, you name it—lined up like books on a shelf. He also had wild boar heads mounted to the walls of his office. To me, killing a wild pig is like shooting ducks in a barrel. Although they are certainly mean, boars are also about the stupidest animals on four legs.

As I sat there with those revolting boar heads staring at me, I recounted the chain of events of the last two days for Farish and concluded with my belief that my marriage was on the road to reconciliation and that I didn't need a divorce lawyer. Because I certainly believed that to be true, I was extremely convincing. To his credit, Farish encouraged the reconciliation. He also told me that he was available if I needed anything. We shook hands, and I left with Jacquie. That was the last I ever expected to see of Joe Farish. I was wrong.

Over the next weeks, I did need Joe Farish, though for such minor details—at least in my mind—that I continued to absolutely believe that Herbert and I were reconciling. Depositions were being filed, my answer to Herbert's petition was filed, his answer to *my* answer was filed, but we were still sleeping together every afternoon at one o'clock —he loved sex after lunch—and continuing with Ed McCabe's counseling sessions. I felt that McCabe was fair in pointing out mistakes we had both made. Incredible as it may sound, despite all this frantic activity, I thought things were fine.

During those sessions, Herbert and I would sit there and listen to Ed's advice. Ed pointed out that in never spending a day apart in six years, we had logged in more time together than most couples married for twenty years. He told us not to do any more drugs. He said that Herbert must make an effort to include the children in our traveling; that he should let me stay home on short business trips; that I certainly had no right to keep Herbert from his daughter; that he had no right to keep me from my best friend. However, in spite of Ed's efforts, the sessions and our relationship would end at a stalemate.

I kept pressing Herbert to move back in, and he kept being vague about when and his reasons for putting it off. He would stop by the house for a drink dressed in his tuxedo, and this was very hard for me to swallow. I was so tightly wound emotionally over the counseling sessions and my growing jealousy that I found myself blowing up at him or the children over the least little thing, which certainly didn't help the situation. However, with Herbert gone, I experienced a relief from having always to split my time and attention in my roles as wife and mother. It was nice being able to devote so much time to Mac and Zac. We ate dinner together, and we all slept in my bed. I had no social life at this time, so the three of us became very, very close. They were just three and a half years old at this time. They never asked about their father's absence. They didn't understand what was happening.

I believe that because he sensed I was on the verge of cracking, Herbert phoned my mother and asked her to come to Palm Beach. As soon as she arrived, however, he began trying to get her to take his side. That, of course, only made things worse. He told her that I was going off the deep end on cocaine, which naturally horrified her. And he told her that Jacquie was a terrible influence on me. Since my mother never had liked Jacquie, she was only too quick to agree with him on that. At one point, Herbert even tried to get my mom to go off to his divorce lawyer, Ronnie Sales, to give a statement about my emotional condition. By then, Herbert had persuaded her to believe the worst about me. The only reason she resisted going to the lawyer was that she felt the situation was as volatile legally as it was emotionally.

In March, Herbert moved back into the house. But if I had been really honest with myself, I would have realized then that the reconciliation and our marriage were doomed. While packing up his things from the boat with my brother and sister-in-law, I discovered a nude photograph of Paulette Lewis—a friend of mine—in one of his drawers and flew into a blind rage.

With the photo clutched in my hand, I ran back to the house, where Herbert was sitting in the living room reading a magazine. I threw the photo in his face and started screaming at him. He sat there impassively without the slightest trace of guilt or contrition in his face, waiting for me to stop screaming.

Then he said with that tone of fatherly condescension that he used so effectively with me, while patting me on the head, "You're making too much out of this, Roxie. It's just an old photo that she gave me. You know how much I admire nude photography. But if you're going to make a big thing about this, I'll just move right back to the boat." He then told me to rip it up, which I did. At the trial, he denied ever having a nude photo of Paulette—and because of my blind obedience, there was no proof otherwise.

This was a turning point in my mind. I couldn't get the picture of Paulette out of my mind. My jealousy was very difficult to keep inside. I felt betrayed. I know that I should have been grateful just to have him back home, but something seemed very wrong.

I should have realized then that if our marriage was going to work it was up to me to shoulder the entire responsibility for it, that making it work was a question of how much I was willing to put up with. I wanted so desperately to retrieve what we had lost between us, and Herbert knew this. I couldn't face the fact that the marriage was over. I wanted to believe that I could single-handedly make it work by being a good enough wife.

With my self-deluding task mapped out, I threw myself into this impossible mission. Over the next weeks, I stopped seeing Jacquie and devoted myself to doing everything I could to please Herbert—both in and out of bed.

The next month, when we made our semiannual trip to Paris, I felt that we were beginning to turn the corner. Paris was exceptionally beautiful that April, and Herbert was more romantic and considerate of me than he had been in months. We visited all our favorite places, took long walks along the Champs Elysées, shopped in Les Halles, bought antiques in "Les Puces," and just talked about us and our future. Herbert told me that he had decided to add on to the house and that he would give me $50,000 to decorate it. This was the first time Herbert had ever given me a dime for the house. I shopped all over Europe for our bedroom. I had never had such fun, and I decided I could finally feel that the house was *our* home.

For me, this was the first sign from him in nearly a year that he wanted to please me too, that he believed we had a future together. And on our last night there, Herbert, who hated discos, made an even more remarkable concession for him.

"We're going to dinner tonight and out dancing at Regine's afterward," he told me that morning. "I want you to go get your hair done and buy a new dress."

I went out and spent the whole day shopping and in the hair salon, more excited about an evening out than I had been in a long time. Regine's had always meant a good time for us, and Herbert opened up only when he was a little bit drunk, so I hoped we could discuss a few of our problems.

We had a fantastic champagne dinner at Maxim's, and I was really looking forward to our night on the town. But just as Herbert was paying the check, suddenly his whole expression changed, as if something was terribly wrong. "I'm not going dancing," he said with an air of finality that left no room for my thoughts about the change in plans. "I just want to go back to the hotel and go to sleep."

I couldn't believe he was changing his mind, taking away the one gesture he had made just for me when I had been knocking myself out for months trying to do everything his way. It reminded me of a child taking a toy away from a playmate because *he* doesn't want to play with it anymore. The Indian giver!

We quarreled bitterly and didn't speak for the rest of the night. He read his *U.S. News & World Report* and I went down to the lobby to telephone the children.

The next day we flew to New York together, barely talking during the six-hour flight. Originally we had planned to spend a few days in New York. I was missing Mac and Zac very much—especially since Herbert and I were fighting.

"I think you should go on back to Palm Beach and see the children, because that's what you really want to do," he said. "Go out and have a good time. It's only fair. I'll see you tomorrow night." I absolutely couldn't tell if he was being a nice guy here or sarcastic.

I was not sure if I should go. We had separate plans that morning; I went to Clive Summers and he went to his financial adviser. When I arrived back at the St. Regis, he had left me a note on the bed which sounded to me as if he was never going to see me again. When I was on the plane alone the next morning, I began to feel that he had said goodbye to this "new" Roxanne that he had helped create. I knew he wanted the twenty-two-year-old back.

We had grown into two entirely different human beings, and we no longer knew each other.

Before getting on the plane, I phoned the nanny to have her meet me at the airport with the children. After I got home, I phoned Jacquie and we agreed to go out that night with a group of friends. It ended up as one of those Twilight Zone nights, and I returned home late. I didn't know that Herbert had been phoning me all night.

I took the children to the park the next morning, and when we came home, Herbert was there. We had the worst fight ever. He stormed into the house and started yelling at me in front of the nanny and Mac and Zac, which he had never done before. He accused me of sleeping out the night before. And then he picked me up under the arms and held me against the kitchen wall, screaming that I was a no-good slut and calling me every name in the book. I retaliated just as venomously with namecalling and screaming. We raged on for what seemed like hours. Then he walked out with the parting words: "I'm divorcing you and that's it."

As awful as that fight was, the scene that followed a few days later, Mother's Day, was even worse. This is the way I described it when I testified at the trial:

"He just told me that I was going to check into the hospital or he was going to kill me and himself. Upon which he put the gun at my temple and cocked the pistol. And I just closed my eyes and sat there and then he didn't do anything. He sat down and then he turned and he put the gun in his mouth with it cocked and he said, 'Do you want me to kill myself or are you going to go to the hospital?' And I said 'I'll go to the hospital. I don't want you to kill yourself.' "

I *believed* he would shoot me, there was no question in my mind about that. Yet I felt an amazing calm; I knew it would be painless.

But I couldn't believe what I was seeing, that we had come to this. It was really for fear he would kill himself that I agreed to check into the hospital, although at the trial, of course, Herbert flatly denied my version.

LAWYER'S QUESTION: "Now, you've heard this story about you taking the gun and pointing it at your wife's head and threatening to kill her and you if she wouldn't go to the hospital. Did that happen?"
HERBERT: "That's not true. That is *not* true."

After the incident with the gun, as incredible as it may seem now, I still couldn't imagine my life without Herbert. I walked back into the nursery, where Mac and Zac were sitting on the floor watching Scooby-Doo—they were sitting identically. I started to cry and tried to find the words to tell them that I would be gone for a month. I just hugged them both, and they hung on to my neck for so long. It was as if they knew.

We drove to Miami and the hospital that afternoon in silence. During that hour-long drive, I felt that I was seeing Herbert in a new light; egotistical, manipulative, selfish, demanding. That day there was nothing about him that I liked, nor could I even remember what good I had once seen in him. I was going along with him now only because I was too tired to resist. I didn't know which one of us was going off the deep end, but I was very scared by what lay ahead of me.

When we arrived at Highland Park, I signed the admission forms without even reading them, I was so eager just to get to my room and away from him. He told me that he was going to speak to the doctors and that he wouldn't be able to see me for a few days until I was permitted to have visitors, and then he left. Alone in my room, seeing the bars on the windows and the locks on the doors like in some insane asylum, I began to cry. I felt as though I were on the verge of insanity. I had never felt more alone in my entire life than I did that day.

That dismal introduction to Highland Park Hospital was soon followed by my official orientation, when a series of staff doctors, psychiatrists, and others breezed into my room and proceeded to explain to me how I would be spending the next thirty-six days: physical examinations, psychiatric evaluations, group therapy, incommunicado. Dinner that night was served on a plastic tray with little plastic utensils. I had the distinct feeling that real forks and knives were potentially too dangerous in the hands of my fellow inmates at Highland Park Hospital. That made me cry even more.

By the next morning, however, I had resigned myself to making the best of my weeks there. If there was anything to be gained or learned from this dreadful place, I was going to gain it and learn it. By the second day, I actually began to like it there. Nobody hassled me. In contrast with the past months at home, there was no arguing, no feeling that I was walking a tightrope. By the third day, I was actually enjoying the group-therapy sessions and focusing on other people's problems for a change. And there were some very interesting problems in my group.

Take Benny, for example. He was into speedballing—shooting a combination of heroin and cocaine. But he had no intention of going off drugs. He was there to appease his parents, who were threatening to wrest control of his considerable trust fund unless he cleaned up his act. Then there was Sally. She had a bit of a Quaalude problem—thirty a day, to be exact. This was her second time in Highland Park. Another girl had overdosed the month before on heroin.

When it was my turn to talk about my cocaine addiction—for by now I was viewing myself as being addicted, too—I held back nothing. I told them all about my worst night—the time I consumed three-quarters of a gram and most of a bottle of champagne, how I once or twice snorted coke two or three evenings in one week, how I liked it because it made me feel confident, in control, uninhibited, and unfettered.

When I had finished recounting my shocking shamefulness I was braced for the group's censure. Instead, their reaction was one of disbelief—gee, is that all? One of the group members even told me that he wished he had my problem. I felt as though I had disappointed them. But I began to realize how Herbert had manipulated me into thinking that my drug problem was much worse than it actually was, manipulated me into this place. I began to wonder if Herbert wasn't the sick one.

That night I phoned Jacquie, the first phone call I had been permitted to make since my admission. I told her I couldn't wait for her to come visit, because I had so much to tell her about Herbert and the program. I needed desperately to talk to someone about the frightening thoughts I was having, now that I was cold sober. Had Herbert been trying to convince me that I was an addict or even mentally unbalanced for some ulterior motives? Was he trying to line up witnesses? Could he be capable of this?

The next day I was totally unprepared when my counselor, Roberta Cusumano, told me that Jacquie wasn't coming. I phoned Jacquie again, and she told me that she couldn't visit me because she couldn't afford being seen going into a drug hospital, that the potential for negative publicity was too great and Jim wouldn't allow it. I couldn't believe what I was hearing. My best friend, I thought, and all she's worried about is her publicity. I was depressed for the rest of the night, because everyone had a visitor except me. This was Mother's Day weekend, and I was very lonely.

The next morning, on my sixth day there, I was called into the office of Dr. Stephen Kahn, the medical director of the recovery center at Highland Park General Hospital. He began by telling me that the staff had just finished a meeting about my case. I was half expecting him to tell me that I was going to have to stay for an additional thirty-six days. Instead, he said they had all concluded that I was a "social abuser of cocaine and alcohol" but was definitely not addicted.

"This hospital is for people who have very serious problems, Mrs. Pulitzer," he said. "And we need the beds for them. We've called your husband, and he's coming for you this afternoon."

I started to cry, because suddenly I didn't want to leave. As much as I missed Mac and Zac, I didn't want to go home to all the problems. I felt safe here after the gun episode, and it was somehow peaceful. I asked Dr. Kahn if I could stay anyway and complete the program, because it could help me in my everyday life.

"Mrs. Pulitzer," he said, "this is a drug and alcohol program. You have a marital problem."

I knew, of course, that he was right.

When Herbert came for me that afternoon, he gave me a very stiff hello hug. I could tell he was not happy that I was being released. I later learned that he had tried to get the hospital to keep me.

In the car on the drive home from Miami, he asked, "Well, did you tell them everything?"

I told him, yes, that I had told them about my worst night, the most drugs I had ever done, the most champagne I had ever drunk.

"Well, maybe they're right," he said, sounding more resigned than convinced. "But you've got to promise me that you'll never do drugs without me and that you aren't going to be seeing Jacquie or go out dancing anymore."

I agreed, even as I thought, Here we go again: more demands, more rules, more doing things Herbert's way.

One funny example of this submission was my subsequent breast implants. During one of the many physical exams at Highland Park, the doctor informed me that my nipples were pointing the wrong way, which Herbert had subtly been trying to tell me since the twins were born. They gave me the name of an excellent plastic surgeon in Miami, Dr. Lawrence Robbins.

Herbert and I went to his office to discuss the operation. While we were sitting there, Herbert asked me if I might consider having larger breasts. I wasn't thrilled by the thought, but once again, I found myself meekly watching Herbert pick out the size of the silicone implants that he wanted for me. He picked up a few, handled them, patted them, and finally declared, "We'll take this one."

Dr. Robbins was so booked he couldn't operate until the fall. By that time, Herbert had moved out. I decided to go ahead with it anyway. So eventually I was left with big boobs and no husband.

After a few weeks back home, I began to miss the counseling I had received daily at Highland Park. I called the hospital to ask if Roberta Cusumano took any outside patients and was told that she had just moved to West Palm Beach. I made an appointment and went to see her by myself the next day. I saw her from then on, once or twice a week over the next year. I felt very comfortable with her. Her counseling helped me tremendously that year and has stayed with me ever since.

In June, Herbert and I went fishing in the Bahamas. Although we slept together on the boat, we had very little time alone beyond that. And the moments we did have were tense ones. I felt that I was doing everything I could and that he was contributing nothing. The tension between us was made even worse by the presence of the captain's fourteen-year-old daughter. She was supposed to be helping out with the kids, but instead she usurped my usual job of making Herbert's drinks and generally catering to him.

One night, on the island of Eleuthera, he went off with her and some of the other young mates with baseball bats to kill rats. I decided I had had enough. After another big quarrel, I told him to arrange a plane for me, the nanny, and the children so we could leave and go home.

Herbert returned home about two weeks later. By now the new master bedroom suite that he had agreed to build when we were in Paris was completed. I had it decorated with Trisha Guild fabrics from London, and I was very excited about it. But he never slept in it. Instead, he packed up his personal belongings, taking everything this time. He told me that he was going to file again for divorce.

I felt sad and disappointed. I remembered how good things had once been. Over the next month we spoke only when he came to visit the children every other weekend. I knew that he was still being seen around town with other women, but I was too distraught and discouraged to be dating anyone, although I did see Jim and Jacquie occasionally.

As fall went on, Herbert went hunting out west and in British Columbia, and Mac and Zac saw him less and less. I felt I had to compensate for this lack of interest by talking to the children about him so they wouldn't feel left out.

Then one day, totally out of the blue, Herbert proposed that we go together to one of Ed McCabe's group-therapy sessions saying that he had just joined the group and felt that it had done wonders for him. He told me how several couples whom we knew were going there to work out their problems. I didn't want to go, because I felt it was like walking into a Palm Beach cocktail party and telling everyone your problems. But I relented because Herbert told me that if I came to the group with him, he would move back into the house and we would try living together again.

When we walked into Ed McCabe's office for the session there were so many people there whom I knew I felt I just wanted the ground to swallow me. I had also learned around town that these people were fast becoming Herbert's new friends and part of his entourage. He was now exclusively dating one girl called Janie Dean, who was the "queen" of the group, having been there the longest. My insecurity was nothing compared to the humiliation that followed, as Herbert delivered a scathing indictment of me, my wanton ways, and my terrible transgressions. He told the group that I had lied my way out of Highland Park Hospital by denying that I had a drug problem, when in fact I was an incorrigible drug addict. And all the while, he said, he had been doing his best as the long-suffering and supportive husband to keep the marriage together.

He concluded by saying there was no point in my trying to reconcile with him and that our marriage was over.

I couldn't believe what I was hearing, and I was too stunned to say anything, much less defend myself. Ed McCabe must have picked up on my shock.

He turned to Herbert, shaking his head, and said, "I hope you know what you are doing."

I drove home alone, sobbing all the way, jumped into the shower, and shaved every hair off my body, not only my armpits but below my belly button as well. This would teach him! Unfortunately I later found out he loved me that way.

Herbert turned up at the house, to my surprise, half an hour after "group." I was in my dressing room playing with the boys, and he began to cry. "I just had to do that," he said. "Forgive me." He kept crying, "Forgive me."

I was so confused about his motives, I didn't know which end was up. I didn't know whether he was just playing some kind of manipulative game that I didn't understand or whether he really believed all those things he had said about me. In any case, I was fed up with and exhausted by all his machinations.

The next week, I went back to the group-therapy session and delivered a speech of my own directly into Herbert's eyes.

"As I understand it," I said, "people are supposed to

come to 'group' because they want to help themselves, not because they are being lured here under false pretenses. I just came to say, 'Fuck you.'"

And with that, I marched out of the office.

❧ *Thirteen* ❧

Although Herbert and I lived apart over the next couple of months, I continued to desperately hope that we could still salvage our marriage, a hope that was underscored by the approaching Christmas holiday and the annual family ski trip to Snow Mass in which Herbert told me he wanted to be included. So when I was served with divorce papers a second time in November, I was even more confused than the first time. But instead of bolting for the closet and falling apart, I felt a crushing sense of resignation so powerful that I no longer wanted to resist it. I felt like a death-row inmate who had just learned that her stay of execution was up.

About an hour after the divorce papers arrived, I spoke to Herbert on the phone, and then he stopped by. I told him about being served. I don't know what I expected him to say. At this point, I was prepared to hear and believe anything, no matter how incredible or painful.

"Can you believe this?" he said, hitting his forehead with the palm of his hand in a gesture of incredulity. "I told the lawyer to drop that. I filed those two months ago in September. I can't believe you're getting these papers now. Christmas is coming. We're going skiing. We'll probably reconcile so just throw them away. And even if we don't reconcile, we certainly don't need lawyers. We'll work things out. So throw the papers away. They don't mean anything."

So into the wastebasket went the papers. And that was the last we spoke of it. As usual, I fell head first into yet another trap. The biggest trap yet.

Early in December, after dinner on a Friday night, there was another knock at the front door. This time it was a notice to appear in court at eight forty-five on Monday morning for my final divorce hearing. *Final Hearing for Dissolution of Marriage.* The words jumped off the printed page as though they were written in neon. What *was* this?

I was absolutely panic-struck. I phoned Jacquie, and she gave me Joe Farish's phone number. I phoned Farish, and his secretary told me he was out of town for the weekend and couldn't be reached.

"This is Roxanne Pulitzer," I told her. "He knows who I am. I've got to reach him. I've got to have a lawyer by Monday morning."

Then I phoned Herbert. No answer.

The next day, Farish returned my call. As I proceeded to explain my predicament, the court summons, the thrown-away divorce papers, I began to feel embarrassed about just how unbelievably stupid I had been.

"What is he asking for?" Farish demanded.

Since I hadn't even bothered to read the papers before throwing them in the trash, I didn't know what Herbert's side was proposing. But remembering the first suit papers, I told Farish that I supposed Herbert was asking for everything—the kids, the house.

"You suppose?" he shot back, his voice tinged with scorn. "Well, let me tell you, he is probably going to get it. Because legally, he's right. By not answering the first summons, you are conceding and you are in default. That is the law. I really don't think there's anything I can do for you. But you can come to my office on Monday morning and I'll go over to the courthouse with you. It's a real long shot, but maybe—*maybe*—I can persuade the judge to give us an extension."

As slender as the thread of hope that Farish held out was, it was all I had to go on. I allowed myself to feel a measure of relief. All weekend I tried to reach Herbert, with no success. I was still thinking that this might just all be the lawyer's mistake.

Finally, on Monday morning, moments before I left for the courthouse, Herbert answered his phone. I told him about the summons. He told me that it was not a mistake.

"How can you do this?" I pleaded, my voice cracking. "It's not fair."

With a tone of cold finality that was like a slap in the face, he replied, "Life's not fair, Roxanne." Then he hung up.

On that note, I walked into the courtroom a few minutes later with Joe Farish. With his lawyer, Ronnie Sales, Herbert was already seated at the plaintiff's table almost within arm's length of me in the small conference-size room. Herbert did not acknowledge me. He didn't even look at me, not even when his lawyer was arguing for a final decision in the case on the grounds that I had willfully ignored the suit. When I saw that Herbert couldn't even look me in the eye, I wondered again whether all the pain and anguish he had put me through over the past year had been one big manipulation game, setting me up for this moment.

Under oath, I explained why I hadn't answered and that I was not in agreement with the terms. The Judge ruled in my favor.

Christmas came and went. Herbert stopped by for only an hour to exchange presents with us before leaving on a ski trip with friends. We barely spoke to each other. It was a very sad Christmas. Mac and Zac and I spent the day alone trying to assemble their toys, a job their father and I used to share. Once again I tried as hard as I could to compensate for his absence.

Since the beginning of our separation, I had become acutely aware that my Palm Beach friendships were fading fast. While Herbert was continuing to lead an active social life and was being seen around town with Janie Dean, I wasn't even receiving the courtesy of condolence phone calls, much less invitations. When *Town & Country* magazine phoned to tell me that I had been cut for space reasons from a photo spread on up-and-coming Palm Beach hostesses for which I had posed in happier times, there was no question in my mind as to why I hadn't made the cut.

One of the few people who was reaching out to me at all during this period was a kind, sympathetic man named Jamie Murdoch, who had been in Ed McCabe's therapy group.

After Herbert's embarrassing speech before the group about me and my wanton ways, Jamie phoned me to say how wrong of Herbert that had been and how bad he felt for me. Our friendship grew from there. He took me to a couple of opening nights at the Poinciana Playhouse, but he was never anything more to me than a supportive friend and a sounding board for all the craziness that was going on in my life. Nevertheless, during those dark times he helped keep me from going over the brink of sanity by simply listening and being supportive.

Holed up alone at home in virtual social isolation, I was beginning to feel almost paranoid, a feeling that was reinforced by the private detectives Herbert had tailing me. At one point, a couple of Palm Beach police officers showed up on my doorstep to warn me that I could be in physical danger and ought to be locking my car, just in case someone tried to plant drugs on me. I called the police several times convinced that somebody was on my roof trying to collect incriminating evidence on me.

To that caveat, a friend further suggested that I gather up all the drugs and drug paraphernalia in the house—grinders, papers, bottles, water pipes—and give them to her for safekeeping. I did and later, with her inimitable flair for the dramatic, she told me that she had buried them one night in a safe place.

I met a psychic, Janice Nelson, and in my loneliness

and isolation, I turned to her, too, as a friend as well as a spiritual guide. I was so desperate that I actually believed that through her psychic powers, she could help straighten out my marriage. I was willing to go along with anything, even magical potions. So when she hit upon a crazy plan to turn Herbert around, I went for it. I know it sounds ridiculous now, but I was as desperate as a person can get.

The plan was to get Herbert to drink a few drops of a love potion in the belief that this would make him fall in love with me again. Nutty, sure—but I tried it. We had a little ceremony; she chanted mystical love rites and she read me the Tarot cards.

Late one night, I sneaked onto the *Sea Hunter*, while Herbert was away, and stole off with a bottle of his red wine. I brought the bottle back home and poured the love potion into the wine. Then I stole back onto the boat and set the bottle in an obvious place where I hoped Herbert would see it and drink it. I never found out whether he did or not. But he never came running back into my arms.

What really put me over the edge, though, was overhearing the nanny I had then, Estelle Godbout, arranging an appointment with Herbert's lawyer one afternoon in late January. I felt as if I had a spy living in my house and this was the last straw. It was too much pressure on me. I flew into a rage and told her to get out of my home.

With a defiant, hateful glare, she replied, "I don't work for you. I work for Mr. Pulitzer. This is his house, not yours, and I'm not moving."

I phoned the Palm Beach police and demanded to have her physically removed. They came; she went.

My firing the nanny sparked Herbert's side to file for an emergency child custody hearing. The date was set for late January.

I am guilty of many mistakes, but I do not carry the responsibility for the ugly tone the trial was given right off by Herbert's lawyers in their opening statement.

To quote Ronnie Sales:

MR. SALES: If it pleases the Court, Your Honor, this is a dissolution of marriage proceeding.

We are here on the Husband's application for temporary child custody.

The Husband is the petitioner in the dissolution of marriage proceeding.

He is Herbert Pulitzer, Jr. He is 51. He is a hotel operator.

His wife is Roxanne Pulitzer. She is 30 years of age and she is unemployed.

The parties are married six years. They have twin sons, McLean and Zachary, age four, who were born August 28, 1977.

We are here on the Husband's prayer for temporary child custody which is contained in his petition, Docket Entry 1.

The proofs will show that Mr. Pulitzer is a gentleman; he is a loving father.

The proofs will show that Mrs. Pulitzer is addicted to dangerous drugs, cocaine, Ritalin, and that she is also an inebriate.

Until around a month ago she had an adulterous relationship with another man.

She sleeps until late in the day and she stays out all night, carousing with men and abusing herself with drugs and alcohol.

Sometimes she is absent for several days at a time.

Mr. Pulitzer owns the house at 410 North Lake Way in the Town of Palm Beach where his wife and sons reside.

Mrs. Pulitzer is not domesticated and she has never taken care of the children.

From birth the children have had two nannies. Until April of 1981 the children had two live-in nannies and from April '81 until January 13, '82, the children have one live-in nanny.

The way that went is, from ten days from the time they were born she had a baby nurse, and then she had two live-in nannies until she fought with them and ran them off in April—since April of '81, that is.

Since April '81 until January 13, 1982, she had one live-in nanny.

She is not domesticated, the proofs will show.

She cannot cook, sew, clean, make a meal, or take care of a child and makes no effort to do so.

The parties were separated at the end of August 1981. At the time the parties were separated there was living in the house a woman named Estelle Godbout, a loving and responsible nanny.

On Wednesday, January 13, 1982, Mrs. Pulitzer in a fit of rage—because the ingestion of these drugs had altered her moods, the proofs will show—fired Estelle Godbout, and Mr. Pulitzer is fearful that the children may come to some harm.

He was content to leave them in the house because Mrs. Pulitzer had abdicated her responsibilities to this woman, with whom you will be impressed. She is a good Christian devout woman.

But just a few days ago Mrs. Pulitzer ran her off because she thought she was a spy, and now Mr. Pulitzer is fearful that his children may come to some harm.

The proofs will show that Mrs. Pulitzer's man friend who was or is the drug pusher, threatened to kidnap the Pulitzer children at one point, and Mr. Pulitzer had to go to the Town of Palm Beach police over that.

Mr. Pulitzer has attempted to take the children into his custody, and Mrs. Pulitzer refuses to let the children see him.

Mrs. Pulitzer encourages the children to call her new lover "Daddy."

Incidentally, Mrs. Pulitzer's new lover keeps his boat at Mr. Pulitzer's dock, and his gear inside Mr. Pulitzer's house.

Mrs. Pulitzer may deny she is an addict—she may also deal in drugs—and being an unfit mother, and that she stays out all night with her boyfriend, but the overwhelming proofs will show that she was hospitalized in April or May of 1981 for cocaine abuse.

The hospital records are under subpoena.

Her first cousin and former nanny will testify that she is a cocaine abuser.

Now, I understand that this woman has proved adverse, but she gave us a tape, and it may be that we will introduce a prior inconsistent statement, but I can promise you if you hear it you will hear a recording from her own first cousin, and one of the two nannies who took care of the children from ten days after birth, that she is a cocaine abuser and an unfit parent.

A witness, a person, will testify that she got religion for a few days, a couple months ago, and attended an encounter group, and she told 17 people at the encounter group she was a cocaine addict and needed help.

A witness will testify that while sitting in the neighbor's yard—the witness being a neighbor—she heard Mrs. Pulitzer testify or say to a man that she was so strung out that she couldn't wait until her next fix.

The yard man will testify that he found a vial of cocaine in her car seat.

Actually, he will say he found a small bottle, and he will describe it to you, with a little spoon in it.

He says he doesn't know what it is. It had a white substance in it.

The housekeeper will testify that she found drug paraphernalia in Mrs. Pulitzer's closet; that is to say mirrors, razor blades, spoons, and rice.

I'm not sophisticated about these things, but I understand that they use rice to keep the cocaine dry.

The maid will testify that Mrs. Pulitzer stays out all night and returns home in the early morning hours.

The last nanny whom she recently fired will testify that she stays out all night, stays absent for days at a time, that she brings her lover in the house where the children are, and is intimate with him there.

Mr. Pulitzer will testify that Mrs. Pulitzer tried to leave her boyfriend Brian Richards, claiming that—a drug pusher—he had threatened to kidnap her children.

So it just won't be from Mr. Pulitzer's testimony that the Court hears that Mrs. Pulitzer's personality has completely degenerated, and that she is totally out of control.

She believes that she can do anything that she cares to do, and the paramount concern that the Court ought to have is the welfare of the children.

Mrs. Pulitzer enjoys a presumption that she is the more fit custodian of the children of tender years—underlined—all things being equal, but all things are not equal here.

THE COURT: Does that complete your opening?
MR. SALES: Yes.

What else could they add? I would find that out six months later in the big trial.

I was branded a drug addict, an "inebriate," an "adultress" who "deals in drugs," and as "not domesticated," an "unfit mother."

I was stunned. I thought I was having a nightmare.

Their first witness was a perfect example of how testimony can be twisted by smart lawyers. Her name was Fran Howe and she was one of the new friends Herbert had cultivated in group therapy. I hardly knew her. She testified, "The conversation I overheard was in connection with they had to make a connection very soon, that they were getting very low in their dope and would, whoever it was, please go in the house and get whatever was left." The lawyer asked what we were getting low of and Fran responded, "Smack, coke and pot."

This wording implied the notion of heroin. It became an immediate rumor around town that I had been caught lying in my driveway screaming for a fix.

Herbert's side brought on many witnesses, including Estelle, the nanny I had just fired, and culminating with Herbert. Here is a sample of his questions and answers:

QUESTION: Who has taken care of the children from birth?
ANSWER: Nurses.

QUESTION: Has Mrs. Pulitzer ever taken care of the children?

ANSWER: No, *never*.

QUESTION: As between the two parents, who has taken care of the children?

ANSWER: I have.

QUESTION: What do you do for them?

ANSWER: I take them to the ranch, I bathe them, clean them, wipe their bottoms, dress them, feed them, cook for them . . .

QUESTION: What are your fears now?

ANSWER: Without Estelle being there, nobody being there, and Roxanne staying out all night and taking drugs, I don't even know where the kids are half the time. I'm worried to death about them . . .

QUESTION: Does Mrs. Pulitzer take dangerous drugs?

ANSWER: Yes, she does.

QUESTION: What drugs?

ANSWER: I know she takes cocaine and Ritalin and I have seen her drink in excess.

QUESTION: Is she a cocaine addict?

ANSWER: Yes.

QUESTION: How do you know that?

ANSWER: She admitted it to me on two occasions.

QUESTION: Are there some people out there (indicating) from an encounter group?

ANSWER: Yes.

QUESTION: What is that called?

ANSWER: Ed McCabe's . . .

QUESTION: Did you go to one of those encounter groups?

ANSWER: Yes.

QUESTION: What did she tell the seventeen people?

ANSWER: That she was a cocaine addict . . .

QUESTION: Do you love your wife?

ANSWER: With all my heart—I would do anything for her.

Well, thank God he loved me! What if he'd *hated* me? Because the picture painted by Herbert's side was so horrible, I created my own rationalization for the motives behind it.

I *had* to believe that it was the lawyer behind all this, not Herbert; that Herbert was being manipulated by them and didn't know what he was doing. How else could I cope with this? I *had* to tell myself that the man I had loved for seven years would never do this to me if he had been thinking straight. I *had* to tell myself that he was utterly confused and as emotionally drained as I was, that he would come to his senses and realize that despite all the pain and anger of the past two years, I still loved him and wanted him back. However, the thought that kept nagging me was that I was the mother of his children and by allowing such testimony against me, he was ruining Mac and Zac's private security for years to come, possibly forever. This is the one point I must admit I am still working on to forgive him for. I need to remind myself of the saying John had taught me years ago, when we were both teenagers: "He who cannot forgive burns the bridge over which he himself must pass."

The emergency child custody hearing lasted a few hours and was heard by Judge Carl Harper, a gruff authoritarian bear of a man who was later to preside over the big trial.

When his decision came in a few days later and I was awarded the children, it gave me a false sense of security —I came to believe that the truth would prevail no matter how cleverly the lawyers played their game.

Having lost this round, Herbert retained the huge firm of Gunster Yoakley in place of Ronnie Sales. Within a few weeks, it would be my turn to get caught up in lawyers' games.

Farish filed for emergency financial support when Herbert cut off my credit. I had no money to buy groceries or gas for the car. To me, this was further proof of Herbert's craziness, since he knew I didn't have any money for the house and the children.

But if the emergency child custody hearing set the ugly tone for Herbert's side, the financial-support move by mine certainly set the image of me as a gold digger who was holding out for the bucks. Looking back, I realize that the emergency financial support statement made it a lot easier for Herbert's side to portray me as money-hungry.

At the time, however, I didn't appreciate any of this. Farish handed me the financial-statement forms, which included idiotic details for household expenses, such as carpet shampooing and pet care and pet toys, and told me to fill it out. It took me days to gather all the information, since Herbert had always been the one who ran the household and paid the bills.

When I brought back the completed form, carefully itemizing everything down to the last penny, the monthly expenses for me and the children and the house came to about $4,000.

Farish glanced at the total and explained the facts of life to me.

He told me that the average financial award by a court ends up being a third of what you ask for. It seemed to me that if I wanted $4,000 a month, I had to ask for $12,000.

Well, of course, I couldn't get by on a third of $4,000 a month. So I padded it, asked for $12,000 a month. The court ruled that Herbert had to continue paying all the usual household bills and family expenses—things like the cook, pool maintenance, the children's medical and dental bills —which amounted to about $5,000 a month. He also had to give us an extra $2,000 a month cash as additional temporary alimony and child support.

In the early spring, I was surprised to see Herbert coming by the house more often. Our relationship, which had been on ice all winter, was beginning to thaw. The four of us were actually sitting down to have dinner together and talking. Yes, yes, I know—but I was still susceptible to his charm.

During this time, I received notice to appear for my deposition. I met Joe Farish that March morning at the office of Herbert's new lawyers, Robert Scott and Mark Luttier.

"Don't volunteer anything," Farish told me as we rode up in the elevator to the offices of Gunster Yoakley.

I had no idea that I was walking into a carefully laid minefield. The deposition, which was taken by Robert Scott and Mark Luttier, took several hostile, tense hours. I was shocked by many of the questions. They were so personal. They involved things that I knew only Herbert could have told them. But why? Why would he tell them these things? I had thought we were just starting to get along well again. I became very indignant and protective of my marriage. I felt that our sex life was no business of theirs.

"Tell us about Herbert as a father," they asked. "Does he abuse them physically in any way that you are aware of?" I was angry that someone was even insinuating such a thing. I rushed to Herbert's defense. I did this several times as the result of their clever questioning.

I left the session thinking it hadn't gone too badly, that I hadn't said anything against Herbert to particularly provoke his anger. I was very happy with the recent progress of our relationship. In the back of my mind, I was thinking that even the lawyers would see that he was wrong about me and that they would tell him that his divorce and custody battle was all a mistake. I believed that they might even urge us toward a reconciliation. How stupid I was! This deposition was crucial to the trial—more so, possibly, than anything else. I buried myself that day.

Once the lawyers got involved, there was no real hope for reconciliation. The battle lines were drawn. From then on, Herbert and Roxanne's dispute became a lawyers' game that had nothing to do with who was the better spouse, or parent, or person, nor did it have anything to do with fairness or the truth. It had to do with using every possible tactic to win. It was war.

I was never truly prepared for this. I should have gone into my deposition fighting for my life and children instead of holding back in the desperate hope of saving my marriage. My priorities couldn't have been more wrong.

My positive feelings about the deposition were reinforced by Herbert's increasing friendliness toward me. He told me that of course he knew I was a good mother, and repeated that suing me for the custody was just a standard divorce tactic that lawyers used all the time to gain a financial advantage. He acted as though this was just a legal exercise over which he had no control. We started going out on dates. One night, in April, over dinner, he began talking about working out our problems together and reconciling. Herbert proposed going back to Martinique, where we had honeymooned, and starting all over. I was thrilled, of course.

But my hopes were dashed a few days later when Herbert told me that his lawyers were against our going to Martinique together. Hearing that really threw me for a loop. How could anyone be opposed to a couple reconciling? What kind of person or people could argue against holding a family together? It just didn't make sense to me. But I didn't say anything.

Herbert continued, "Even though my lawyers don't want me to go, they agreed that I could go, if your lawyer will draw up an agreement saying that no matter what happens during the trip, say for instance that we sleep together, it can't be used against me in court. Because Bob Scott told me if I don't have that agreement, he's dropping me as a client."

This was especially hard to take—even as Herbert was talking about working it out, he was concerned about how he was going to look in court. That should have told me something about the man and the impossibility of the situation. But I was too desperate to pick up on the message, too desperate to let go.

I phoned Joe Farish and asked him to draw up the agreement. He sent it over to Herbert's lawyers. But we never made it to Martinique. A few days later, Herbert told me that despite the drawn letter of agreement, his lawyers still wouldn't permit him to go. That was our last attempt at reconciliation.

Shortly after that, Herbert's side proposed an offer of

settlement, revised from the postmarital agreement of two years before. The offer, as I recall, was $200,000 in cash, plus another $400,000 spread out monthly over many years. But it stipulated that I had to give up custody of Mac and Zac.

Herbert knew that I would never agree to give up my children, whatever the money.

But, to my horror, Farish suggested I take the offer.

"I don't think you've been hearing me," I told him. "This divorce isn't about money; it's about custody. You're telling me to sell Mac and Zac!" I couldn't fathom any of this.

Farish argued that Herbert didn't really want custody of the kids, that they didn't really fit into his life-style, that he was using custody as a bargaining chip and that if I signed, he would probably give me the kids.

I told him bargaining chip or not, there was no way I was going to sign any such agreement.

I felt I would have been selling my children to Herbert. In retrospect, given the outcome of the trial, Farish's advice was probably sound. I probably should have taken this offer. Financially, it certainly was a mistake. My reputation also would not have been dragged through the mud. The most important element, of course, was Mac and Zac, and I have had many sleepless nights since when I have wondered whether Farish was right, whether Herbert would have gladly given up the children if I had only agreed to the proposed financial settlement. Unfortunately I'll never know.

During the preceding fall, Lorraine and I had become very close, spending long afternoons with our four children, swimming or shelling on the beach with them, walking on the Lake Trail.

I found that I could talk to her openly. Nothing ever seemed to shock or surprise her. Little by little, I told her my whole story, leaving out no details. It felt great to know that she accepted me totally for what and who I was.

In view of her family's position in Palm Beach, and her own sheltered upbringing, I was amazed at how understanding and free she could be in her attitude toward me.

I had heard that she was incredibly hospitable and gave small impromptu parties that were known as being select yet casual and fun at the same time. She and her husband, Christian, a French movie producer and director, were often visited by various artists, singers, writers, and other movie directors who enjoyed the young international atmosphere as well as Christian's great culinary talents.

One morning during the spring, Lorraine called me up and invited me to dinner—the first social invitation I had had in months.

I was feeling very low, but at her insistence I accepted —to pull myself out of my lethargy and to make the friendly effort to show up. Lorraine was entertaining some longtime family friends and introduced me to a tall, lanky Frenchman named Hubert. I was immediately drawn to his gentle, soft-spoken manner. Although he was a couple of years younger than I, he seemed much more mature. There was an air of relaxed confidence about him that I found attractive and reassuring. He had a pleasant sense of humor and a great deal of French charm.

I learned that he had come to Palm Beach some months earlier with another Parisian (a duke or a marquis) to open a French bakery just off Worth Avenue.

Hubert's family had owned an impressive percentage of the prestigious French publishing company Hachette since after the war. His father, a onetime polo player, had been president of Tele Hachette, one of Europe's largest television production companies, until the Hachette Companies were sold in the seventies. Hubert's father had been a close friend and admirer of Walt Disney and had had the flair to be the first in Europe to publish Disney books.

Hubert and I were immediately attracted to each other. This was the first evening in months that I felt included and totally accepted. We all laughed and joked a lot, and I was surprisingly lighthearted as I drove home later that night.

The next day, Hubert called me up to ask me out to dinner.

We went to a Mexican restaurant, then on to a discotheque. We sat and just talked for a long time. He told me he wanted to go out with me, but he knew all about the oncoming trial, and would this hurt my case?

I replied that although I had been living alone for many months now, I was still legally married to Herbert, that I couldn't get involved with another man until the court had ruled a final divorce.

I suddenly felt years younger as we laughed at our predicament.

During the difficult months that lay ahead, Hubert was always there for me, patient and considerate. The attraction between us grew deeper, as did our friendship, and we waited anxiously for the trial to be over.

It's ironic that one publishing magnate's son was totally supportive of my cause, even as another was trying so hard to destroy me.

Over the late spring and into the summer, I became acutely aware that the legal wheels of *Pulitzer* v. *Pulitzer* were rolling inexorably toward a September court date. The word on the street, fueled by newspaper stories, the origins of which I still don't know, hinted that this was to be one dirty domestic dispute, even by Palm Beach standards.

Herbert's side was subpoenaing half the town; 102 people were on his list to give depositions in the attempt to make their case for my drugged-out, debauched life-style. A lot of people couldn't get out of town fast enough nor far enough away—some even left for Australia.

Farish was busy working on a personal multimillion-dollar estate settlement against John D. McArthur, and he assigned one of his young assistants to deal with me. When the assistant asked me to provide a list of character witnesses who would testify for me at the trial, no one would help me except Lorraine. All the others I asked, including

Jacquie, told me they didn't want to get involved.

"Listen, Roxanne," she said. "You're heading into a very messy divorce, and I can't afford to get dragged into it. I'm afraid that we can no longer be friends. Jim won't allow it."

As crushed as I was to hear her say that, I didn't reply. What could I say? That was the end of our friendship. I couldn't ask people to ruin their own lives and marriages over my divorce.

Over the summer, I began to be dissatisfied with my relationship with Farish. With the trial just two months away, I wanted to meet on a regular basis with him to discuss strategy. Instead, I was still dealing mostly with his assistant. To my way of thinking, this was not acceptable.

I decided to go see another lawyer, John Christiansen, who came highly recommended. In contrast with Farish, this man had a serious, button-down demeanor, and I felt much more comfortable with him. I explained my concerns about the preparation of my case and asked him to represent me. He declined.

"This is going to be a big, big trial," Christiansen said, "and there's no way that I could prepare for it adequately in only two months. When I go into a trial, I go in to win. There is no way I can come in at this late date when the other lawyers have been working since January and do you justice as a client. I'm sorry."

In August, Lorraine invited me to visit her chateau in France, knowing that Mac and Zac were leaving for their summer vacation with their father. I needed to get away. I was dreading those weeks alone without them. Hubert accompanied me on the trip. He wanted to visit his parents, then go on to St. Tropez. On his way back, he stopped at Lorraine's home in the country in St. Georges.

Christian surprised us with a delicious dinner set out on the terrace overlooking the river. He made a lobster soufflé and served it with a bottle of excellent white wine, followed by a casserole of pigeons with truffles and another bottle of excellent wine. He then brought in a crystal bowl filled with fresh wild strawberries, raspberries, and a sprinkle of mint, all from the garden, topped with a touch of Champagne Rosé Dom Ruinart. Later, under the Normandy stars, we tasted a bottle of Calvados 1928.

It was the nicest time I'd had in months, possibly even years.

Since Herbert and I had been living apart on and off for more than a year, I didn't think my going would have any bearing on the upcoming trial. But they ended up dragging poor Hubert into it, too, as another example of my torrid trail of adultery.

⟨ *Fourteen* ⟩

When I entered that West Palm Beach County courtroom on September 20, 1982, I had no idea what I was walking into. It was going to be a long trial, twenty days in court stretching over a period of three months with recesses. I thought I was braced for it. Farish had even warned me that there would be reporters there, adding that I should just stick close to him and everything would be okay. But you don't know what it's like to walk down a courthouse hall with a few hundred news and TV cameras flashing in your eyes until you are there. And even worse than seeing them is having to endure the kind of invasion of your life that they bring with them.

It wasn't a trial, it was a circus. The ringmaster, Circuit Judge Carl Harper, gave me the feeling that he thought he had better things to do than preside over a sordid battle over money between two crazy people. This was one of his first divorce cases. He had been a criminal judge for many years. I never got the feeling that he understood what was really at stake here: two five-year-old boys being separated from their mother and their world torn apart. I later learned that he was childless.

In retrospect, I think he made up his mind about me right from the start. I was a brazen young hussy and fortune hunter. I think he made up his mind from the start about Herbert too. Harper bought Herbert's hardworking, self-made, local-boy-made-good image lock, stock, and barrel. "A man's man."

But even worse than not being prepared for the circus scene surrounding the trial, I never seriously considered what the possible outcome might be, that I might, in fact, lose my boys. Throughout the earlier legal rounds and the preparation of my case, Farish kept telling me not to worry, that this was a trial about money and power and that he liked Judge Harper, who had hunted at his ranch. He kept reassuring me that there was no way Herbert wanted the children because they would never fit into his life-style. In view of Herbert's paternal track record, this was one piece of advice from Farish that actually made sense. The worst that would happen, I imagined, was that I would end up with little or no financial support, a working mother with her kids in a day-care center.

I was certainly not in there at first to dish the dirt or financially bleed Herbert Pulitzer, but unfortunately, I ended up in the gutter with everyone else. I wondered about the motives of Joe Farish, and Herbert, and his lawyers. To them, I think, this was as much a battle for publicity. I often had the feeling that they were all playing out their Perry Mason fantasies.

Herbert's side fired the first shot in its opening statement.

I thought I had heard plenty during the emergency child custody hearing, but once again I was wrong. Robert Scott's opening statement announced that he was going to show I was: "A pathological inveterate, irrepressible and continuous liar." He promised to show that I "experimented in lesbian relationships" and that my religious beliefs were founded "in the strange and nonreconcilable." He also listed all my adulterous escapades, those later tagged in the press as the "drugpusher," "handyman," "salesman," "race-car driver," "French baker," and "Kleenex heiress."

I was called to the stand as the opposition's first witness. I was feeling extremely apprehensive. The lesbian accusation kept running through my mind. To think that Herbert could take this very private thing I had done to please him—out of love!—and twist it into lesbianism. Since I had won the previous child-custody round, I wondered if this was the additional ammunition they needed to win this round.

Part of me was scared, the other part couldn't help but see the ridiculousness of it all. I hate to disappoint anybody, but perhaps this was overestimating me just a wee bit! I mean, I didn't have the *time* to indulge in all of those affairs, never mind the inclination.

So with mixed feelings, I started my testimony while national news cameras rolled in my ear and the press took notes.

I looked over at Herbert, whom I had known for ten years, for some small sign of warmth or eye contact, but his side was united in portraying a well-oiled machine at work—ice-cold.

I was on the stand for two days. As an outlet for my nervousness, I started doodling on my yellow legal pad. I didn't want to show too many signs of weakness, nor did I want to break down emotionally. I knew that if the lawyers could prove mental instability, the little white men would come after me with their straitjacket.

Each day was getting harder. I now knew where we were headed. The newspaper headlines were getting bigger and better. We were fast becoming the only soap opera in town. I couldn't wait to get off the stand.

Finally, Mark Bloom, Herbert's accountant, was called as their second witness. He was a long time proving that Herbert was worth very little—$2.6 million. Later, Farish counteracted with Everett Nolan, our financial expert, who testified that Herbert's net worth was $25 million. Judge Harper ruled that "a fair estimate of the husband's net worth is in the neighborhood of $12,500,000 [a nice neighborhood, to say the least]." During the financial testimony, I would have the only emotional contact from Herbert in the entire trial. Herbert hid both sides of his face with his hands and stuck his tongue out at me vehemently with a look of "I told you, don't mess with me." I sure got the picture then!

I had told Farish all along that I felt there was too much emphasis on money. Luttier's closing statement clearly reiterated this. "The relief sought by Peter [Herbert] is very simple, he seeks custody of his children. The relief sought by his wife is custody of the children and money." Herbert's side separated the financial battle from the custody issue, whereas I felt that we were fast falling into the money trap. I came off as a gold digger. For the first time, my intuition was correct. Instead of following it, I took my lawyer's advice.

Next, my ex-boyfriend Randy Hopkins, then Lyman Bradford, one of the private detectives who had followed me for months, were called to the stand.

Bill Cheatham, Herbert's new friend from group therapy, whom I barely knew, testified that I had said that I used to take Dilaudid, a drug I had never heard of. He also testified that Jamie Murdock had bragged to him of an affair with me and that I was a "very powerful woman"—whatever that meant.

The court found Bill Cheatham a credible witness.

Next was called Jamie Murdock, who became known as my "salesman." He disputed Cheatham's testimony and said he had never had a sexual relationship with me.

Then Herbert's side put on the Highland Park psychologist, Roberta Cusumano, to talk about my stay at the alcohol and drug center.

Next came the "baker," Hubert, who had cut off his long hippie hair and shaved his beard at Farish's request. I almost didn't recognize him. He denied that he ever "lay on the couch" with me.

Tim Whisner was called next. He was just a vague acquaintance from parties and had been Brian Richards's roommate until they had had a severe falling out. The issue of lesbianism came up:

QUESTION: Had you and Mrs. Pulitzer ever discussed her sexual experiences?... Has she ever mentioned to you that she has engaged in or experimented with lesbianism?

ANSWER: On one occasion.

That was the extent of his testimony on this issue.

Next came my favorite, Liza. She claimed we had never been close from the start and that I was jealous of her. But then she also added to the lesbian issue, her own little surprise. She announced that I had propositioned her.

QUESTION: Now, did you ever have any discussions with Roxanne Pulitzer about the subject of lesbianism?

ANSWER: Yes, I did.

QUESTION: Would you tell the judge what that discussion was?

ANSWER: That took place the same night. We had come back to the table and she said to me that if I ever felt that I ever wanted to have a lesbian relationship to please let her know because she would like to be the one that I got involved with.

QUESTION: Can you explain to the judge then why, if you didn't get along with her and she didn't get along with you, she would ask you to have a sexual relationship with her?

ANSWER: I can only say that possibly she was attracted to me physically.

Robert Reid, Herbert's boat captain of many years, told how I had told him that I would sit in the dark while a spirit would come down and take over my body and move me to draw. Prior to this testimony, in arguing that Reid should be allowed to testify, Robert Scott self-righteously demanded, "Should somebody who wants custody of a five-year-old child or two five-year-old children . . . be a person who tells somebody . . . that the spirits guide them when they draw drawings in the dark?"

I started to see what all this was heading toward. I remembered having to turn in all my metaphysical books from Rainbow Bridge before the trial for evidence. They were going to use my spiritual beliefs and psychic experiences to paint me as some kind of sexually kinky religious weirdo who carried on "strange and bizarre" rituals in her home. They produced, as evidence, my drawings, checks I had written to psychics for readings, and the infamous trumpet that had been given to Herbert following the seance we had attended together in Lily Dale—at his urging! Herbert's side testified that I had taken the trumpet home and kept it in our bedroom.

The court clerk held the four-foot aluminum trumpet for everyone to see. They also produced pictures of one of Herbert's eight-point trophies that was mounted on the wall because I had stuck the trumpet to the deer's nose along with a big red ball on the end of it, under which Mac and Zac and I had sung "Rudolph the Red-Nosed Reindeer" during the previous Christmas season. This was part of their case against me. I guess they didn't approve of our caroling.

But whether relevant or not, it made great grist for the hundreds of news reporters covering this trial. The *New York Post* seized on this tidbit, embellishing it into the headline "I Slept with a Trumpet." The reasoning was that since the trumpet was stored in my closet and my closet was in the bedroom, I must have used it to have sex. I would forever more be known as the "strumpet with the trumpet."

Nothing was making any sense. Maybe Hunter Thompson had the answer in his interview with the *Palm Beach Post*: "We all sleep with trumpets. The real question is, is Peter Pulitzer jealous of the trumpet?"

Next came surprise witness Janice Nelson. She was the "psychic" who had given me the love potion. She also, it turned out, had a few aliases. On the stand she said she was also known as Cassia Donovan, Jessica Smith, and Janice O'Brien. Joe Farish referred to her as "the swami."

My side hadn't a clue about what she was going to testify on. I hadn't seen Janice since the late summer when she had asked me if she could be a character witness for my side because she wanted the publicity. Farish had turned her down. As far as I knew, she had left town. She had called me from the west coast of Florida to ask for money. I had wired her $100, but I guess that wasn't enough, because on the stand she said I owed her $57,000 for all the hours of psychic counseling she had given me and that I'd promised her a new car. It was a shock to see her on the stand.

She testified to witnessing a great deal of immoral adulterous conduct on my part with the "French baker" and Brian, the "handyman."

While she was on the stand, a staring contest began which lasted seven or eight minutes.

I can remember telling Janice, when I thought she was a friend, how bothered I get when people stare at me, so when Mark Luttier started the contest, I foolishly felt I had to stare back and not give Janice the benefit of this play.

Herbert took over where Scott and Luttier stopped, and I locked eyes with him. I didn't want to show weakness—after all, my head was the only trophy not up on his wall. Joe Farish picked up on this and asked the court to have them stop. Judge Harper answered, "I didn't notice anybody staring," upon which Farish replied, "They're doing it constantly—that's some of Janice the Swami's psychic tactics, sir."

Judge Harper's final judgment comments that he "closely observed the appearance and demeanor of the witnesses, and in particular, the parties, throughout the trial. As to the husband, this court could readily observe the embarrassment, painful hurt and frustrating concern exuding from his doleful eyes and aging face. By contrast, the wife nonchalantly sat at the table "doodling" on a note pad as though unconcerned. As the husband and his witness, Janice Nelson, were testifying, the wife engaged them in vitriolic stares, eventually staring them down."

Janice was considered by the court a credible witness.

Herbert's side put Dr. Myrl Spivey, our family physician, on the stand to testify to his good physical condition. Then they brought on Estelle Godbout, the nanny I had fired and Herbert had hired to do his ironing after the emergency child custody hearing. She testified to my "questionable relationship" with Jackie Ickx, the "race-car driver."

Herbert and I had met Jackie Ickx at the Kimberlys' several years before. We had become very good friends. We invited Jackie and his wife, Catherine, to stay with us at the Hotel Pulitzer in Amsterdam. Another time, they invited us to their home in Brussels, where they showed us pictures of Ickx's five wins at Le Mans.

Estelle claimed that Jackie Ickx and I were kissing in "amorous embrace" on the beach a short way away from Mac and Zac. She was referring to the public beach directly at the end of Worth Avenue, beach-blanket heaven —such a secluded, private place to pick for an illicit love affair!

She also testified that she had observed us lying in bed together while Mac and Zac were in the room. Now, where else were we all supposed to watch cartoons from, when there are no chairs in the room?

The court considered Estelle a credible witness.

I couldn't really understand how all these alleged "lovers" who had come into my life *after* Herbert had moved out had anything to do with the deterioration of our marriage.

I knew that Florida was a no-fault state; however, I feel the court found a dual meaning in the no-fault law. Herbert's infidelities with Jacquie Kimberly and Janie Dean were not taken into consideration. Judge Harper saw me as committing "flagrant acts of adultery" and other "gross moral misconduct" and destroying the marriage, but he saw Herbert in a different light. "The husband testified that well subsequent to the final separation of the parties he began a relationship with Jane Dean. While that relationship was meretricious, it had no causal connection with the marriage breakup, but rather was a by-product of the broken marriage."

Many times, after this, I have been aware that mothers have a definite disadvantage when engaged in custody disputes. *We* are the ones on trial, *we* are criticized for every imperfection, while a father who simply wants his kids is given credit for having that wonderful desire.

Herbert's side called to the stand Sheri Rifenberg, a social investigator for the county. During the summer, when she began her investigation, Joe Farish had told me not to worry about this; she was simply going to see how I interacted with the children and I should just be myself. She called me to make an appointment at her office and told me to bring a list of no more than five or six character witnesses who had been around Mac and Zac and me. I spent approximately an hour with her at her office and brought my list, which consisted of Sandy, my cousin who had lived with us for three years; Pierrette Barr, our nanny for the last nine months; Annie, the maid; Maria Schultz, Mac and Zac's schoolteacher; Roberta Cusumano, my counselor for the past year; and Terry de la Valdene, a girlfriend whose house Mac and Zac used to go swim at.

A few days later, Sheri Rifenberg came to observe the children and me for approximately forty-five minutes, during which she spent most of the time quizzing me about all the men in my entire life, from John to the present. Had I lived with them? Had they supported me? What did I do with them? And on and on.

As Sheri Rifenberg was testifying on the stand with her report in front of us, I was astonished to see Herbert's list of character witnesses. It consisted of Robert Reid, his boat captain; Peter Benoit, one of Herbert's closest friends, who had just married Liza's best friend; Johnny Capers, his cook-gardener for thirteen years; Minnie Pulitzer, his oldest daughter, whom I hardly knew at all; Lilly Rousseau, his ex-wife; Tim Whisner, the ex-friend of Brian Richards; Ronnie Sales, Herbert's previous attorney; Janie Dean, his new girlfriend, the "queen of group"; Estelle Godbout, the "fired in rage" nanny; Dr. Paul Jahnig, the marriage counselor I had seen twice in 1980; Bill Cheatham, Herbert's new friend from group therapy; Enid Cheatham, wife of Bill, Janie Dean's best friend, new friend from group therapy; and last but not least, Liza.

Rifenberg's report revealed she had spent two hours face to face with Bill Cheatham, longer than she'd spent with me, and fifteen minutes on the phone with Sandy, who had spent three years with Mac and Zac. I knew then this was trouble.

I was right. Her report concluded that Herbert was the preferred custodial parent.

The court found it a "cogent objective custody investigation report."

Dr. Theodore Blau, a child psychologist, argued in this case against the application of the "tender years doctrine," which normally awards children of a young age to their mother.

Instead, Dr. Blau referred to something called the Warshak Study, a comparison of children who were raised by the father as primary custodian compared with children raised by the mother. Dr. Blau said that the studies showed that boy children, beginning at age two, tend to prefer time with the father. He said the studies showed that boys with fathers as primary custodian did better in their academic work, were better adjusted and were better accepted by their friends than boys raised with mothers as their primary custodian. He had observed Mac and Zac interacting with Herbert on one or two occasions, and he brought up the fact that they were well-adjusted children.

Dr. Blau never came to observe *my* interaction with Mac and Zac, yet I felt their adjustment should logically have been traced to their having spent the last year and a half with *me*.

Judge Harper, in his final judgment, decided the case based upon "the testimony of Sheri Rifenberg and the very impressive testimony of Dr. Theodore H. Blau, child psychiatrist, both of whom recommend the husband as primary custodian of the children, in preference to the wife." The judge's final judgment continued, "To do otherwise would continue to be adverse and detrimental to the moral and social health, safety and welfare of the children." As for the "tender years doctrine," Judge Harper found "the doctrine is inapplicable under the facts of this case. As noted hereinabove, all other factors are not equal because of the wife's flagrant adultery and other gross marital misconduct; the wife has abandoned the primary caretaker role to nannies and the husband; and the children are well beyond the bonding age."

I knew all along that we'd made a mistake in concentrating on financial experts instead of bringing in child experts.

Johnny Capers, Herbert's cook-gardener, testified to my cooking abilities, saying I couldn't even make bacon and eggs for my children's breakfast.

Dr. Paul Jahnig's testimony surprised me, because much of it was based on his separate meetings with Herbert, rather than our two meetings together in April 1980. In my two meetings, I had talked mostly about my problems with Liza. Now I found out that Herbert had gone back to see him a few times without me in January 1981 and had discussed other things—such as *my* drug problem—with him.

Herbert was called as the last witness for his side's direct testimony.

Of course, this was the most painful witness for me, especially since almost all of the fond memories of our marriage were being destroyed one by one. He said that I had tricked him into getting me pregnant, and, most painful of all, that he had no love left for me.

I thought I was braced by now for Herbert's testimony, but I was not prepared for the pain I felt that day.

Every afternoon at five o'clock, drained and weary, my ears still ringing with accusations and lies, I would drive by the Little French Bakery and spend a few minutes with Hubert before going home. He invariably met me with a warm welcoming hug and a few light jokes. I needed Hubert's unquestioning support and these brief moments not just to wind down but to find the strength to become a mother again.

It was imperative that I discard all trace of the courtroom's daily frenzy and filth before entering my home and encountering Mac and Zac's sweet innocence. As soon as their arms were around me, the last painful remains of the day would fade away and I would enjoy making our evenings together as special as ever. But this, for reasons beyond my control, was fast becoming a very difficult task.

I couldn't allow the children to watch their favorite TV programs any longer for fear my face might suddenly flash onto the screen.

Similarly, I was afraid to take them on the Lake Trail or to public places lest we meet with reporters or photographers. It was my primary concern to shield Mac and Zac at all times from the ugliness of the trial. The media were unrelenting in hounding me. They had picked me for their newest victim and they were having a heyday.

I was a trollop, a gold digger of extremely unsavory background, a small-town "strumpet with a trumpet," a "nympho dyke," a "cocaine slut," a "black-magic voodoo queen," who had lied and weaved her infamous way into upper-class Palm Beach. Herbert Pulitzer could do no wrong. He was the kindly, trusting pillar of society whom I betrayed and deeply wronged. Indeed, the roles were reversed and *I* had perverted *him*, a man of fifty-two!

The publicity surrounding the daily sensational events

of the divorce poured on and on in this vein. It brought to my mind how hard Joseph Pulitzer had worked to elevate his newspapers out of the realm of yellow journalism. Ironically, his grandson Herbert was now feeding the media's baser appetites. It had come full circle.

At Lorraine's suggestion, I carefully avoided the newsstands and the evening news broadcasts. "Why bother with any of this, Roxanne? It's all trash anyhow—not worth the heartache," Lorraine had warned me as soon as Scott's opening statement made it obvious that Herbert's lawyers had picked the sewer to fight in.

To this day, I still haven't read most of the articles concerning the trial.

But everyone else in Palm Beach and indeed many people throughout the world were thoroughly enjoying the sizzle and drama in the morning papers.

It became increasingly difficult for me to do my grocery shopping or to run any errands around town. People would stop and nudge each other or smirk. Others would turn their backs and pretend I didn't exist or simply look offended. Everywhere I could hear the whispers and feel the condemnation. I felt I was the Scarlet Woman of the South.

Mac and Zac were still living with me, so the teachers at the Palm Beach Private School had little choice but to talk with me when I needed to confer with them about the boys' progress or behavior. However, the other parents were quite a different story—the mothers particularly. Without fail they would all race by me with not so much as a glance, and retreat with their offspring as if I were spreading the plague.

One Sunday morning, it was my turn to be "helping mother" at the kindergarten Sunday school class at Bethesda-by-the-Sea, Palm Beach's stately Episcopal church.

I had been assigned this date to attend the class back in September at the start of the Sunday school year. For Mac and Zac's sake, I didn't cancel out, although the preceding court day had just blasted out more dramatic and sordid revelations for Palm Beachers to feed on.

I had brought cookies, and although I was a little nervous at being out in public, I was quite ready to relax with the children and help them with their drawings or lessons.

But one after another, as each mother walked into the little kindergarten room and recognized me, trying to blend with the walls and look efficient, they rushed to grab their children and make a hasty exit.

So that Sunday, most of Palm Beach's future staunch Episcopalians had to make do without religious education.

The nastiest shock, however, came when I drove by a Worth Avenue shop, Donald Bruce, one afternoon. To my horror, this shop's window displayed a naked mannequin partly covered with mink, reclining on a large bed with a champagne glass in one hand and a trumpet in the other. I was hurt and insulted. I also was so startled that I very nearly collided with a Rolls Silver Cloud.

My French friends, however, went off into gales of irreverent mirth when I indignantly related my story. They laughed until the tears rolled down their cheeks. I still haven't heard the end of it—I suppose I never *will* hear the end of it. What *did* I do with that trumpet?

The next morning back in the courthouse, where the press coverage had grown to over three hundred reporters, who had been given their own room with several special TV monitors, I pushed my way down the hall to my chair to listen to Joe Farish start his case for my defense.

Herbert was called back to the stand; I just remember how cold and hostile he was. Then Farish put on Pierrette Barr, our nanny of the past nine months, who was very close to Mac and Zac. I thought she gave a very positive testimony.

So did Annie Knowles, the maid; Marie Schultz, Mac and Zac's schoolteacher; and Lorraine. These witnesses were exclusively concerned with the custody issue and my role as a mother. Unfortunately, none of their testimonies were ever picked up on, not even in the final judgment, so I won't bother relating them now. The nicer the person, the less interested the media was—not juicy enough!

Jacquie Kimberly took the stand in her flamboyant style. Her attorney sat so close to her that they looked as if they were joined at the hip. Herbert's lawyer questioned her.

QUESTION: Now, Ma'am, have you ever had sexual intercourse in a lesbian way with Roxanne Pulitzer?
ANSWER: No.
QUESTION: Have you ever been in the first-floor bedroom in a bed located in that bedroom naked with Roxanne Pulitzer who was also naked at the same time?
ANSWER: You're disgusting.
QUESTION: Will you answer that question?
ANSWER: No.

I agreed with Jacquie. For the life of me, I couldn't see any connection between a brief threesome fling and lesbianism. I think she gave an honest and proper response. And furthermore, what was supposed to have taken place in this first-floor bedroom? I was very confused. Had there been a threesome that I'd forgotten? I only remembered the Holiday Inn and the boat!

This testimony took place late in the afternoon, and when Scott wanted Jacquie back the next morning, she had taken to a hospital bed with some undisclosed illness—but not before telling the reporters her feelings about the trial and Herbert: "It's ludicrous. Pulitzer is definitely deranged and desperate for the almighty buck."

We called my cousin Sandy, because she had spent three years with us helping with Mac and Zac.

All the good things she had to say about me as a mother were totally negated by her previous tape, in spite of her explanation for making it.

QUESTION: Tell the court the circumstances of going to Mr. Sales's office to make that statement.
ANSWER: At that time, the circumstances surrounding that statement is the day after we left Pulitzer's. I

was extremely, very emotionally upset, because
number one, Mr. Pulitzer had said I could no longer
see the children, which I found out later was not
true, and secondly, he had promised me that he
would never, ever, use it in court, that it was strictly
a scare tactic to try to patch up his marriage.

The court relied on the tape—rather than Sandy's positive testimony in the courtroom—in the final judgment.
Judge Harper referred to the tape, but never even *mentioned* Sandy's testimony, which refuted the validity of the
tape. "... from the inception of the birth of Mack [*sic*] and
Zack [*sic*], the wife has all but abandoned the raising of the
children to various nannies employed for that purpose. See
for example the tape recorded sworn statement (in evidence
as husband's exhibit number 22) made by Sandra Andreasen, the wife's cousin."

We called Brian Richards, my "paramour," to refute the
allegations about our love affair.

Roberta Cusumano came on next to testify about my
stay at Highland Park. At the time, she had summed it up
across the top of her file as "Seems to be a Pawn in the
Marital-Palm Beach divorce game." This was shown to the
court. They also asked her about my psychological state of
mind over the last year.

QUESTION: And what did you find her problem to be?
ANSWER: The initial, the diagnosis that was made? ... I
felt her problem was marital counseling, that she
needed marital counseling, that the problem was
more marital.
QUESTION: In your counseling with Mrs. Pulitzer, was it
ever presented to you any problems of a psychological abuse on either side?
ANSWER: Yes, I guess the psychological abuse basically
revolved around the vacillating back and forth in the
divorce situation, especially, we are going to get a
divorce, we're not, let's get back together, let's settle

out of court, let's go to court, da, da, da. Back and forth, this kind of pendulum going, seesaw, seesaw, and Roxanne kind of not being able to deal with that.

Next, we brought on Dr. José Almeida, another marriage counselor Herbert and I had gone to see after Dr. Jahnig. He felt that we had been living out a master-servant complex. But like everyone else who had to take the stand, the tension was a bit much. Dr. Almeida was so nervous his *hair* was shaking. When asked "Are you married," he replied, "Yes, I do."

Dr. Almeida also went on to say: ". . . she was getting a double message. You are my wife but you don't have any needs. I don't respond to your needs. You respond to my needs. . . . The impression that I got and that I was working on was not that Mrs. Pulitzer was sick but that the marriage was sick. Their relationship was kind of a structured relationship in terms of marriage. That is the reason why she was constantly getting what she perceived as a double message. On one hand you marry me and be my wife but you are not supposed to have any children, you are not supposed to have any needs, you are to respond only to my needs."

Then we called Dr. Stephan Kahn, the head of Highland Park Hospital, and he reiterated that my problem was a marital one and that he had dismissed me from the hospital because I was *not* addicted to drugs.

I was brought back on the stand as we were heading into the third week. By now, we had national television coverage, *Time* magazine, *Newsweek*, *Playboy*, Hunter Thompson covering for *Rolling Stone*, *Paris Match*, the *Daily Express* in London, and various other publications; some were even trying to snatch my doodles to have them analyzed!

So by the time I took the stand in my own defense, I was a nervous wreck. I was asked very personal questions. I testified about Mac and Zac and our deep relationship, but then after the next few questions, I broke down on the stand.

QUESTION: Do you love Herbert here?

ANSWER: I will always have a special love for him, because he's the father of my children.

QUESTION: In what way has he expressed his love and affection towards you and the children?

ANSWER: I think he has shown the world what kind of love he has for us by this lawsuit.

QUESTION: . . . How do you want the children to look towards their father?

ANSWER: I want the children to always love and respect their father and their name.

QUESTION: Now Ma'am, you heard Dr. Almeida describe what he observed, that your husband Herbert was in a position of master and you were in the position of servant. Looking back, now reflecting back, can you help the court in filling in details in that respect?

ANSWER: Well, I don't want to put the blame on this man totally, because obviously, if I were in this relationship, I was going along with it. Also, I would have done anything this man wanted me to do.

I broke down sobbing, and the court had to call a recess as I was whisked away into the closet outside the judge's chambers to recover.

I had tried so hard in this trial to hold myself together. I guess I should have listened to my lawyer, who had been urging me to cry throughout the trial.

Evidently, that is what the courts like, because to quote Judge Harper's decision, "Frankly, the court was somewhat relieved, when, toward the end of the eighteen day trial, the wife finally broke into tears, necessitating a brief recess, indicating that she was, after all, capable of human emotion and concern."

I then had to go back into the room to resume my testimony.

This concluded my side's defense case.

Later, David Roth, Jacquie's attorney, and Dr. Kaupe testified that Jacquie couldn't take the stand again. "She looked thin, she looked tired and she had a hacking cough."

Herbert's side came back on with Richard Hurly, a former bartender at Herbert's restaurant. He testified that he had seen Jacquie and me having lunch at the Yacht Club.

QUESTION: What activities were they engaged in?
ANSWER: Talking . . .
QUESTION: Was there any physical contact between the two?
ANSWER: Some.
QUESTION: What contact?
ANSWER: Affection.
QUESTION: What exactly were they doing?
ANSWER: The kind of thing you see a boy and a girl do—touching each other—holding hands—physical touching—holding of hands—maybe touching each other's shoulder or arm.

Since then, I haven't dared pat another female on the arm.

At this point, Scott and Luttier produced the bomb. Steve Anderson, Herbert's previous mate aboard the *Sea Hunter*, was called as a surprise rebuttal witness.

What I was about to hear nearly made me fall off my chair. Now I was to find out the mystery of the first-floor bedroom.

QUESTION: Would you now tell Judge Harper what you observed.
ANSWER: I came up from the boat, from behind the home to make a phone call, which we normally did, entered the front door, and heard voices from the bedroom. And I recognized Mrs. Pulitzer's voice. I stepped aside, looked into the bedroom there, glanced, and observed four legs protruding from the

end of the bed. At that point, I just kind of hesitated for a minute, and a set of legs . . . Anyway, I noticed four legs protruding from the end of the bed. Subsequently one set of legs slid off and up stood a woman totally naked, for a few seconds. She then returned back to the bed. The other set of legs then slid off the end of the bed and out came Roxanne in a very sheer nightgown. And she asked as to what I was doing in the house. And I said I was making a phone call and she asked if I was finished and I said yes. She returned to the bedroom, closed the door, and I left.

Farish cross-examined Steve Anderson.

QUESTION: When did you first tell about this incident to anyone?
ANSWER: This year . . .
QUESTION: So you kept it a secret for three years, is that right?
ANSWER: More or less . . .
QUESTION: Well, to whom did you tell this first, after three years?
ANSWER: To Peter Pulitzer.

It was a sensational story, but why had we left the door leading directly into the living room/kitchen wide open in broad late-morning daylight? And where were my children, the two nannies, the maid, the cook-gardener, when they were needed?

I really thought that Herbert's side had gone too far with this one. The trial had taken on such proportions and the insinuations were so preposterous and farfetched, I felt that Herbert's attorneys were not only too far out on a limb, but had now fallen off!

I couldn't believe the lengths to which everybody was going.

So many witnesses had poured out their dreadful tales and the lawyers had selected and twisted and edited each testimony to such an extent that I wondered if this whole trial retained any credibility at all.

Judge Harper found Anderson a credible witness.

From then on, the trial was virtually over. Lawyers' fees were discussed, and we got ready for the closing arguments.

My side blamed him, his side blamed me. The last thing I wanted to do at this time was to hear all the charges all over again.

But as Luttier was speaking, I realized I wouldn't have to hear them *all* again: "There is no doubt that Mrs. Pulitzer lied at this trial, we have counted them up and there are a hundred lies. I'm not going to go through them, that would be nit-picking."

Well, that was a relief. At least I didn't have to hear him nitpick!

But seriously, how could such unsubstantiated statements be allowed in a court of law?

I returned to reality as I heard Luttier say: "Peter had to file this lawsuit, he was forced to and he was forced to for the simple reason that his one goal, that he felt that it was absolutely necessary to obtain primary physical custody of his children in order to assure their safety and well-being in the future."

We both knew perfectly well this wasn't true. Two weeks before he sued for child custody, he had offered the children to me—if I had signed the postmarital document he wanted me to sign.

Luttier went on for forty-five minutes. One more time I tried to look over at Herbert but to no avail. The last thing I remember is Luttier saying, "And lastly, Peter Pulitzer does not apologize to Roxanne Pulitzer for what has been said in this trial."

The trial concluded in early November. In the two months waiting for Judge Harper's decision, I had a long time to think. I was becoming aware of a much bigger picture.

Here I was, branded with labels that didn't apply to me, yet which would stay glued to me for the rest of my life. The truths that no one had really bothered to look for during this farce of a trial were becoming much clearer to me. I was slowly recognizing the willful, stubborn behavior that had been my contribution to the failure of our marriage.

Because I had needed more space, more autonomy in our life as a couple, I had convinced myself that Herbert should change *his* ways. I had also demanded he choose between Liza and me and had become adamant he do so. This was totally unrealistic, and unfair since, after all, Liza was his daughter.

Just as Herbert had decided to make me over into a more suitable Palm Beach type, here I had been unreasonably determined to impose my will on a man of his age and habits.

So I had allowed this devastating head-on collision to occur.

A few spurts of jealousy, a few tantrums on both sides, added to a few months of high living in social Palm Beach and a great deal of paranoia, and the result was this chaos in our lives.

At this time, I couldn't foresee who would pay the highest price for these mistakes, but already I knew that we would all carry scars—deep ones—that would not fade rapidly.

There lies the true tragedy of this overpublicized trial. There had been too much dirt, too much anger, and the four of us, as a family and as individuals, would have to bear the stigma of this divorce forever.

Now I was at last fully facing my share of the responsibility in the mess we had made of our potential happiness.

For many a soul-searching night, I was to battle with my guilt and lonely regrets.

I could see all too clearly where I had been blind and willful and childish and where I had traded compassion for my pride.

To give credit where it is due, Herbert had been the first to pick up on the negative effects cocaine had on our lives, but instead of cooperating, I had only resented the way he was handling the problem. I am bitterly aware that had I listened to him then, I would have avoided many mistakes and pitfalls.

Why hadn't Herbert and I been adult enough to meet each other halfway? Why hadn't we been able to compromise for each other? All this pain for ourselves and our children—would it ever end? And was there a way to overcome the waste of our marriage and of our lives?

For the second Christmas in a row, Herbert and I went through the motions of celebrating it together with the kids, as we waited for the judge's final decision. As saddened as I was about what we had come to, Herbert looked just as sad. I felt such overwhelming sorrow, such shame, over how we had both behaved, I wanted to salvage one gesture of kindness, humanity, from our shredded past.

I knew that Herbert was leaving for the ranch the next day, and he had not spent much time with Mac and Zac these last months. I suggested that he take the kids with him.

"They're really becoming great little boys," I told him. "Take them with you for two or three days and they'll cheer you up."

Three days later, December 28, the judge issued his final decision.

I can still remember the scene as vividly as if it were yesterday. I was staring at the television in Mac and Zac's room. I missed them very much while they were away with Herbert and had gone into their room because it made me feel closer to them. The phone rang; when I put my hand down on the receiver to answer it, I got this dreadful feeling inside, and the receiver was stone-cold to my touch.

Why was my intuition so strong at this moment, the intuition which had totally failed me for the past two years?

On the other end of the line was a secretary from Farish's office. "The decision has just come down," she said. "Joe would like to see you in his office right away."

I told Pierrette where I was going. She hugged me, and there was a sadness in her eyes that made me turn away from her.

"I will say a prayer for you and the children," she said, as I walked out the door.

I had promised Lorraine and Hubert that I would call them immediately when the decision came in. They both wanted to be with me, but at the moment it finally happened, I needed to be alone.

❧ *Fifteen* ❧

As soon as I climbed into my car and pulled out of the driveway, I felt a rush of negative thoughts. I kept telling myself to think positively, think positively.

Although Farish's office was only a few minutes away, just on the other side of the nearest bridge leading to West Palm, I purposely drove over to the second bridge because I wanted to have the extra minutes to get my thoughts on a positive track. My subconscious knew what was coming, but I needed to fool myself.

When I walked into the reception area, all the secretaries were huddled, whispering, over the Xerox machine. The door to Farish's office was ajar, so I walked in unannounced. Farish's back was to the door and his feet were up on the desk, and he was reading a copy of Judge Harper's final decision while talking on the phone.

"Can you believe it, I only got one hundred two thousand five hundred dollars, and for a case like that?" he was telling the person on the other end of the conversation.

It crossed my mind that if he was complaining about money, everything else about the decision must be all right.

He continued with his conversation for several more minutes, while I sat there, staring at the boar heads on the walls and the alligator briefcases lined up next to his desk.

Finally he put the phone down.

"What happened to Mac and Zac?" I asked. "Who's the primary custodial parent?"

"He is."

I was too stunned to say anything. My chest got very tight, and I felt dizzy. I couldn't focus at all. I just wanted to run, to escape, to make this go away.

He started paging through the document with one hand as he dialed the telephone with the other.

He looked up at me for a minute as the phone number rang and said, "Well, he bought this case. He bought it."

I felt a sense of shame so excruciating I thought I was going to be sick. All I could think of was, *Get me home. Get me home.*

I got up from that chair and I ran. I ran out of that office, down the elevator, and out the door to my parked car. Reporters and TV cameras were already gathering outside the courthouse. I was speeding so fast that I flew over the bridge. And the whole way I kept repeating over and over to myself, *Get me home. Get me home. Please, God, get me home.*

The TV reporters were already waiting for me in my driveway. I ran into the house, where Pierrette was waiting to hear. She just looked into my eyes.

"I lost my children," I said, brushing past her as I headed for my room. I remember the pain searing her face, for she had loved them, too. I told her that I was going to my bedroom and that to please understand I had to be alone. There was nothing anyone could do for me now.

I drew the curtains and collapsed on my bed in the cool, dim room, still strewn with Mac and Zac's Christmas toys which I had left there purposely as a sort of comfort in their absence. I stared at those toys for a long time and wondered how or where I could find comfort now. I reached for the phone to call my mother at work at the restaurant.

"Frawleys," she answered in her bright, chirpy way. I can still hear my own anguished voice echoing in my ears. "Mom," I moaned, struggling to gather the strength to tell her about her grandsons.

But my long, long speechless pause must have said it all. She knew. "Oh my God, no," she said. "You lost your boys."

"Yes," I breathed, my voice cracking.

After talking to my mother, I took the phone off the hook and put on my old blue bathrobe. The loss of the children felt like an amputation, as though my body had been severed from the neck on down. What made it worse was that my brain would not shut down and block all this out for me—not even for a second. I immediately started punishing myself with pictures of the boys' tear-stained little faces looking sadly out the window, peering at my car driving away, as they would always do whenever I had to leave them. This played like a broken record over and over again for hours in my mind. I felt I had lost my children because I had put my husband first. It seemed unbelievable that in trying to save my marriage, I had lost my children.

Pierrette must have called up Hubert. He came in and just lay next to me on the bed, hugging me as I cried. We didn't talk. There would be no sleep for me that night.

It wasn't until my mother and sister arrived the next day that I could even bring myself to read Judge Harper's final judgment word for word. As bad as it had been having to sit in the courtroom and hear all the lies and terrible things said about me publicly, reading that heartless decision in cold black type in the privacy of my own bedroom was even worse. It was so final. Judge Harper didn't even manage to spell the children's names correctly. He wrote:

> Based on the totality of the credible evidence, both direct and circumstantial, this court finds that the wife's gross, moral misconduct involved more than isolated, discreet acts of adultery. . . .
>
> Regarding the allegations of the wife's lesbian infidelity, a credible witness [Steve Anderson] testified to having observed the wife and her female companion, Jacqui [*sic*] Kimberly, lying together on a bed in the marital home in the Spring of 1979. . . .

In addition to the above, from the inception of the birth of Mack [sic] and Zack [sic], the wife has all but abandoned the raising of the children to various nannies employed for that purpose.... Much of the wife's abundant idle time is spent on her own personal pleasures such as visiting numerous nightclubs and discotheques, dancing and snorting cocaine, as well as consuming alcoholic beverages, until the wee hours of the morning. For a time, the husband participated with the wife. However, it was not long before the fast pace nightlife began to take its toll on the early rising husband who is 21 years older than his wife. For a time, the husband turned to cocaine, as a crutch, to give him the stamina to keep pace with his younger, energetic wife. When that failed, at the request of his wife, the husband began to leave his wife at the disco so that he could get some restful sleep before having to go to work....

At this time, the court feels it appropriate to comment on the demeanor of the parties as it relates to their credibility and in weighing the evidence.... As to the husband, this court could readily observe the embarrassment, painful hurt and frustrating concern exuding from his doleful eyes and aging face. By contrast, the wife nonchalantly sat at the table "doodling" on a note pad as though unconcerned....

The wife's exorbitant demands shock the conscience of this court, putting the court in mind of the hit record by country music singer, Jerry Reed, which laments, "She Got the Gold Mine, I Got the Shaft."...

The wife entered this marriage with limited financial resources, a used automobile of unknown value and a $7,000 interest in a mobile home. Upon departing the marriage, which she destroyed, she takes with her a $20,000 Porsche automobile purchased with the husband's funds; about $60,000 in jewelry purchased in large measure with the husband's funds; $48,000 in rehabilitative alimony; $7,000 cash equity in the husband's boat; and $102,500 in attorney's fees.

When I got to the part about the children, it was too cruel to even comprehend. How do you emotionally deal with the fact that you no longer can see your children at any time? How do you cope with the fact that from here on, you can no longer just wander into their room in the middle of the night and kiss them? Who's going to comfort them when they are sick? Who's going to tuck them in at night?

The words on the document seemed blurry, and I could hardly grasp them. My visitation rights were limited to four weeks out of the twelve in the summer and two weekends a month the rest of the year, with every other Christmas day, Easter, and Thanksgiving. Roughly a total of eighty-five days a year.

I soon learned that except for the summer weeks, there is no time during the year when the visiting parent can have a sense of family life with the child. The weekends are simply not long enough. No sooner has the child adjusted to the Friday-night transition than it is time to deal with another separation on Sunday night.

The visitation agreement filled an entire page of legal-size paper and seemed to cover every possible contingency for taking possession and relinquishing possession of the children except one: simple human need and a mother's love.

That afternoon, Lorraine came over and held me for a long time as I sobbed. She kept telling me that the children and I would be fine one day, that I would pull through.

"You've got to hang on, Roxanne. You're going to make it through this. You are, for the children's sake," she repeated over and over. I wasn't minding her—I kept imagining Mac's and Zac's hurt, bewildered faces. I was fully aware that they were not close to Herbert then. They would be scared. I thought of their little arms around my neck—I knew they needed me now. I couldn't let myself dwell on what they must be going through. The three of us had been living alone for the past eighteen months, and I knew they were not at all prepared for this. I wished I could have helped explain things to them. They were not ready for this. And now I had let Herbert take them with him for a few days just at the worst time imaginable.

I couldn't face life without Mac and Zac. "I might as well be dead," I moaned over and over to my sister Pam. But way down deep inside a tiny voice emerged through the grief for an instant telling me that I would go on and fight for them until the bitter end—whatever it took. I knew then that this would have to be my only road, all the way to the Supreme Court, if necessary.

During those first few days, I was desperate to see the children so that Herbert and I could sit down together to discuss the judge's ruling. I kept calling the ranch, calling the boat, and the phone was either off the hook or no one answered. My sister even went to see Herbert to plead with him to allow me to see the children, but he wouldn't permit her on the boat and refused to listen. She wrote him a letter, but he ignored it.

I couldn't believe—even after all that had happened—that he was behaving this way. I just didn't understand it. I knew that if I had won custody, no matter what conditions had been set in the visitation agreement, I would have given him open visitation. He could have seen them whenever he wanted to. Herbert knew this; I had testified to this during the trial.

I was so worried that Mac and Zac would feel I had somehow abandoned them. I couldn't erase from my mind the night, during the period of the trial when little Mac had turned to me as I was tucking him in for the night and with the most heartrending look in his eyes had asked, "Mommy, we're always going to be together, right?" Never doubting that we would, I assured him not to worry, that, yes, we would always be together. Now it turned out I had misinformed him, something I will regret forever.

I felt so helpless, so filled with despair.

Pam would just pace the floor for hours, and I remember telling her, "There is no God," because I didn't understand how the God I had believed in would let this happen. I completely dismissed Him from my life. For months afterward, I didn't pray or meditate or seek the help of psychics. I didn't believe in anything or anyone.

I felt an incredible hate welling up in me. I thought of murdering Judge Harper and Herbert and the lawyers. I thought of killing myself.

No doubt because she sensed this, my mother doled out sleeping pills one by one for fear that I might take the whole bottle. I probably would have.

For several nights I slept, as best I could, with a gun next to my bed. Subconsciously, I think that I derived a measure of reassurance from knowing it was there, that if the pain ever got too bad, I could end it.

My mom kept telling me she didn't like the gun so close, that it wasn't safe. One night I overheard her talking to my stepfather about it, so I took the gun and hid it in the closet in one of my boots. A few nights later, I really hit bottom. I thought about the gun and went to the closet to retrieve it. The gun was gone.

I flew downstairs like a crazy woman and started shouting at my mother and stepfather. "Who's got my gun? Who's got my gun? Whoever it is, you'd better give it back. Otherwise I want you all out of my house, because you're taking my things and I won't tolerate it in my house!"

My stepfather took me by the shoulders and tried to calm me down. I can still remember the fearful look in his face, mirroring my momentary insanity.

"I've got the gun right here," he said. "I took the bullets out of it because I didn't think it was safe."

"Put that gun back right now," I snapped. "I'm not going to shoot myself. But I want that gun put back there."

The gun, though empty, was returned to my night table. I never got any closer to using it on myself, although I'm not really sure that I ever intended to. The gun represented a choice, if I ever needed that outlet.

In the midst of the emotional shock of the final decision and custody agreement, I was also forced to deal with moving. Although it had been my home for more than eight years, it was Herbert's house. Judge Harper's final decision was no more generous in this respect than in any other—he gave me less than two weeks to vacate with only my clothes, my car, and my personal belongings. I found it eerie that I had married Herbert on January 12, 1976, and I was ordered out of the house January 10, 1983, the end of a seven-year cycle. Within five days of the court's decision, Herbert stormed into the house and up to our bedroom, where I was still crumpled on the bed in a disheveled emotional heap.

"When the hell are you going to get up out of this goddam bed?" he raged. "You've got to start packing. You've got to be out. Start acting like an adult and get up off your ass and go get a job."

I was stunned by his venomous excoriation. I thought he might have shown some compassion. Even more than stunned, I was confused by his anger. *He* had won. Why was *he* angry with *me*?

For several seconds, I just lay there on the bed looking at him, saying nothing, trying to absorb this scene. He was a man I didn't even know.

Then I asked him when I could see Mac and Zac.

"It's in the agreement," he said with a cold arrogance. "Your first weekend is January seventh."

"You can't be serious," I said. "We have to sit down with the children as parents."

"I'm very serious," he said. "You pick up the kids at six P.M. on January seventh. I told you what you were in for if you tangled with me. You got what you deserve. This is what you get for hurting my baby."

By his baby, I knew that he meant Liza. I had talked about her in court.

I asked if I could talk to the boys on the phone, and he refused. I kept thinking of that cold woman Estelle looking after them, being their mother from now on. What could Mac and Zac be thinking, not hearing from me? I had never let a day go by without calling them at least two or three times when they were away from me.

Herbert was right about one thing, however. I couldn't only dwell on the emotional pain of losing the children. I had to get about the business of securing help with the legal appeal of the decision.

Since I had no money to hire another lawyer, I called Farish first, figuring that he knew the most about the case and had already invested a considerable amount of time. But I had lost a lot of faith in him. I hoped he would offer to help me free of charge out of guilt, if not sympathy. I was desperate to put in my appeal within the thirty-day period that was allowed. Farish came to my bedroom with his secretary. My hopes were in vain. He told me that legally he didn't think I had a chance, that the odds of overturning a custody decision, coupled with Herbert's name and power, were nearly impossible ones.

I was truly desperate. So desperate that I listened quite seriously when a friend came over and outlined an elaborate getaway plan for me and Mac and Zac. He told me that I should wear a black wig to disguise myself and dress up Mac and Zac as little girls, but not twins, and that he would have a private plane waiting for us at the airport with phony passports.

In my desperation, I was ready to try anything. But if I had been caught, I probably would have ended up in prison, once again separated from my kids. Even if I had managed to flee the country with the children, there's no doubt in my mind that Herbert would have followed me to the ends of the earth to find us.

Later that night, though, I asked Hubert if I could take the children to his parents' house in the south of France.

Hubert just shook his head and said, "Rox, that's the first place they would look for you."

I never gave up trying to call Mac and Zac, but every day the phone would either be off the hook or Estelle would answer that the children were out, and hang up in my ear. My sister stayed at home with me, while my mother and Lorraine searched for an apartment for me. I did not care what they found as long as it was close to Mac and Zac.

A few days before I had to move, Hubert stopped by with the first hopeful suggestion for help with my legal appeal. He told me about a conversation he had had with one of the customers of his French bakery shop. Her name was Princess Sumair. Her lawyer was Marvin Mitchelson, the self-styled Beverly Hills divorce bomber best known for having won the palimony case of Michelle Triola, the former live-in girlfriend of actor Lee Marvin.

Princess Sumair told Hubert that Mitchelson had been following my case and that he felt the decision was disgraceful to a mother. She gave Hubert a news article quoting Mitchelson to that effect, along with a letter of recommendation for Mitchelson, and asked him to relay them both to me.

I immediately phoned Mitchelson's office in Los Angeles and was surprised that I was able to get through to him right away. I explained that I was calling at the suggestion of Princess Sumair and because he had made a comment about my case in the local paper. He told me that he would like to help me, but that I should first send him a copy of my final judgment. I had been turned down, at this point, by several lawyers in town because I didn't have the $25,000 to $50,000 retainer fee they were asking. In fact, I was still paying off Christmas credit-card purchases and I wasn't to receive my first $2,000 monthly payment before the end of January.

I told Mitchelson right off that I didn't have a dime to pay him.

"I'm aware of that," Mitchelson said. "I'm not taking

this case for the money. I don't know if you know much about the Lee Marvin versus Michelle Triola case. But I'm a big believer in women's rights. That's why I'm taking this case."

I told him that I didn't have much time, that I had to be out of the house in a few days.

"In that case," he said, "I'll put one of my secretaries on the phone and you can read the final judgment to her."

He called me back that evening. "I've read the final judgment," he said. "I can't believe it. It's the worst judgment I have ever read in all my years as a lawyer. Do you want me to help you?"

At this point, getting Marvin Mitchelson for free seemed like the answer to all my prayers. Yes, of course, I told him.

"You won't be sorry," he said. "I'm a fighter, and I'll take this all the way to the U.S. Supreme Court if I have to. I've been there before. In the meantime, don't grant any interviews or talk to anybody."

I had no intention of granting any interviews at that point, despite offers from several publications of $20,000, $30,000, even $50,000. I wasn't about to cooperate with any interviews, I was too numb.

Mitchelson arrived a few days later. We had asked for a hearing asking for an extra thirty days to vacate Herbert's house. When he pulled up in a stretch limousine a group of photographers huddled in front of the courthouse began snapping his picture. He was dapperly dressed in a perfectly tailored three-piece suit, looking every part the big-time barrister with his shock of silver hair and personable manner. I was immediately impressed and heartened by his reassurances.

"Don't worry," he kept telling me. "After this hearing, we're going to work on getting your kids back. We should be able to turn this decision around. No court should uphold this decision."

On the way into the courthouse, I told him again that I didn't have any money to pay him.

"Don't worry," he said, sounding as though money were the least of his concerns. He said that he would not charge me anything until the decision had been overturned and that he would take his fees from that.

"Even if we never get anything from Herbert, you won't owe me a dime," he said as we entered the hearing room.

Waiting for us there were two other lawyers, whom Mitchelson introduced to me. They were Melvin Frumkes —a tall dark-haired man—and his partner, Cynthia Green. This came as a surprise to me; I'd thought only Marvin was to represent me. Mitchelson explained that Frumkes and Green, who were from Miami, were going to be helping him with my case because they were members of the Florida bar. Mitchelson told me that they had worked together on several other cases, including the then highly publicized and ongoing Mohammad al-Fassi kidnapping case. Mohammad al-Fassi, who was related by marriage to the Saudi royal family, had been ordered by a court not to leave the country with his several young children, pending the outcome of his marital dispute. In the dead of night, he had spirited them off on his private yacht to Paradise Island, where they were holed up in the penthouse of a hotel. Mitchelson was representing al-Fassi's wife, Deena.

As we waited for my old friend Judge Harper to show up, Frumkes put a typed document in front of me, saying, "You have to sign this before we go in."

"What is it?" I asked.

Before Frumkes could answer, Mitchelson handed the paper back to him, saying, "Not now, Melvin. We don't need this."

"Yes, I do need it," insisted Frumkes.

"Look, I'll take care of this, Melvin," Mitchelson said soothingly. "She doesn't need to sign this."

"She needs to sign it," said Frumkes, refusing to budge.

"We can talk about this later, Melvin," said Mitchelson. "I have a suite at the Breakers and we can meet over there later and talk about it then."

Then the two of them stepped outside into the hall. I didn't have a clue as to what was going on.

After the hearing, which granted me an extension of only four days, and a pause on the courthouse steps so that Mitchelson could pose for more photographs, we climbed into the limousine and headed for the Breakers. On the drive over, Mitchelson told me about a conversation he had had with an editor of *People* magazine.

"They said that they are going to run you on the cover," Mitchelson said.

I told him that yes, they had already called me several times and told me that they would run me on the cover whether I posed or not. They would simply use an old photograph. But I had no intention of cooperating with them; publicity was my least concern.

"I've given this a lot of thought," he said, "and I think a *People* magazine cover would really help our strategy, as well as being great publicity. I'm not going to charge you to handle this case, but I would really appreciate it if you would let me pose with you for the cover."

It sounded fair. So I agreed.

When we arrived at Mitchelson's hotel suite, Frumkes and Green were waiting for us. Frumkes resumed his efforts to get me to sign the document and insisted I read it. I leafed through it. It was a retainer agreement, requesting an initial $5,000 plus additional fees to be determined as the case progressed.

I explained to him that I didn't have $5,000. I didn't have any money. There was no way I could pay this.

With a conciliatory air, Mitchelson said, "As part of the final judgment, you will be getting at the end of the month that seven-thousand-dollar reimbursement from your interest in Herbert's boat, Roxanne. Why don't you just give that to Melvin."

Having no furniture of my own, I had planned to use this money to buy beds, silverware, and other necessities. However, Mac and Zac were more important, so I agreed and signed the document. In the years since, Frumkes has billed me for additional money for his services, which I have been unwilling—and unable to pay. But in June 1986, he sent me a letter saying: "We wish to advise you that we will not pursue or 'press you' with respect to the fees owed to our firm nor will we do so as long as you remain in financial hardship." I never anticipated that Mitchelson *would*, however, bill me. Despite the fact that the law firm of Frumkes and Green received over $26,000 for handling my appeal—the court awarded it to them; under Florida State law, Herbert had to pay the fee—at the end of 1986, I received a bill for $7,000 from Marvin Mitchelson. I wrote to him, reminding him of my understanding of our agreement—his services in exchange for publicity. He wrote back to me telling me that this $7,000 was not, in fact, for his legal time. It was to cover his *personal* expenses involved in the appeal. I suppose it's possible that, in the state I was in, I could have misunderstood the agreement. But I sure was shocked to find that he expected me to pay for his hotel and car and other personal expenses while he worked on my case.

The next day Mitchelson and I posed for the *People* magazine cover, standing on the balcony of his suite at the Breakers Hotel, overlooking the ocean. Mitchelson couldn't have been more accommodating as the photographer fiddled with lights and tripods for what seemed like hours. I was anxious to get it over with, because that evening was to be my first visit with Mac and Zac since they had left for the ranch with Herbert. Finally, I told the photographer I had to leave and went for a long walk by the seawall to think about how best to handle my meeting with the children.

I had been so looking forward to my reunion with Mac and Zac, but I was unprepared for all the healing that would have to take place and all the scars that had built up—and could probably never be totally erased.

As soon as I heard Herbert's Bronco pull up, I ran out to the balcony overlooking the driveway. "I'll bring them up," Herbert called to me.

I waited in the bedroom. It had been more than two weeks since they had played here, but the room was still scattered with their Christmas toys, because I couldn't bring myself to move them. Everything in the bedroom was exactly as they had left it.

As soon as they entered the room, I sensed that it was going to be a lot harder than I had thought. My first look at their little faces gave me an uneasy feeling. Zac came over to me, put his arms around my neck, and said, more as a gesture to help me, "Oh Mommy, we missed you." But when I went to hug Mac, he backed up and extended one little hand which he wrapped around his father's legs.

Of the two, he had been the most outwardly upset and questioning throughout the trial. Zac seemed to have extra strength.

Mac's hesitation was devastating. Not knowing what else to do and not wanting to force myself on him, I backed up too.

Then to my horror, Herbert said pointedly, "The kids aren't really happy about having to stay here for the weekend. So, I'll call at eight P.M. and check, in case you have any trouble tonight." I couldn't believe that he was saying this in front of the children. I knew that this kind of talk would confuse and upset any five-year-old. I wondered what he had told them about our situation.

As Herbert turned to leave, Mac began to cry, and Herbert, setting the scene for a dramatic parting that I would helplessly witness again and again in the years to come, got down on one knee and put his arms around Mac, as though he couldn't bear to leave him with me.

I felt terrible, as if I were hurting my son. I almost wanted to tell Mac that it was okay for him to go with his father if he wanted to.

"Don't worry, I'll call you from the boat," Herbert reassured him. Then turning to me he added, "Maybe I should come by and see them tomorrow."

Again, I couldn't believe how cruelly Herbert was manipulating them and me. I had no choice but to agree. "Yes, it's all right for you to come by," I said.

The three of us stayed up in the bedroom playing with the toys for quite a while. Zac immediately went to his new remote-control robot. As I watched him, I could see his struggle, but he was a very brave little boy, constantly climbing on my lap the entire weekend. Mac was having more trouble. He was pretending to play with a remote-control fire truck, but his mind was somewhere else. He acted as though the weight of the world was on his little shoulders. I wanted to reach out to him, but for the first time in his life, I didn't know what to say to my own son. I didn't know what their father had told them, and I certainly didn't want to cause them any more stress.

Eventually, when I felt Mac warming to me, I began to ask him how he had enjoyed his time at the ranch, groping for some shared past experience between us. With a heart-piercing look, as though he were looking right into my soul, he said: "You told me you'd never lie to me. But you did. You told me that we would always live together." My heart sank. I knew immediately he was referring to the night when I had promised him we would always be together.

I didn't have an answer for him. There were no answers.

Then he turned away from me and walked over to the other side of the room. I didn't know how to comfort him. I felt tears welling up and struggled to maintain my composure.

Fortunately, at that moment my mother entered the room, creating enough of a distraction for me to collect myself. As both boys rushed over to embrace her, the problem of how to cope with Mac was temporarily tabled.

But Mac's mood hung over the whole first night, setting me back two weeks in my own depression. I don't think I could have made it through the weekend without the help of my mother, sister, and stepfather.

My mother kept telling me, "Pull yourself together.

Make a good weekend *for your boys*." I knew she was right, but I couldn't look at my poor children without breaking into tears. It took me weeks, months, to get to the point where I was able to put aside my own grief over losing them and focus totally on how best to help them get through theirs over losing me.

The first weekend together brought an even more heart-wrenching blow. At my mother's suggestion, I took the boys over to see the tiny studio apartment that I had rented on Brazilian Avenue. It was a hole in the wall and had no furniture, but it was all that I could afford within bike-riding distance of Mac and Zac's house.

My mother felt, and I agreed, that seeing my new home would reassure the kids that I would remain close to them, and that they would be able to picture in their little minds where I was living since I could no longer live with them. I tried to be enthusiastic as I showed them around the cramped, empty space. I told them that we would be cozier than ever here, all sleeping together, and showed them a closet where they could keep their toys.

When we returned to the house, Mac asked me for the key to my apartment. I gave it to him and went over to the kitchen to help my mother prepare dinner. A few minutes later, when I glanced over at the children, Mac was lying in front of the fireplace curled up in the fetal position, rocking back and forth and sucking his thumb, something he hadn't done in years. In his little hand he was clutching the key to my apartment.

I went over to him and put my arms around him. I told him everything would be all right and not to worry. That I would be close by, that we would still have our special moments to be together, and more important, that I loved him and Zac more than anything else in the world "all the way to the moon, the stars, and the sun." He listened, looking directly into my eyes, clutching the key, which he refused to give up.

That first weekend together, while by far the most painful for all three of us, was by no means the end of my heartache in defining my relationship with Mac and Zac as a part-time parent. The process continues even today.

It took months for me to understand and learn to cope with the pain that goes with living apart from them. The adjustment was especially difficult for me because I am a person who greatly needs emotional intimacy with the people I love. I knew I had had that with Mac and Zac before our separation. But I felt that had now changed.

At times, usually by the end of their two-day visits, we recaptured those bonds. But then it would be time for them to leave. It was as hard for Mac and Zac to say goodbye to me as it was to leave their father. They would cry and hang on to me starting early Sunday afternoon. I dreaded those transition times for them. After some weeks I sat down with them and explained that such moments were part of our lives now and we had to accept them. So whenever I drop them back at their father's, they try to handle their hurt; when they can't, I remind them of our talk. I wish Herbert would do the same on his end, so they wouldn't have to live through all that stress each time he performs his melodramatic goodbyes.

There isn't a day without them when I don't feel sadness and loss. When I see children running on the beach or riding their bicycles in the street, I'm reminded of everything I'm missing. At times it still throws me into night-long depressions.

I made a promise to myself never to speak negatively of Herbert in front of the children. That has been difficult for me sometimes. When we were finally on speaking terms again, Herbert told me how he had explained the divorce to Mac and Zac. "Yes, I told them we had gone to court for a judge to decide who was the better parent, and the judge ruled I am the better parent."

They have asked their father to let them spend more time with me, and although he has occasionally relented, he uses those extra days like a cudgel, another tool for controlling me. I depend entirely on his whims and moods for any additional visits with Mac and Zac; therefore it has been hard for me to develop my autonomy.

Of course, I am nervous about Herbert's reaction to this book. I'm afraid he may use it to hurt me even further, at least as far as my children are concerned.

Nevertheless, in grappling with the situation, I feel I have come a long way. I'm getting better at taking steps to get on with my life. I'm beginning to define it in broader terms than the visitation schedule.

I have come to realize that I don't need to feel guilty about having to work and sometimes missing a few hours with the boys. That's a healthy part of being a parent under any circumstances. I have to learn. I *am* learning, to cope with life without them.

I think that Herbert has grown better at putting the boys' interests over his. I believe that he is a much better father today than he ever was to his first children. I also believe that he is probably a much better father to Mac and Zac than he could have been if our marriage had stayed together. Although I have no doubt that his initial motive in wanting custody of them was a financial one—as well as a spiteful one—I think he has discovered a measure of satisfaction and gratification through fatherhood.

A year or so after our divorce, I returned home to Cassadaga for a visit with my family. I had just broken up with Hubert after many months of dating. He had had his own problems with his business. Sadly, the timing had been all wrong for us. While I was in Lily Dale, I consulted a psychic, the first time I had been able to bring myself to rekindle my lost faith in God and my metaphysical beliefs. I knew in my soul that there must be some message, some lesson, to be learned from the trial and the loss of my children. Now I felt that if I could just find the answer, I was ready to transcend the pain and suffering of the past year, and accept my road in life.

That meeting proved to be the turning point that enabled me to come to grips with the terrible guilt and unworthiness I had felt and with the awful stigma of having been branded an unfit mother. It gave me hope for myself, for Mac and Zac, and for Herbert.

The message, said the psychic, was not to blame myself. As painful as losing my children had been and would continue to be, he reassured me that eventually I would find the strength to see that there was a reason for all of this. Now I would have to try to achieve the things in life that I needed in order to grow. It was up to me to realize this and to seize that opportunity for fulfillment.

He said that Herbert, on the other hand, had been given a second chance at being a parent, provided he could bring himself to grasp the lessons that were there for him. In winning custody of Mac and Zac, the psychic said, Herbert was being given the tools to understand and experience love between parent and child. This could not have happened without the divorce.

The psychic predicted that it would be a difficult lesson for Herbert, because he himself had never really experienced the love of his parents in a truly meaningful way. That was why he had already failed once as a father in his relationships with his first children. Now he could turn his failures into success.

Back in Palm Beach, a few days after this meeting, Herbert and I had our first dinner together since the divorce. He asked how my trip home had gone and whether I had consulted any psychics. I told him that I had and I relayed the psychic's message that he was being given a second chance to be a father. I told him why it would be difficult for him, but to not lose hope or faith in himself.

It was one of the few times that I ever saw Herbert Pulitzer cry.

[Sixteen]

As I look back today on my years of many mistakes, two failed marriages, and a lot of broken hearts—including mine—I realize more than ever that I could never have made it this far without these mistakes. Experience has been a good teacher. No one is perfected without trials.

Today, I can't help but feel that my marriage to Herbert could have been saved, and should have been, for the sake of our family. The problems were not insurmountable. There is a certain laziness in not trying to work things out no matter how much water is over the dam.

As is true of so many other couples, ours was a failure of communication and of perspective, not love.

Each of us should have assumed responsibility for nurturing the other.

Eventually, I believe that Herbert came to understand this too. One night, shortly after my visit to the psychic in Cassadaga, Herbert stopped by my apartment unexpectedly. I was alone and watching TV.

"Can I just come in and hug you for a while?" he asked.

"Sure," I said, surprised to see him.

We lay on the bed together, watching TV and just hugging.

"I'd love to stay here with you for a few hours and just

go to sleep," he said. "I can't do anything, so don't worry. I'm having a real tough time sexually."

I knew what he meant, because I had had a difficult time myself after the divorce. Hubert had been loving and patient, but I had felt too emotionally drained to give our relationship a chance. The trial had made me feel so invaded, so dirty and cheap.

I also knew that Herbert's admission was a difficult one for him to make. I told him not to worry; when the right girl came along, he'd be fine. In the meantime, I said it was okay for him to sleep here. Then I kissed him on the cheek and turned off the light, and we cuddled like spoons, the way we always had gone to sleep.

Next thing I knew, it was just like old times and Herbert was having no difficulty. Afterward, he acted very nervous, as though he wished this had happened with anyone else but me.

"I think I should go," he said sadly. And he left.

Over the next four months we continued to date and occasionally sleep together. I knew it was foolish, but like steel drawn to a magnet, I was unable to resist. I missed my children and the house where we had lived for eight years as a family. The possibility of getting back together and the security of the past lifted my spirits—even in light of what had happened at the trial. The only brightness my future seemed to hold at that point was the continuance of my legal appeal. Herbert kept trying to convince me the appeal was an unnecessary waste of time and money. I told him I would reconsider this if he would give me, in writing, more visitation. He said, "No, Roxanne, you'll just have to trust me." Of course, I could not trust him. I had made a promise to Mac and Zac and myself that I would try and change the visitation rights. I couldn't take the gamble with Herbert without a written agreement.

At Herbert's open invitation, I was coming to the house daily to see the children. Herbert even lent me money to repair my car and then tore up the IOU as a birthday gift. When I needed money to pay my taxes that year, he bought back from me two diamond bracelets, then surprised me with them as Mother's Day gifts.

The final date for pressing the appeal to the U.S. Supreme Court was looming just a few days ahead. Earlier that week, Herbert had mentioned we should go away together to the Bahamas. It was so tempting, but I had the nagging suspicion that once again he was attempting to trick me into missing the final filing date for the appeal. After all, he had been a master at tricking me.

One evening, Herbert and I met for dinner. I sensed that this would be our last date, for I intended to tell him my decision to file—absolutely—for the appeal.

Up to then, we had never discussed anything having to do with the trial. But that night, knowing that I had nothing to lose, I posed the one question that I had been burning to ask ever since we had begun speaking again. How, I asked, had he managed to get Steve Anderson to say he saw Jacquie and me nude together in that first-floor bedroom?

Shaking his head in dismay as he looked down at the tablecloth, Herbert replied, "Roxie, you've got to let go of this. This is why you're having trouble getting on with your life. This is the past, and you just have to forget it.

"Divorce is a war," he continued. "And in a war, there can only be one winner. When I go into a war, I go in to win. Like anybody does. You lost and I won and that's it. It's over. You never had a clue how to win that game."

I knew that no matter what question about the divorce I had asked, the answer would have been the same. There was no more room for discussion. He was right. It is a cruel game, and no concessions are given to beginners.

In the car on the drive to my apartment, I told him about the appeal.

"It's a waste of money," he said. "A waste of effort. You lost. You're always going to lose. You're just ignorant when it comes to this. Completely and totally ignorant."

He let me out at the curb without even opening my door. That was the last time I saw him on a date. We had

had our meeting of the minds and we both knew it. We had nothing left to offer each other. It was over.

Some months later, I lost the appeal.

Over the years, I've lost three appeals. In the District Court of Appeal, Fourth District, they upheld Judge Harper's ruling. The Supreme Court of Florida and the U.S. Supreme Court refused to even hear the case. That was the end of the line.

I had lost.

My hope is that from here on in, I will find the insight to get through the critical moments in life and that I'll be able to apply some of the lessons I have learned.

One of those lessons is that the body has to be in shape as well as the mind. Aerobics actually helped pull me through the difficult months after the divorce. I put a tremendous amount of energy into the physical side of my well-being—so much so, in fact, that I eventually became an aerobics instructor. There's no question that this helped lift me out of the depressed doldrums I was in.

I also now feel I'm beginning to make some progress in my quest to climb the spiritual ladder. I don't think I could have reached the level I've reached if I'd remained in my marriage. And if I can share what I've learned and help others along the way—and laugh a little, too—then all the better.

One of the reasons I agreed to pose for the June 1985 issue of *Playboy* was to laugh at all this. The other, frankly, was for the money. Reg Potterton, who had previously covered the trial for *Playboy*, was clever enough to approach me for the third time just at the point when my alimony was one month from running out. I was scrambling to figure out how to juggle my need to support myself with my need to continue to spend as much time with Mac and Zac as I could. *Playboy*'s $70,000 offer was one I couldn't refuse.

When Potterton came to Palm Beach to discuss the deal,

he assured me that the magazine had agreed to do the photo story my way, with a sense of humor and hyperbole. Editorial control was important to me, because I didn't want to come off as just another Playmate.

Together, we came up with the idea of doing a series of photos parodying some of the most fantastic scenes, real or imagined, from my life with Herbert Pulitzer. The cover, for example, had me posed in a blue sequined bathing suit, holding a trumpet. Inside, there was a shot of me lying on the bed with the entire brass section. Another showed me lying on a Kleenex-strewn bed with my back to a Jacquie Kimberly look-alike model.

Posing nude, within the bounds of good taste, was fine with me. I have always been open-minded about nudity and believe there is nothing offensive about it. Of course, I know that many people are uncomfortable with *Playboy*, but I figured that was their problem, not mine. I never worried that Mac and Zac would feel threatened by their mother posing nude, because I've brought them up to be open-minded about nudity, too.

I consider *Playboy* to be a top-of-the-line, mainstream magazine, not some sleazy pornographic publication. In a way, posing for *Playboy* was my first step toward my autonomy.

In truth, as the mother of two, I was flattered to be asked to pose and was determined to measure up to the challenge. I dieted and taught twice as many aerobics classes to get myself in shape.

However, when I actually had to take all my clothes off for the photo sessions, I was petrified.

My first scene was in the shower, and I hoped the splashing water was hiding me. All went fairly well until the water turned ice-cold and I lost my confidence. The photographer, Arny Freytag, offered me a glass of white wine to loosen me up, but it was only nine o'clock in the morning.

The shooting covered several weeks, including breaks for me to fly home for my weekend visits with Mac and

Zac. We started out on location in Antigua. Although they ended up scrapping all those shots, they were my favorites.

Three weeks later, they flew me to *Playboy*'s photo studio in Hollywood, where photographer Richard Fegley and I would go from eight-thirty in the morning till six-thirty at night. This went on for four weeks. He must have shot thousands of frames of film. I emerged from that experience with a sincere appreciation for the hard work involved in photographic modeling and the amazing wonders wrought by expert makeup artists. I hardly recognized myself.

Most nights I collapsed in bed, exhausted and in pain with muscle cramps from holding the same pose for hours while Fegley fiddled with his camera or adjusted lights.

The fun part was the off-camera pampering by the smoothly oiled *Playboy* public-relations machine, headed by one of my favorite people, West Coast editor Marilyn Grabowski. Even though they may be exploiting you to sell magazines, they never make you feel that way. They are masters at building up your ego, laying limousines at your disposal, putting you up in luxurious first-class hotels (my suite was at the Bel Air), and giving you carte blanche for expenses. They made me feel like a star.

I also gained my first glimpse of what it's like to be a star *maker* in Hollywood, when I was invited up to the Playboy mansion to meet Hugh Hefner. I found Hef to be personable and sympathetic, and well briefed on the events of my divorce trial. I attended many dinners and movies over that month at his house. We hit it off right away. Within the first five minutes, I liked him very much. He was very interested in how badly my publicity had gone during the trial and he compared it to his own bad press in connection with the story of Dorothy Stratten, the Playmate of the Year who had been brutally murdered by her estranged husband.

During those lavish gatherings at the mansion, I was amazed at how everyone deferred to Hef, hanging on his every word as though he were the great sage of our time. Ironically, the only other men I had ever seen command such deference were Herbert and Jim Kimberly.

The photographers follow Hef, clad in his pajamas, snapping shots of every celebrity that he honors with a chat, from Clint Eastwood to Tom Cruise to Grace Jones. I have also never seen so many beautiful girls in my life. They by far outnumber the men, whether in the game room, or in the Jacuzzis, or in the zoo, or in the saunas. Everywhere I looked, there were always beautiful single girls.

It was fun watching Hef in command. Dinner was served, only by men, within minutes of his entrance from his upstairs chambers.

There was a certain time allotted to eat, after which Hef would boom, "It's showtime!" and everyone would come to attention and follow him into his private screening room. There he would sink into his Chesterfield sofa with his girlfriend, Carrie Leigh, while the rest of us would sit in our little fold-outs. During the screenings we were served bowls of popcorn, peanuts, M&Ms, and drinks. This was what I loved best about staying at the mansion—the twenty-four-hour room service. Menus weren't necessary because anything in the world you wanted was available.

Over the month that I was in L.A., I became friends with Carrie Leigh. I was one of the few people invited to the upstairs chambers of the mansion. We spent hours up there talking; Carrie showed me all her modeling pictures, home-movie collection, and closets, the size of small bedrooms, filled with clothes.

In April, upon receiving my advance copy of *Playboy*, I decided to sit down with Mac and Zac and explain to them my decision to pose for the magazine. Very carefully, I explained that I needed to make some money to pay my bills and that I had accepted a job posing without my clothes on for *Playboy*.

"Oh, that's the magazine Daddy gets," Mac said.

Zac asked to see the copy, and I showed it to them. I explained that some people might not agree with my decision and warned them that some kids might come up at school and say bad things about me or the magazine pictures. But I told them that I felt that there was nothing embarrassing or bad about showing your body.

Mac looked at me with a couldn't-care-less look. "Well, if anybody says anything bad," he said, "we'll just walk away and ignore it." As the two of them were leafing through the pages, the only comment was when Zac said, "Mummy, your eyes look so blue."

I wish that Herbert had taken it so well. Although I had intended to tell him about it before the photos were published, I didn't know that subscribers received their copy a week in advance of the publication date.

I found out, though, when I dropped the kids off one weekend. Herbert was standing in the driveway with his copy. He was absolutely livid. The veins in his forehead were pulsing, just like old times.

"Have you told your children this disgusting thing you've done?" he said, holding up the magazine in front of Mac and Zac. I found this amusing, because some years before, Herbert had asked me for a nude photograph of myself as a Christmas present. I was tempted to say, "This is a belated Christmas present." But I held my tongue.

I told him that I had talked to Mac and Zac and they were fine. Then, as Zac put his arms around my neck to hug me goodbye, Herbert yanked him away from me. The children stood there for an anxious moment, unsure of what to do next.

Grabbing their hands to pull them into the house, Herbert shouted at me, "You're never going to see these kids again."

For the next two weeks, I didn't. Then, returning from

New York, my plane was delayed and I was half an hour late picking the children up on my Friday night. Even though I had called, Herbert made me forfeit my weekend. He then kept the phone off the hook so that I couldn't even reach Mac and Zac for our daily phone chats. I was frantic, desperate to get in touch with them, but there was nothing I could do. It was two weeks before I could see them again, so I tried to keep busy preparing for a talk-show appearance.

Posing for *Playboy* brought me to *The Phil Donahue Show*. This was going to be the start of a new chapter in my life. Suddenly people realized for the first time that there were two sides to my story.

I received hundreds of positive letters following the show, and I saw the beginning of a change in the public's opinion.

Viewers started to see me as an individual rather than a newspaper headline. Many letter writers apologized for having preconceived ideas of me, and others supported my views on child custody.

At first, I was afraid of doing the show, but I had great respect for Phil and it obviously was the right choice. This first TV show and the next thirty or so that ensued over the next couple of years launched me into child-custody lectures all over the country.

Funnily enough, people who before would not have given me the time of day were now asking for my advice, not only on child custody, but on divorce, the judicial system, my spiritual values. Some were also trying to reap some kind of undefinable strength from me.

I slowly began to see that perhaps my divorce had had a purpose—it was a stepping-stone to understanding a much broader canvas. Spiritual truths cannot come until one is ready for them. I chose this path and this lesson, and now it is my responsibility to turn the negative into a positive, or at least put it on the road toward the positive. For truly, there is no negative experience, only a lack of understanding of the lesson involved. There is no failure except in no longer trying to make things better. The defeat comes from within.

We must all survive with and for the ones we love.

I'm trying to share with Mac and Zac some of the truths I have learned. I want to help them to become independent and free, and to use their own wisdom. I want them to think for themselves and not to worry about the mistakes they may make along the way.

I'd like to teach them through my misfortunes that outer appearances cannot be judged, because no one knows the purpose of the spirit.

As an adult, I still have a hard time myself not judging Herbert when he excludes me from shared parental responsibilities and denies me frequent visitations. Every other weekend is absolutely inappropriate for achieving balance for the child's best interest. I feel custody should be fifty-fifty everywhere in the world. It is in Mac and Zac's best interest to have frequent access to both mother and father. There is no such thing as a disposable parent.

No one—not fathers, mothers, lawyers, judges, counselors, child psychologists, or court investigators—has the right to deprive a child of either parent. Unfortunately, in the past few years, the use of the custody issue to gain financial leverage has escalated. In the past, some women bled their spouses outrageously; now men have learned to strike back. The children are used as pawns.

I feel it is urgent that a law be enacted forbidding men or women to fight over ownership of another human life. Good intentions are not sufficient; positive decisions have to be made into laws. This is not a female or a male issue, it is a *human rights* issue. It affects millions of children.

Both parents must work together to ensure that the child has *frequent* access to each of them. The recent work of Jean Piaget indicates that emotionally and intellectually, small children cannot stretch their waiting time between visits for more than a few days without feeling overwhelmed by the absence of a parent. A two-week absence is traumatic and cruel. When a child's bonding has been disrupted, as is frequently the case when parental responsibilities are unbalanced, the survival mechanism for the child is anger and withdrawal. The child will say to himself or herself, "I trusted that I would be taken care of and now I feel that I have been dropped, so I will trust no one and do what I must do to survive."

I remember all too well my own little boy's accusation after the divorce that I had lied to him.

It is very clear to me that if the shared parental living arrangement is not tailored to the child's time perspective, he or she feels a sense of abandonment, and cannot handle the transition periods well. The "separation anxiety" that occurs at these times is devastating and can cause permanent psychological damage. The important issues of bonding and attachment can *never* be dismissed.

The custodial parent has the responsibility to ensure that the child is aware at all times that the absent parent loves the child as deeply as ever.

I feel that children are capable of loving *both* parents *more* when they are not pressured into loving one more than the other.

Every other weekend, when I see Herbert collapsing to his knees, crying and hugging Mac and Zac goodbye as if it were forever, and see the look on their little faces, I am reminded of the story in the Bible of Solomon and the two mothers. Both women profess to be the rightful mother of the child. After listening to them, Solomon asks for a sword to cut the child in half—and the true mother walks away. Was there a time when *I* should have walked away? Maybe . . . though I can't accept that emotionally.

At any rate, Herbert and I must accept that we are forever connected through Mac and Zac. When both of us can face that, we will have made a giant step forward for our boys.

So if this book reaches but *one* parent, so that he or she can find compassion in his or her heart for the other parent, or if somewhere one child and one parent are kept together, this book—and all that's happened to me—will have been well worth it.

IN RE: THE MARRIAGE OF
HERBERT PULITZER, JR.,
    Husband
and
ROXANNE D. PULITZER,
    Wife

_____/

FINAL JUDGMENT

THIS CAUSE was tried before the court over a protracted period of approximately eighteen days, commencing on September 20, 1982 and concluding on November 9, 1982. The husband, Herbert Pulitzer, Jr., was present and represented by able counsel, Robert T. Scott, Esquire and Mark T. Luttier, Esquire. The wife, Roxanne D. Pulitzer, was also present and represented by able counsel, Joseph D. Farish, Jr., Esquire and Louis L. Williams, Esquire. The court has heard the extensive testimony of the parties and their witnesses, received numerous exhibits in evidence, and heard the closing arguments of respective counsel. The court has also reviewed the husband's Memorandum of Law received on November 16, 1982; the wife's Memorandum of Law received on November 29, 1982; and the husband's Reply Memorandum received on December 7, 1982, all of which shall be filed of record in this cause. The court has also considered, but hereby rejects, the proposed final judgments submitted on behalf of each party.

Our so-called "no fault" divorce law was ostensibly enacted, in part, to eliminate the emotional and financial blackmail made possible by the continued threat of mental torture by way of embarrassing harassment through public washing of dirty linen as was noted by Judge Letts in Linda v. Linda,

352 So.2d 1208 (4 DCA 1977). In spite of that laudible goal, section 61.08(1), Florida Statutes, expressly authorizes evidence of adultery on the part of a spouse who seeks alimony, and further provides that "the court may consider <u>any other factor</u> necessary to do equity and justice between the parties". Also, section 61.13(3) (f), Florida Statutes, expressly provides, among other criteria, that trial courts shall consider "<u>the moral fitness</u> of the parents" in order to determine the best interests of the minor child whose custody is an issue.

Throughout the trial of this case and in writing this judgment, this court was ever mindful of its obligation under <u>McAllister v. McAllister</u>, 345 So.2d 352 (4 DCA 1977), not to mention this court's own human compassion and empathy for the parties and witnesses, to limit such evidence of misconduct to gross situations so as to avoid "the effect a detailed probe into the private lives of the parties might have on the innocent children involved, not to mention the disruptive effect such an inquiry might have upon the married lives of third persons involved in the illicit conduct and their children," <u>Claughton v. Claughton</u>, 344 So.2d 944 (3 DCA 1977). However, that is a difficult task that is more easily said than done, under our law.

This hotly contested trial was duly reported by two court reporters, televised gavel to gavel and was highly publicized on the front pages of many newspapers throughout the world. No useful purpose would be served in detailing the sordid evidence herein, except to unnecessarily add to the grief and shame already endured by the parties and witnesses, and their families, and to unduly lengthen this written judgment. Nevertheless, this court is legally obliged to make written findings of fact, based on the evidence presented, in support of its judgment, in compliance with <u>Beville v. Beville</u>, 415 So.2d 151 (4 DCA 1982) and <u>Vawter v. Vawter</u>, 419 So.2d 747 (4 DCA 1982).

Therefore, based on the greater weight of the credible evidence presented at trial, after having closely observed the parties and their witnesses and having considered their appearance and demeanor, and having weighed their credibility; and after giving due consideration to the arguments of respective counsel; and being fully advised in the premises, the court makes the following

FINDINGS OF FACT AND CONCLUSIONS OF LAW

This court has jurisdiction of this cause and of the parties in that the parties have been bona fide residents of the State of Florida for more than six (6) months immediately prior to the filing of this dissolution action. The parties were married on January 12, 1976 in the Town of Palm Beach, Palm Beach County, Florida where they cohabited until their last separation in late August or early September, 1981. There were two children born of this marriage on August 28, 1977, twin boys named MacLean Simpson Pulitzer and Zachary Simpson Pulitzer, more affectionally known as Mack [*sic*] and Zack [*sic*], each of whom is presently in the temporary custody of the wife pursuant to this court's order dated February 1, 1982, residing in the marital home located at 410 North Lake Way, Palm Beach, Florida.

This was the second marriage for both parties. The wife's first marriage ended in divorce in 1973 or 1974. There were no children born of that marriage. The husband's first marriage ended in divorce in July, 1969. There were three children born of that marriage, the custody of whom was awarded to the former wife. Subsequent to that divorce, the husband maintained a close personal contact and relationship with the children, all of whom are now emancipated and living on their own. The husband has enjoyed a good relationship with his former wife who is a well known, highly successful business woman in her own right.

The husband is 52 years of age and is in excellent health, both emotionally and physically. He completed high school at a private boarding school in Massachusetts, one year college at Stanford University and one year college at the University of Virginia. Throughout his adult life, he has been a hard worker and has invested his money wisely, with much financial success. He is a self-made millionaire, several times over. He refers to himself as a "hotel executive," and owns many properties and other investments, both real and personal, too numerous to catalogue herein, not the least of which are a resort hotel in Miami Beach, Florida and a fifty-one percent controlling interest in a resort hotel in Amsterdam, Holland. He is very active in overseeing his investments, early to bed and early to rise, but has still found time to enjoy his family life and hobbies. He has travelled extensively with his wife and children throughout Europe, the Caribbean and South America. He is a sportsman and enjoys diving, boating, hunting and fishing, particularly in the company of his two boys, Mack [*sic*] and Zack [*sic*]. In short, he is a "man's man."

The husband's net worth is in hopeless dispute. Much time has been unnecessarily spent, in pretrial discovery and at trial, in an effort to resolve the dispute. The husband estimates his net worth to be about $2,618,475, whereas the wife estimates his net worth to be about $25,000,000. After considering all the financial evidence, a fair estimate of the husband's net worth is in the neighborhood of $12,500,000 (a nice neighborhood, to say the least) with an annual spendible income of about $240,000, except for the year 1982 when he experienced a $180,000 shortfall due largely to this lawsuit. In any event, the husband's net worth is more than adequate to meet the financial obligations that will be imposed upon him in this judgment.

The wife is 31 years of age, attractive and is in apparent excellent physical health. She has experienced some emotional problems in the past relating to the marital discord for which she has been treated by medical care, hospitalization and therapeutic counselling, mostly at the insistence of the husband in an effort to save the marriage.

At the request of the husband, the wife has remained unemployed throughout this marriage in order that she might be available to travel with the husband on his business and pleasure trips. However, she has a two year degree from Palm Beach Junior College and has done secretarial work in the past, prior to this marriage. With some self-motivation and rehabilitation, the wife is capable of gainful employment. In time, she can become self-supporting, but not to the extent she could afford the same lavish lifestyle she enjoyed during this marriage. Even when (as here) there is no financial problem, it might well be thought improper to permit an errant spouse to destroy a marriage and then to claim benefits equal to those which would have been provided had it remained intact. Smith v. Smith, 378 So.2d 11, 15 (3 DCA

1979). Also, habituated living standards is but an element to be considered (among others) and is not the equivalent of need. Quick v. Quick, 400 So.2d 1297 (1 DCA 1981).

THE DISSOLUTION ISSUE:

As to the dissolution issue, under our no fault law, fault in causing the marriage breakup is not relevant. Suffice it to say that the voluminous evidence clearly demonstrates that this marriage of relatively short duration is unfortunately irretrievably broken and has been for well over a year now.

THE CUSTODY ISSUE:

As to the paramount issue in this case, i.e. the child custody question, the moral fitness of the parties is a factor, among others, that must be considered in determining the best interests and welfare of Mack [*sic*] and Zack [*sic*]. Section 61.13 (3) (f), Florida Statutes. In doing so, the court will make findings as to each party individually as follows:

(a) As to the wife

In the trial of this case, this court heard considerable testimony concerning the wife's alleged adulterous conduct with various male paramours, her alleged illicit relationship with a female family friend, and her alleged frequent and progressive abuse of cocaine and alcohol in combination.

To prove adultery, in a civil case, the law does not require that specific acts be attested by eye-witnesses. Because adultery usually takes place in secret or seclusion, proof thereof in most instances is by circumstantial evidence, through showing desire, by evidence of mutual affection or otherwise, coupled with opportunity under conditions or circumstances from which a reasonable judge of human nature would be led to conclude that adultery was committed. Leonard v. Leonard, 259 So.2d 529 (3 DCA 1972). Under Florida law, adultery is not merely confined to extra-marital heterosexual union, but also includes homosexual relationships as well. See Patin v. Patin, 371 So.2d 682 (4 DCA 1979).

Also, under Florida law, proof of adultery, standing alone,

is not sufficient evidence upon which a trial court may base a finding of moral unfitness for child custody purposes. See for example Farrow v. Farrow, 263 So.2d 588 (2 DCA 1972), where the appellate court held that although the adulterous wife was a bad wife, she nevertheless was a good mother. Clearly then, under Florida law, in order for adultery to disqualify a spouse as a custodial parent of minor children, the evidence must also demonstrate that the adultery had a direct, adverse bearing on the welfare of the minor children. See McAnespie v. McAnespie, 200 So.2d 606 (2 DCA 1967); Dinkel v. Dinkel, 322 So.2d 22 (Fla. 1975); Brock v. Brock, 349 So.2d 782 (1 DCA 1977); and Solly v. Solly, 384 So.2d 208 (3 DCA 1980). But see also Smothers v. Smothers, 281 So.2d 359 (Fla. 1973), where the Florida Supreme Court upheld a custody award to the husband where the trial court based the award on the adulterous wife's overall "relationship with Moore" (her paramour), not just her sex life with him.

Based on the totality of the credible evidence, both direct and circumstantial, this court finds that the wife's gross, moral misconduct involved more than isolated, discreet acts of adultery. She openly engaged in a continuing adulterous relationship with her male paramour, Brian Richards, both before and after the final separation of the parties and prior to the filing of this dissolution action. During that period of time, the wife frequently and progressively abused cocaine and alcohol in combination. As a consequence, the parties previously separated and a prior dissolution action was filed. The parties remained separated from January to March, 1981. However, upon the wife having agreed to end her relationship with Brian Richards and to undergo treatment for her cocaine and alcohol abuse, the parties reconciled and resumed cohabitation in March, 1981, whereupon the husband dismissed the prior suit. They made a reconciliation trip to Europe, but upon her return to Palm Beach County prior to the husband, the wife immediately resumed her adulterous relationship with Brian Richards and continued to abuse cocaine and alcohol as before, directly leading to the final separation of the parties in late August or early September, 1981 and to the ultimate filing of this dissolution action on September 4, 1981.

As if that was not enough the wife thereafter began an adulterous relationship with James Murdock III who bragged of the affair to the witness, William Cheatham, but now denies having done so. In spite of Murdock's denial, this court finds Cheatham to be a credible witness.

The wife also began a questionable, meretricious relationship with Hubert Fouret and Jackie Ickx under circumstances that would lead a reasonable judge of human nature to conclude that adultery was committed. Leonard v. Leonard, supra. The court heard testimony, believed to be credible, about an occasion where the wife and Jackie Ickx were observed lying on a beach adjacent to the marital home, in the presence and view of the minor children, Mack [*sic*] and Zack [*sic*], in amorous embrace, kissing each other. The credible evidence further showed that the wife and Ickx were also observed lying in bed together in the marital home where Ickx spent the night. Both children expressed some displeasure over the wife's behavior with Ickx.

As to Fouret, another credible witness was present on an occasion and observed the wife and Fouret lying on a couch in the marital home engaging in amorous sexual foreplay. The minor children were present in the home but did not witness that conduct. Brazenly, just prior to this trial, the wife and Fouret accompanied each other on an extended trip to Paris, France in August, 1982. En route, they spent 3 days and nights in New York City. The minor children were on court ordered visitation with the husband. The wife had informed the children's nanny, Pierrette Barr, that she was going to New York state to visit her mother, leaving a phone number where she could be reached in case of an emergency. The nanny's attempts to reach the wife at that number were unsuccessful, of course. Fouret testified that the wife has spent the night in his Palm Beach residence on two separate occasions, ostensibly because of robberies in her neighborhood. The children were not present, however.

Regarding the allegations of the wife's lesbian infidelity, a credible witness testified to having observed the wife and her female companion, Jacqui [*sic*] Kimberly, lying together on a bed in the marital home in the Spring of 1979. According to the witness, Kimberly was nude and the wife was wearing a sheer negligee. Upon perceiving the presence of the witness, the wife inquired as to the purpose of his presence and, upon receiving a satisfactory explanation, the wife closed the bedroom door.

In addition to the above, from the inception of the birth of Mack [sic] and Zack [sic], the wife has all but abandoned the raising of the children to various nannies employed for that purpose. See for example the tape recorded sworn statement (in evidence as husband's exhibit number 22) made by Sandra Andreasen, the wife's cousin. Much of the wife's abundant idle time is spent on her own personal pleasures such as visiting numerous nightclubs and discotheques, dancing and snorting cocaine, as well as consuming alcoholic beverages, until the wee hours of the morning. For a time, the husband participated with the wife. However, it was not long before the fast pace nightlife began to take its toll on the early rising husband who is 21 years older than his wife. For a time, the husband turned to cocaine, as a crutch, to give him the stamina to keep pace with his younger, energetic wife. When that failed, at the request of his wife, the husband began to leave his wife at the disco so that he could get some restful sleep before having to go to work. As would be expected, the wife began to stay out later and later, coming home after the husband had left for work and on occasion not at all.

The court also heard testimony from the husband's witness, Randy Hopkins, who testified to certain relations he allegedly had with Roxanne Pulitzer prior to this marriage. The wife's attorney timely objected to the testimony, but the court overruled the objection subject to striking the evidence before entry of this judgment. At this time, this court hereby sustains the wife's objection and strikes the testimony of Hopkins as being irrelevant and immaterial to any of the issues involved herein. Accordingly, that testimony has played no role in the entry of this judgment. Furthermore, the evidence relating to the wife's alleged belief in spiritualism and the occult has played no role in the entry of this judgment.

(b) As to the husband

The credible evidence has clearly demonstrated that since the inception of this marriage the husband has been faithful and loyal to the wife. He has been a good husband to the wife and father to the children. In fact, the wife has made no allegations of the husband's marital infidelity prior to the final separation or of his moral unfitness as custodian of the children.

Nevertheless, the husband has not survived this trial unscathed and without blemish. The wife testified that, prior to this marriage, the husband had allegedly engaged in an incestuous relationship with one of his daughters by his prior marriage. Both the husband and the daughter vehemently denied the uncorroborated allegations. Also, the wife had made pretrial statements that she did not believe such allegations. After weighing the evidence and credibility of the witness, this court gives no credence to the unfounded allegations either.

The husband testified that well subsequent to the final separation of the parties he began a relationship with Jane Dean. While that relationship was meretricious, it had no causal connection with the marriage breakup, but rather was a by-product of the broken marriage.

At this time, the court feels it appropriate to comment on the demeanor of the parties as it relates to their credibility and in weighing the evidence. Although the court was busily engaged in taking detailed, copious notes during the lengthy trial, the court nevertheless closely observed the appearance and demeanor of the witnesses, and in particular the parties, throughout the trial. As to the husband, this court could readily observe the embarrassment, painful hurt and frustrating concern exuding from his doleful eyes and aging face. By contrast, the wife nonchalantly sat at the table "doodling" on a note pad as though unconcerned. As the husband and his witness, Janice Nelson, were testifying, the wife engaged them in vitriolic stares, eventually staring them down. Frankly, the court was somewhat relieved when, toward the end of the eighteen day trial, the wife finally broke into tears, necessitating a brief recess, indicating that she was, after all, capable of human emotion and concern. The husband's testimony and evidence had the ring of truth, whereas the denials of the wife and her paramours were patently false and knowingly given.

Applying the above evidentiary findings to the criteria

enumerated in section 61.13(3) (a) through (j), Florida Statutes, which became effective on July 1, 1982, this court hereby determines that the best welfare and interests of the minor children would be served by ordering shared parental responsibility, but provided that the primary physical residence of the minor children shall be with the husband, subject to the right of reasonable visitation to the wife. See the cogent objective custody investigation report of Sheri Rifenberg, counselor of the Juvenile and Family Division of this court, in evidence as husband's exhibit number 20; the testimony of Sheri Rifenberg and the very impressive testimony of Dr. Theodore H. Blau, child psychiatrist, both of whom recommend the husband as primary custodian of the children, in preference to the wife. To do otherwise would continue to be adverse and detrimental to the moral and social health, safety and welfare of the children.

The husband is likely to allow the children frequent and continuing contact with the wife. There is love, affection and other emotional ties existing between the husband and the children in spite of the wife's disparaging statements to the children designed to alienate their affection for the husband. As between the parties, the husband has the greater capacity and, more importantly, the disposition to provide the children with food, clothing, medical care or other remedial care recognized and permitted under the laws of this State in lieu of medical care, and other material needs. The children have spent their entire lives in the marital home owned by the husband. Unlike the wife, the husband has strong family ties and vast financial investments in Palm Beach County and South Florida thereby insuring the permanence of the children's residence and continuing educational needs.

In so ruling on the child custody issue, this court has given due consideration to Florida's so-called "tender years doctrine." Under that doctrine, mothers have historically been the preferred custodian of children of tender years when all other factors are equal. The doctrine is predicated on the premise that the child between the age of six months and three years establishes a bonding attachment to the mother, as a primary caretaker, and the bonding is essential to the wholesome emotional development of the child; and that to deprive a child of the primary caretaker during the bonding period has a destructive effect on the child's intellectual, physical, and psycho-social development. See Agudo v. Agudo, 411 So.2d 249 (3 DCA 1982).

However, the tender years doctrine has from time to time been eroded. See for example the recent legislative amendment to section 61,13(2) (b) 1, effective July 1, 1982, which now provides, "upon considering all relevant factors, the father of the child shall be given the same consideration as the mother in determining custody regardless of the age of the child."

Nevertheless, even without regard to the effect of that amendment on the "tender years doctrine," this court finds that the doctrine is inapplicable under the facts of this case. As noted hereinabove, all other factors are not equal because of the wife's flagrant adultery and other gross marital misconduct; the wife has abandoned the primary caretaker role to nannies and the husband; and the children are well beyond the bonding age.

THE ALIMONY ISSUE:

At the outset, it should be noted that according to the proposed final judgment submitted on behalf of the wife, the wife, in addition to seeking custody of the children, also seeks a total of $6,000 per month child support; full ownership and possession of the marital home and its contents as lump sum alimony, which she estimates has a value of $1,500,000 according to her financial affidavit filed on February 16, 1982 (she wants the home free and clear of the outstanding mortgage); in addition to $6,000 per month as permanent, periodic alimony; a one-third special equity interest in the husband's boat, Sea Hunter, which has a present fair market value of $169,000; and $300,000 attorney's fee, plus court costs. The wife's exhorbitant demands shock the conscience of this court, putting the court in mind of the hit record by country music singer, Jerry Reed, which laments, "She Got the Gold Mine, I Got the Shaft."

Section 61.08(1), Florida Statutes, as noted above, expressly provides (among other factors) that "the court may consider the adultery of a spouse and the circumstances thereof in determining whether alimony shall be awarded such spouse and the amount of alimony, if any, to be awarded"; and the statute concludes by expressly providing that "the court <u>may consider any other factor necessary to do equity</u> and justice between the parties." Therefore, under Florida law, adultery and other gross marital misconduct of a spouse seeking alimony are factors, among others, that a trial court should consider within the limits expressed by the Florida Supreme Court in <u>Williamson v. Williamson</u>, 367 So.2d 1016 (1979). See also <u>McAllister v. McAllister</u>, 345 So.2d 352 (4 DCA 1977), for an excellent discussion of all the factors to be considered.

Proof of adultery or other gross marital misconduct is not an absolute bar to an alimony award to the offending spouse. On the contrary, the decision to either grant alimony (and the amount thereof) or to deny alimony outright is a matter resting within the broad judicial discretion of the trial court. <u>Canakaris v. Canakaris</u>, 382 So.2d 1197 (Fla. 1980). The trial court's discretion is not an arbitrary discretion, but is governed by evidence as to the needs of the spouse seeking alimony, the ability of the other spouse to financially respond to the needs, taking into consideration the lifestyle and standard of living enjoyed during the marriage, as well as the other factors enumerated in section 61.08 and discussed in <u>McAllister v. McAllister</u>, supra. Trial courts need not equalize the financial position of the parties, but must insure that neither spouse passes automatically from misfortune to prosperity or from prosperity to misfortune, and, in viewing the totality of the circumstances, one spouse should not be "shortchanged." <u>Canakaris</u>, supra, at page 1204.

In this day and time, women are as well educated and trained in the arts, sciences, and professions as are their male counterparts. The law protects them in their right to independently acquire, encumber, accumulate, and alienate property at will. They now occupy a position of equal partners in the family relationship resulting from marriage. The woman continues to be as fully equipped as the man to earn a living and provide for her essential needs. Therefore, the fortuitous circumstance created by mere recitation of the marriage vows neither diminishes her capacity for self-support nor does it give her a vested right in her husband's earnings for the remainder of her life. <u>Cummings v. Cummings</u>, 330 So.2d 134, 136 (Fla. 1976).

The wife has clearly demonstrated her need for alimony and the husband's financial ability to respond. However, upon due consideration of the criteria enumerated in McAllister v. McAllister and Canakaris v. Canakaris, supra, in order to do equity and justice between the parties, and in reliance upon Patin v. Patin and Beville v. Beville, supra; Pro v. Pro, 300 So.2d 288 (4 DCA 1974), and Oliver v. Oliver, 285 So.2d 638 (4 DCA 1973), this court hereby denies the wife's claim for alimony in all forms except rehabilitative alimony. In so doing, this court finds that while the parties enjoyed a lavish lifestyle and standard of living during this marriage, the marriage was of relatively short duration; the wife is young, attractive and healthy and is fully capable of gainful employment after a reasonable period of rehabilitation; the wife's financial and domestic contributions to this marriage and to the husband's career building were minimal to say the least; and, as fully articulated hereinabove, the wife continuously engaged in adultery and other gross marital misconduct, outweighing all favorable factors.

THE SPECIAL EQUITY ISSUE:

The term "special equity" was created to describe a vested interest in property brought into the marriage or acquired during the marriage because of contributions of funds or services over and above normal marital duties. Canakaris v. Canakaris, supra, at page 1200. A "special equity" in its true term is not a form of alimony nor a substitute therefore. Duncan v. Duncan, 379 So.2d 950 (Fla. 1980) and Ball v. Ball, 335 So.2d 5 (Fla. 1976).

Herein, the wife claims a special equity in the husband's resort hotels in Amsterdam, Holland and Miami Beach, Florida and in the husband's seagoing vessel, the Sea Hunter. The undisputed evidence clearly shows that the husband's substantial assets and properties, both real and personal, were acquired by him through his own blood, sweat and tears well in advance of his marriage to Roxanne D. Pulitzer, and remain titled in his sole name. Any improvements to the properties subsequent to the marriage were made with funds either earned by the husband or with borrowed funds for which the husband is solely responsible to repay. The only assets brought to this marriage by the wife was a used

Lincoln automobile of unknown value and an undivided one-half interest in a mobile home which she acquired in her prior divorce. Throughout this short-term marriage, the wife made no financial contributions (except as noted hereinafter) to the marriage and did not contribute extraordinary services over and above the normal household duties, which were nominal, or in the husband's career building, nor did she sacrifice her own career and educational opportunities.

Nevertheless, the wife did eventually receive $7,000 for her one-half interest in the mobile home referred to above. The wife donated the $7,000 to her husband to be used in the building of his seagoing vessel, Sea Hunter, which was built in 1975 and 1976 at a total cost of $275,630. The wife also assisted in building the Sea Hunter by helping the husband paint and varnish the vessel. However, the wife did not offer any proof as to the extent and value of those services, and for the court to evaluate those services would be pure conjecture. In any event, earlier this year, the husband attempted to sell the Sea Hunter for $169,000, but the sale fell through because the purchaser's deposit check did not clear. The vessel is still on the sales market. Based on the asking price, this court finds that the present fair market value of the Sea Hunter is $169,000, after depreciation. Therefore, based on the formula enunciated in Landay v. Landay, 400 So.2d 43 (2 DCA 1981) now pending certiorari in the Florida Supreme Court, but nevertheless binding on this court pursuant to State v. Hayes, 333 So.2d 51 (4 DCA 1976), this court, in equitable distribution between the parties, finds (and the husband concedes) that the wife has established a $7,000 special equity in the Sea Hunter irrespective of the fact that the Landay formula would apply to the $169,000 depreciated value of the Sea Hunter. Canakaris v. Canakaris, supra.

The wife's special equity claim in the husband's resort hotels in Amsterdam and Miami Beach is based on her assertion that she assisted her husband in selecting material colors and patterns for two suites in the husband's 190 room Amsterdam hotel and one room in his 137 room Miami Beach hotel. However, the wife did not offer any proof as to the value of this minimal service or as to the enhancement of the value of the hotels or any increase in operating profits derived therefrom. This court cannot in good faith conclude that the wife's services materially benefited the husband or his hotels, or that the services were above and beyond the normal marital duties. Therefore, the wife's claim to a special equity interest in the husband's hotels is denied for failure of proof.

ATTORNEY'S FEES AND COURT COSTS:

From the very outset of this lawsuit, the undisputed evidence clearly demonstrates the wife's need for a reasonable attorney's fee, suit money and court costs in her defense thereof, as well as the husband's financial ability to respond without financial disaster to him, and so as to avoid an inequitable diminution of the fiscal sums awarded to the wife herein. Canakaris v. Canakaris, supra. In addition to the testimony of her own counsel, the wife presented the testimony of three well-known, experienced lawyers who practice law in the local community, whereas the husband presented the testimony of one local lawyer of equal professional stature. No useful purpose would be served in summarizing that testimony except to otherwise lengthen this already too lengthy written judgment.

According to the wife's evidence, her lawyers devoted in excess of 800 man hours in preparation of this case for trial and at trial. Her expert evidence indicates a reasonable fee to be in the range of $250,000 to $325,000. By contrast, the husband's expert evidence indicates a reasonable fee to be in the range of $75,000 to $135,000, depending on whether this trial results in a judgment favorable to the wife. Regarding the attorney's fee question, there were charges and counter-charges of vexatious and obstructive strategies on the part of counsel for both parties.

To make a long story short, after giving due consideration to the proofs, and taking into consideration all the factors enumerated in Disciplinary Rule 2-106, Code of Professional Responsibility, and in particular considering that this trial resulted in a judgment unfavorable to the wife on the paramount issues, this court hereby finds that a reasonable attorney's fee to be awarded to the wife is $90,000 in addition to the $12,500 temporary attorney's fee previously awarded to the wife's counsel in this court's order dated

June 2, 1982. In so doing, the court has weighed the quality of legal services provided to the wife against the less probative quantity of those services. While it is true that the husband has a "deep pocket," it is not without a bottom.

Accordingly, based on the above findings of fact and conclusions of law, it is

ORDERED, ADJUDGED AND DECREED as follows:

1. The marriage between the parties, Herbert Pulitzer, Jr. and Roxanne D. Pulitzer, is dissolved because the marriage is irretrievably broke [*sic*].

2. Pursuant to section 61.13, Florida Statutes, the parental responsibility for the minor children, MacLean Simpson Pulitzer and Zachary Simpson Pulitzer, shall be shared by Herbert Pulitzer, Jr. and Roxanne D. Pulitzer (hereinafter referred to as parents). The parents shall retain full parental rights and responsibilities with respect to the children. Both parents shall confer so that major decisions affecting the welfare of the children will be determined jointly. In particular, both parents shall confer and share in matters relating to the religion, education, medical and dental care of the children.

It is the intent of this court that the children maintain and enjoy as close an association with each parent as the circumstances allow, consistent with the best interests and welfare of the children, petty differences between the parents notwithstanding.

Each parent shall conduct himself, and herself, in such a manner so as to cause minimum upset to the children, and neither parent shall alienate, by word or deed, the affection of the children for the other parent, and each parent shall consider the other in the exercise of these rights and responsibilities.

3. The primary physical residence of both children, MacLean Simpson Pulitzer and Zachary Simpson Pulitzer, shall be with the husband, Herbert Pulitzer, Jr., subject to frequent, continuing and reasonable contact and visitation with the wife, Roxanne D. Pulitzer, at such times and places as the parties may agree, as set forth in the companionship schedule attached hereto as Exhibit "A" and subject to its conditions, which exhibit is adopted and incorporated here by reference. Provided, however, that Roxanne D. Pulitzer

shall not remove the children, or either of them, from Palm Beach County, Florida without prior written consent from Herbert Pulitzer, Jr. or upon prior written order of this court. Herbert Pulitzer, Jr. shall not remove the children, or either of them, from the State of Florida for more than thirty (30) consecutive days except upon prior written order of this court.

4. Roxanne D. Pulitzer shall peacefully vacate the marital residence located at 410 North Lake Way, Palm Beach, Florida on or before January 10, 1983. Upon vacating the marital residence, the wife shall remove all her belongings of a personal nature. Provided, however, that the wife shall give the husband at least twenty-four (24) hours notice of the date and time she vacates the marital residence and/or removes her personal effects so that the husband or his agent may be present. Any reasonable moving expenses incurred shall be at the expense of the husband.

5. The husband shall pay to the wife, as rehabilitative alimony, the sum of $2,000 per month for twenty-four (24) consecutive months or until the wife remarries or dies or the husband dies, whichever event occurs first, payable on or before the 10th day of each month following the date of this final judgment. Canakaris v. Canakaris, supra, and Reback v. Reback, 296 So.2d 541 (3 DCA 1974). The wife's claim for alimony in all other forms is denied.

6. The wife is hereby awarded a special equity in the husband's seagoing vessel, the Sea Hunter, by virtue of the $7,000 cash contribution from a source unconnected with the marriage relationship, including her labor and service. The husband shall pay directly to the wife the sum of $7,000 on or before January 10, 1983 in settlement of her special equity interest in the Sea Hunter. In all other respects, the wife's special equity claims are denied.

7. The husband shall pay directly to the wife's counsel, Farish, Farish and Romani, as a reasonable attorney's fee, the sum of $90,000 in addition to the $12,500 temporary attorney's fee awarded in this court's order dated June 2, 1982, to be paid in equal installments. The first installment shall be paid on or before February 14, 1983 and the last installment shall be paid on or before April 4, 1983.

8. This court's previous order dated April 23, 1982, commonly referred to as a "gag order," is hereby vacated. The parties and respective counsel are hereby released from the restraints thereof, within their personal discretion and freedom, except that respective counsel, as lawyers and officers of this court, shall continue to be governed by the letter and spirit of the ethical standards of the Code of Professional Responsibility and in particular Disciplinary Rule 7-107 (G).

9. Except for the dissolution of this marriage, the court reserves jurisdiction of this cause and of the parties to enter such orders as may from time to time become necessary, including but not limited to the assessment and allocation of court costs to the wife upon reasonable notice and proper proof of accordance with the Florida Supreme Court's Administrative Order, dated October 28, 1981, In Re: Statewide Uniform Guidelines for Taxation of Costs in Civil Actions.

In response to those who may find this court's judgment unduly harsh, this court would only state in conclusion that there are three parties to every marriage contract, namely the wife, the husband, and the State that licensed the marriage or in which the marital cohabitation continued. The marriage union, and its concomitant family unit, is the very bedrock upon which our society is built. Flagrant acts of adultery and other gross marital misconduct demeans the sanctity of the marriage and family unit, and will not be tolerated by an enduring society. Where such transgressions are shown, appropriate sanctions must be imposed as between the parties, not to mention the deterrent effect on other spouses so inclined. As noted previously herein, it is improper to permit an errant spouse to destroy a marriage and then to claim benefits equal to those which would have been enjoyed had the marriage remained intact. Smith v. Smith, supra. The wife entered this marriage with limited interest in a mobile home. Upon departing the marriage, which she destroyed, she takes with her a $20,000 Porsche automobile purchased with the husband's funds; about $60,000 in jewelry purchased in large measure with the husband's funds; $48,000 in rehabilitative alimony; $7,000 cash equity in the husband's boat; and $102,500 in attorney's fees.

DONE AND ORDERED this <u>28th</u> day of December, 1982 at West Palm Beach, Palm Beach County, Florida.

_____

Carl H. Harper, Circuit Judge

Copy to counsel

COMPANIONSHIP SCHEDULE*

Liberal visiting arrangements are encouraged, as contact with both parents is important to the children. Specific items in the Final Judgment take precedence over this schedule. Changes or modifications can be made by the Court if need for such is shown.

1. <u>AT SUCH TIMES AND PLACES AS THE PARTIES MAY AGREE.</u>
<u>This will Not Normally Be Less Than:</u>

2. <u>Weekends:</u> Alternate weekends from Friday at 6:00 p.m. until Sunday at 6:00 p.m.

3. <u>Holidays:</u> In the odd-numbered years, mother has Easter, July 4th, Thanksgiving and Christmas Day; and father has Memorial Day, Labor Day, and Christmas Eve. In the even-numbered years, the schedules are reversed.

a. A holiday that falls on a weekend should be spent with the parent who is supposed to have the children for that holiday. The rest of the weekend is to be spent with the parent who would normally have that weekend. These do not have to be made up.

b. 48-hour notice should be given by the noncustodial parent to the custodial parent of intentions about the holidays.

c. Mother's Day and Father's Day are to be spent with the appropriate parent. These are as agreed or 10

* Taken from recommended schedule of the Lucas County, Ohio Court of Common Pleas

a.m. until 7 p.m. (any school requirements take precedence).

d. Other days of special meaning, such as Religious Holidays, etc., should be decided together, written down and alternated as above.

e. Hours for parents who cannot agree are as follows: Easter (10 a.m.–7 p.m.), Memorial Day (9 a.m.–9 a.m. the next day, not to interfere with school), July 4th (9 a.m.–9 a.m., the next day), Labor Day (9 a.m.–9 a.m. the next day, not to interfere with school), Thanksgiving (9 a.m.–9 a.m. the next day), Christmas Eve (9 p.m. Dec. 23–9 p.m. Dec. 24), Christmas Day (9 p.m. Dec. 24–9 p.m. Dec. 25).

4. <u>Birthdays:</u> The child shall celebrate his/her birthday in the home of the custodial parent, unless it falls on a visitation day, and the other parent can celebrate at another time if desired.

5. <u>Waiting:</u> The children and the custodial parent have no duty to await the visiting parent for more than 30 minutes of the visitation time. A parent who is late forfeits companionship for that period.

6. <u>Cancellations:</u> If a child is ill, the custodial parent should give 24-hour notice, if possible, so appropriate plans can be made. The noncustodial parent should give 24 hour notice to cancel. The time cancelled by the noncustodial parent is forfeited.

7. <u>Vacations:</u> Four weeks of companionship each year are to be arranged with 30 day advance notice by the noncustodial parent. The custodial parent must give the noncustodial parent 30 day notice of vacations or special plans for the child to avoid planning conflicts.

a. Alternate weekends or holidays which normally would be spent with the <u>custodial</u> parent, and that fall during the <u>noncustodial</u> parent's vacation must be given to the <u>custodial</u> parent or made up at another time. Alternate weekends or holidays which normally would be spent with the <u>noncustodial</u> parent, and that fall during the <u>custodial</u> parent's vacation, must be given to the noncustodial parent or made up at another time. Holidays and alternate weekends that are to be made up must be given/taken within 3 months.

b. Summer school necessary for the child to pass to the next grade must be attended.

c. A general itinerary should be provided for the custodial parent if vacation will be out of town.

8. <u>Moving:</u> For parents residing in different locations that make the above schedule impractical, consult the Court.